D1571802

"OUR MARIE"

"Our Marie" is the story of the life and career of Marie Lloyd, known to her contemporaries as 'the Queen of Comedy'.

She was, however, far from regal in appearance. She was rather short, fair, and decidedly pretty with a wide toothy smile. Her generosity and kindness were legendary and she hated pretence, pomposity and dishonesty. It is difficult for those who never met her, saw her perform, or heard her sing to imagine the impact she made on the music hall audiences of her day. And not simply inside the theatre. Wherever she went she was instantly recognised and greeted, and her popularity would be the envy of many latter day 'stars'.

She was as much the head of her sphere of the profession as were any of the great names of the serious theatre, such as Irving, and to read this book is to grasp and appreciate the essence of her greatness.

"OUR MARIE"
(Marie Lloyd)

A Biography

NAOMI JACOB

CEDRIC CHIVERS LTD
PORTWAY
BATH

First published 1936
by
Hutchinson & Co. (Publishers) Ltd
This edition published
by
Cedric Chivers Ltd
by arrangement with the copyright holder
at the request of
The London & Home Counties Branch
of
The Library Association
1972

SBN 85594 721 7

Printed in Great Britain by
Redwood Press Limited, Trowbridge, Wiltshire
Bound by Cedric Chivers Ltd, Bath

DEDICATION

the many brilliant artistes of the Variety Stage who
have helped me in the writing of this tribute to a woman
we all loved, and particularly to Marie's sisters and
brothers (Johnnie, Alice, Gracie, Daisy, Rosie, Annie,
Maudie and Sidney), and her daughter, Marie.

" There were many things she might have bought,
And did not buy . . .
There were many things she might have sold,
And did not sell."

Adapted from the poem by T. W. H. Crosland.

MY sincere thanks are due to : Alice, Daisy and Rosie—Marie's sisters ; her brother, Johnnie Wood ; and her younger brother, Sidney, for assistance, letters and photographs. Also to Alice McNaughton. To " Brinsworth "—Charles Valvo, Alice Leamar, Leslie Reed, Rose Hervey, Flo Hastings, George Hurley, H. A. Kennedy (Ken) and Jules de Block. To the Editors of the *Stage*, the *Performer* ,and the *Sunday Times* of Johannesburg. Miss Marjorie Lotinga and Mrs. Mabel Thorn, Mabel Dawes, Dorothy Melling, Joan Harrington, Raymond Savage, Langley Levy, Julia Neilson, Mrs. Mary Reynolds, Charles Coborn, A. L. Gibbs (and for the valuable photographs), Sir Seymour Hicks, Harry Marlow, " Mr. E.", Joan Hurley, Jane Stockwood, Ena Grossmith, Walter Brodie, Mrs. Bella Burge, Arthur Prince, Sidney Bernstein, Fred Barnes, Sadie Robinson, George Wood, Harry Hemsley, Winnie Corin, Bransby Williams, Ella Retford, W. H. ("Billie") Boardman, Harry Randall, Tom Fancourt, Mrs. Roma Taylor, H. Carter, Mrs. Martin Adison (Miss Clara Bernard), James Adair, Chrissie Dunbar, George Graves, R. L. Illingworth, Harry Claff, Wilkie Warren, Mrs. John Lawson, Harry Robins, Arthur L. Percival, Edwin Adeler, Clarice Mayne and E. Knox (Mr. and Mrs. Knox), George Mozart, Mr. and Mrs. Coram, Violet Loraine, Nigel ("Willie") Bruce, and others who, although they had no personal recollection of Marie Lloyd wrote to me their generous tributes to her as " Members of Marie's Public."

I thank you.

CONTENTS

CHAPTER FIVE

CHAPTER SIX

CHAPTER SEVEN

CHAPTER EIGHT

BOOK TWO

CHAPTER ONE

CHAPTER TWO

CONTENTS

BOOK THREE

CHAPTER ONE

BOOK THREE

INTRODUCTION

". . . . MY FRIEND, FAITHFUL AND JUST TO ME :
AND THAT THEY KNOW FULL WELL
THAT GAVE ME PUBLIC LEAVE TO SPEAK. . . ."
                    JULIUS CÆSAR

FOR nearly thirteen years I have wanted to write this book. I suggested that I should write it to many people, some of whom agreed that it ought to be written, others who felt that there was not sufficient call for it, and others, probably the wisest of them all, who wondered if I had sufficient ability to do justice to my subject.

They were right for this reason. It must always be difficult to write a book of this type, dealing with the life and work of someone who was supremely loved, without seeming to extol them to such an extent that they lose their human reality. If, on the other hand, one should stress little faults and failings in the belief that this will add to the truthful quality of the book, one lays oneself open to a charge of having been ungenerous and unkind.

So in this book, which I have tried to make honest because Marie hated pretence and dishonesty, if I have seemed to lay too much stress on her generosity, her loyalty and her essential kindness, believe me it is inevitable. She had faults, she had a temper which was roused to boiling-point very quickly, but, somehow, looking back down thirteen years, these things have lost their reality. They are almost forgotten, certainly blurred by the passing of time, and what remains is the recollection of that great heart and that bright and keen mentality.

Some day, years after we are dead, a really brilliant writer will set down for the generation of his or her time the true history of the Tragedy of Marie Lloyd. When that is written, the people who read it will understand why we—as she said of poor Danny Leno—always laughed at her, because the tears were so very near as we listened to her singing.

It is difficult for those of you who never saw her, never heard

her, to imagine all that she meant to her " boys and girls " ;
that is one reason why you ought to read this book ! For those
who knew her—and " to know her was to love her "—this
little extract from something I wrote years ago will " set the
stage " before we actually " ring up " on the three-act drama
of Marie's life.

" There is just a little silence, and everyone sits up and waits.
The band plays ' Tiddily-iddily-om-pom, tiddily-iddily-OM,'
and we see her. Just a rather short, fair, pretty woman with
a wide ' toothy ' smile, and a voice which is most attractively
hoarse—Marie Lloyd. She can't begin for a second or two,
because we go crazy, and the applause is deafening. She is
' Our Marie,' we know her troubles as we know our own, and
we know that she is the greatest music-hall comedienne in the
whole world—and we want her to know that we know."

And here is a later picture, and this is Marie at her most
human, when she was just herself.

" In a car, driving away from the Canterbury Music Hall, I
am seated beside a little fair-haired woman with very bright,
blue eyes. She is talking very fast to me. She began as we left
the dressing-room and is just finishing her homily.

" ' . . . That's how it is," she says. ' Believe me, Micky, I've
had my heart broken so often that when I think of going to take
out a life insurance, I get cold feet because I feel certain they'll
notice the cracks. But it goes on beating just the same—and
you forget about it being cracked to bits. Keep it beating, my
duck, that's the only thing to do.'

" And as we turn into Westminster Bridge Road, I hear a
man on the pavement shout : ' Theer she is ! Blimy, theer's
Our Maree. Goo' night, Maree.' And she looks out and waves
her hand, then looks back at me and says : ' Their hearts beat
all right, don't they ? You know, really, *most* people's do.' "

To show you that hers did, here are two instances which came
to me only this morning—one from Harry Hemsley, the other
from Georgie Wood.

Let's take Harry Hemsley's first, for this goes back to Marie's
first visit to Berlin, when she played the Winter Gardens, with
its huge apron stage. Harry had been sent by his family to
study in Germany. He lived with a German family, knew no
one, and was very lonely and utterly miserable.

" I went to see Marie Lloyd making her first appearance
there. I introduced myself. ' I believe that you know my
father, Miss Lloyd—W. G. Hemsley.'

" ' Know him, of course I know him ! ' That put me at my ease and I began to talk about myself. I told her how lonely I was, how I spoke very little German, and how I was—just miserable.

" ' You poor boy ! ' she said, and all that month while she was in Berlin we went everywhere together. I remember her now—she couldn't have been more than twenty-two, if that— wearing a very wide, spangled dress, and singing cheeky little songs. She was a very light soubrette in those days, and I thought she was the sweetest thing that had ever happened. I saw her many times after that, in England, for my father put on all the scenes for her songs, but I never spoke to her until I was on the Halls myself. Then I felt that I might meet her on common ground. I introduced myself and she said : ' But I've met you before ? ' I said : ' Many years ago.' ' In Berlin ! ' she cried in triumph. ' You're not lonely now, are you ? ' What a wonderful memory she had. Now I have just returned from Berlin, renewing acquaintance with the places we visited together, remembering how kind she—a great star—was to me, an unknown schoolboy."

And Georgie Wood sends his donation.

" I met her at the Pavilion, Glasgow. The whole thing arose through the fact that her name, her real name, was Wood, too, and people used to think that I was her brother. The funny thing was that I gave an impersonation of her, wearing a wig, carrying a diamond-headed stick, and having the same kind of husky voice—I was very like her. I was just a little boy at the time, and I'd never seen her in my life. However, she heard of this impersonation and sent for me. I went to see her in fear and trembling, quite certain she was going to haul me over the coals and probably stop the impersonation. On the contrary, she told me that she had seen my show and liked it. She was sweet to me and set about teaching me a new song— ' The Directoire Dress '—which she had just bought. She showed me all the right gestures, movements and the correct inflections. No one could, and very few people *would*, have taken such trouble over a little boy—as I was then."

These are two stories among the many which have come to me, and which I have inserted here because they are so typical, and are quite literally only two among hundreds. What is there to do, except to record them, and realize what an impression this artiste made on everyone ? Of all the letters which I have received not one had contained anything but good, but admiration, but praise. And why? Not one of all those people who have written to me have an axe to grind. They have nothing to gain in suppressing some amusing but slightly ill-natured story of Marie. Simply, I believe, because, as I have said, the other things are forgotten. More because they never really counted at all—they were not an integral part of Marie Lloyd's character. They were excrescences, they were something which never really " belonged " to her.

I have purposely tried to avoid too much mention of those things which darkened the last years of her life. Not because we didn't all know of them, not because we—her public—did not resent them, not because we did not blame, whole-heartedly the people who caused her unhappiness. I admit that it would have given me a certain satisfaction to have written fully and truthfully of many things, those things might have made many other incidents plain and might have cleared Marie of some of the silly and utterly untrue charges which were made against her. That I have not done so is due to one thing and one thing only—she would have resented it. There was a certain fineness in her mental make-up which made her dislike even allowing other people to wash her linen—and never very dirty linen at that—in public. So I have left out a great many things, refrained from recording all those things which were Marie's " personal property "—poor Marie !

To purposely omit these things is not of necessity to throw my picture of her out of drawing, to make it less true and less real. She was " Our Marie " before these things touched her, she remained " Our Marie " in spite of them.

I should like to feel that this book would reach three types of reader. The first who can remember Marie when she began to " make the managers think that perhaps she might be a clever girl," the second those people who, like myself, knew and admired her when she was holding that position, which she never lost, as The Queen of Comedy, and the third the people who never saw her, to whom she is only a name, someone of whom their fathers and mothers still talk of with affection.

It is a pleasure to be able to record my thanks to everyone who has helped me, particularly as I feel that their help has been given because they wanted to identify themselves with Marie's book. There are names missing—names which ought to have been in the list which follows. The fact that they are missing is not my fault and not due to my negligence. It is because those people have not troubled to reply to letters and enquiries. And there I suppose I ought to take that out, because Marie would have said : " Who cares—anyway ! If they don't want to—well, they don't want to, that's all ! I should worry about it—oh, *you* would ! You'd worry over any damn silly thing ! "

Still—just for once, I'm going to have my own way.

For the rest, I offer my grateful thanks, on Marie's behalf and my own. Her sisters, her brothers and her father have all been the greatest possible help. They have sought out old letters, old and precious photographs, they have entrusted to my care a huge book of cuttings, and have never been too busy to allow my friend, Sadie Robinson, to go and sit in their dressing-rooms and interrogate them with that tenacity and persistence which has produced such admirable and valuable material. For, remember, to write a book in Italy, when all the material you need is in England, and you have only your own memory and various theatrical books on which to draw, is almost impossible but for the splendid co-operation at " the other end."

Then, Brinsworth. Marie was, I believe, Vice-President of the Music Hall Benevolent Institution ; she was, I know, a generous subscriber, and the " old pros " at Brinsworth have certainly been very generous to me. I shall never forget the pleasure it gave me when Mr. Harry Marlow, the secretary, sent along to me a huge envelope full of letters from the people who had once been Marie's brother and sister artistes.

The *Stage*, the *Performer*, and the *Sunday Times* of Johannesburg have been more than kind. The editors of these papers have inserted requests for " anecdotes " concerning Marie, they have allowed my secretary to search their files for information, and have shown me every possible kindness.

There have been wonderful letters, too, from artistes themselves, not only those who belong to Variety, but many others whose work lies on the legitimate stage—Miss Julia Neilson, Sir Seymour Hicks and Mr. George Graves, for example.

Journalists—like James Adair of Edinburgh, and Langley Levy of Johannesburg, who have taken the trouble to search for dates, and spent valuable time writing to me whatever information they could collect which might be useful.

And, lastly—the Profession. Whether it has been Bransby Williams, who could have written this book so much better than I have been able to do, my old friend, Harry Claff (one of the most important officials in Variety Organization), down to some almost unknown little music-hall artiste who is so " down

and out " that even a stamp meant a certain difficulty—they
have been magnificently generous.

One more, and I have finished my thanks. Raymond
Savage and his whole office staff, who have—as always—done
everything they could to help me, not because I was a client,
but because that's how Raymond Savage always behaves to his
clients—who are also his friends.

It has been a very pleasant thing to get these letters, and I
could not help feeling that they were all " gifts " which Marie
would have loved and appreciated as much as she did those
wonderful flowers which were sent to her thirteen years ago.

The music-halls will always have a very warm place in my
heart. If it had not been for the music-halls I might still be
teaching in a North-country town—though I doubt it, because
if I had not " sacked myself ", someone else would have done
it for me.

I knew them when they were booming, when money was
good, when touring was a very amusing and rather gay business. In summer there were picnics, drives, boating parties—
always something going on. Very few real stars on the halls
cared if you were first turn, last turn, or " among the wines and
spirits ", so long as you were a reasonably cheerful person and
a good mixer.

I watched " the Cinderella of the Arts " go to the ball at last,
when the King publicly recognised the claims of Variety—and
spent a pretty dull evening, too, God bless him !

I watched the " movies " come creeping in, watched music-
halls change into cinemas, and almost disappear. I saw the
great artistes pass, and realised that there was no one to take
their place. In those days we had " The Big Five "—for Dan
Leno had already taken his Last Call—Vesta Tilley, Harry
Lauder, Paul Cinquevalli, Harry Tich, and " Our Marie "—
the first has retired, Sir Harry is seen only too seldom, the others
have done with Variety.

In my study hangs the big photograph taken on the afternoon
of the rehearsal of the First Command Performance, signed for
me by all those who took part in it, and who appeared in the
huge tableau known as " Variety's Garden Party."

What a crowd ; how much talent was crammed on to the
stage of the Palace Theatre that afternoon—and how few of
them are left. Barclay Gammon, George Bastow, Fred Emney,
J. W. Tate, Billie Williams, Harry Weldon, T. E. Dunville,
Peggy Pryde, Chirgwin, and many more. The others—retired

INTRODUCTION 19

—finished with their work so far as the halls are concerned, though some of them are as good as ever, if you ever get a chance to hear them. There is talent left—and plenty of it—Clarice Mayne, Dorothy Ward, George Robey—who I heard on the radio, his voice coming right over Europe, over the heights of the Brenner Pass, a few evenings ago—and better than ever—Harry Claff, Charles Coburn (the " Grand Old Man of Variety "), Wilkie Bard, Charles Austin and Florrie Forde, to say nothing of Marie's three sisters, whom age cannot apparently wither nor custom stale their infinite variety in Variety.

The music-halls will come back, they will come into their own again, because Variety is a form of entertainment particularly suited to the British public. They like the " personal " feeling which they have with an artiste, that personal sense which can never exist with artistes who only appear in moving photographs. There is no reason why students of Variety should not exist as much as students of the legitimate stage, there is no reason why such names as Tich, Leno, and Marie Lloyd should be forgotten any more than such names as Salvini, Bernhardt and Henry Irving. Servants of the public all of them—and good servants.

So there is one reason for giving this book of Marie's life to the public—because she was as much the head of her profession as were any of the great names in theatrical history. Which reminds me of a little incident which does show how Marie's mind went direct to essentials, and how she discounted " tosh." Talking about Mrs. Siddons one day to her—for when she was in a quiet mood, remember, Marie loved hearing about such things—I recounted the story that when she ordered a yard of calico she made the shopman turn pale by the tone of her voice.

Marie said : " Who turned pale ? "

" The man who was serving Mrs. Siddons with the calico."

" What for ? "

" Because her voice was so tragic."

" When she ordered a yard of calico ? ' I'll take a yard of that, thank you.' Blimy, wot damned rot ! "

There are other reasons why I personally wished to write this book. One was because of that deep affection which I have for the Variety Stage, because I hate to think that it and its great figures can sink into obscurity. The last is that however badly I may have done my work, Marie Lloyd is too great to be forgotten. Not that she ever will be by those who knew her, who saw her, who listened to her ; but it would be a matter for deep regret if her generous heart, her wit, and her deep—and simple—humanity could become dimmed.

For those who knew her, this book may recall memories which are gay ; for those who did not, they tell, at least, the story of a gallant little figure, a woman who fought her way up to the very top of the ladder of Fame. As Charles Valvo says : " The Star without an enemy, the actress without a mask," carrying with her those two bags, one with silver coins, the other with notes and, in the old days, gold, so that she might be ready to hand practical help to the " under-dog."

Not very cultured, not particularly well read, not very much concerned with art, music, or the political outlook ; loving laughter, resenting the tears of others, making mistakes, but never making that greatest mistake of all, obliterating charity from her life.

She might even swear when she felt like doing so, because she believed that " it was better out than in," but there was something essentially clean about her, and so you will read nothing of her here which can hurt any of you. A little outspoken here and there, but nothing more—because whatever she was, she was—decent.

I have asked from time to time—asked Marie herself, asked Alice, Rosie, Daisy, Sid and Johnnie, what there was about this family of John Wood's that made them carve such a firm place for themselves in the hearts of the public, for, remember, Alice was as great a star in America as Marie was here, and in England they could all hold their own, with something to spare, in their work, and hold their own now. Music-halls have crashed, been closed, but the Lloyds still remain " Bill-Toppers."

None of them have ever answered my question satisfactorily. They have talked vaguely about " being hail-fellow-well-met," of lacking any wish to make " class distinctions," of being " real Bohemians " and so forth, but there was something more to it than that, though I could never put a name to it.

Now—when the book is finished—I have it !

They are England ! They are the English people ! They are the Heart of London. They don't pretend—and Marie never did—for they have no need to. They were born in the very heart of London ; they were poor, but they possessed minds, courage and ability, and those qualities were fostered and encouraged by their father, and that grand mother of theirs.

Daisy used to be billed as " Daisy Wood—on her way to the top "—That's where they all belong—*the top!* Grit brought them from Hoxton to the West End, and ability kept them there.

So, for the second time in my life, I have written a book which " is not my book at all." It's a tribute to Marie Lloyd—Our Marie—from the people who knew and loved her.

I ask you—" Be to her virtues very kind, and to her faults—a little blind "—and if you and I can manage at the end of fifty-two years to have as many virtues and as few faults—well, the world will be a very pleasant place for everyone concerned. Ladies and Gentlemen—Marie's music is playing—her number is shining at the side of the proscenium arch——

" Marie Lloyd, the Queen of Comedy ! "

THE FAMILY

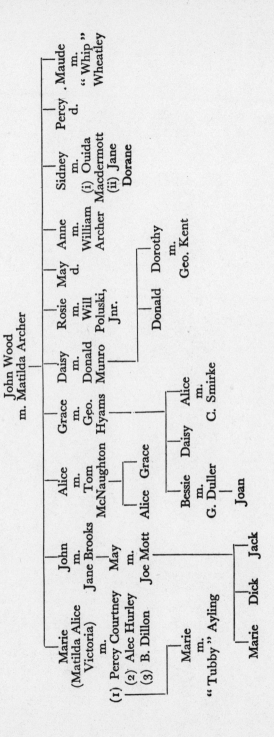

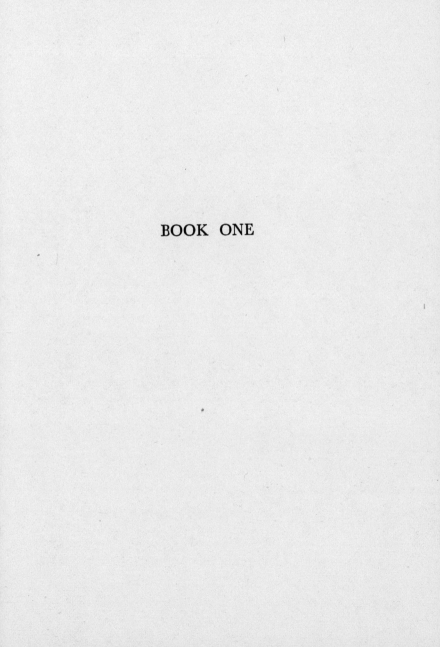

BOOK ONE

CHAPTER ONE

Hoxton—The father and mother—Artificial flowers and Signor
Corti—The family—The perfumed rose—Little Tilly Wood
rules the roost—"She's a caution, that kid!"

NO one lives in Hoxton for choice, no one pays rent
for a house there because they honestly prefer that
locality to any other. People live in Hoxton for two
reasons, sometimes one, sometimes the other, sometimes a
combination of both. They live there because it is cheaper
than the majority of districts, or they live there because it is
near their work and the wages which they earn won't allow
for train, tram or bus fares.

John Wood and his wife, Matilda Caroline Archer, lived
there for both reasons. He was an intelligent, upstanding
young fellow, who originally came of country stock, despite the
fact that he had been born in Bethnal Green. His father had
been a willow-cutter, and his mother a willow-weaver, though
later she abandoned that trade in favour of making "poke
bonnets." His wife, Matilda Archer, also came from Bethnal
Green, where it seems probable that her father did fairly well
as a bootmaker, for there is no record that her mother followed
any actual employment, and in those days—when wages were
even lower and families generally larger than they are now—
that fact argued a certain amount of financial security.

If John Wood was intelligent, which he undoubtedly was and
still happily remains, being an artificial flower-maker and
having to his credit not only making but actual invention, his
wife was in many ways his superior in mentality. John had
one fault—he admitted it later—that was his acceptance of
conditions as they were. His employer was one Luigi Corti,
an Italian from Chiasso. Corti, like the majority of commercial
Italians of the lower class, cultivated an air of careless generosity,

27

a generosity which remained mainly verbal, and which made him perfectly content to pay John Wood about half of what he was actually worth. John had imagination, and was the first person in the artificial flower trade to perfect the yellow centres of daisies, to introduce a scented rose, and various other improvements which added considerably to Corti's bank balance and very little to his own.

Matilda Wood was a remarkable woman. That phrase has been used too often without real cause, in this case it is just. She married when she was very young, she had a large family, one baby following very quickly after the one before, she always managed to keep them not only neat and tidy, but to send them to school looking as if a great deal more money had been spent on them than was actually the case. She was shrewd, possessed not only of considerable humour, but more than an average share of worldly wisdom. I never saw her until 1910. She remained a handsome woman, with a mouth which looked a trifle hard, until you looked more closely and discovered that the corners " turned up " and that the bright eyes were quite astonishingly kind.

There was a streak of the " theatrical spirit " in her family, for her sister Louisa Archer, who took the name of Louisa Patti, was more than usually successful as a dancer, and her brother's daughter became an admirable comedienne—Lily Lena.

However, to get back to the story. John Wood and Matilda Archer met and married. They moved to Number Thirty-six Plumber Street, Hoxton, where John had a workshop adjoining, in which he made the flowers for Signor Corti. Matilda before her marriage had made fancy silk trimmings, a form of work at which she is said to have excelled, because not only were her fingers quick, neat and exact, but she had a great eye for colour and form as will be seen later.

She complained that the house didn't give her enough to do. She hated working at anything but top speed, being filled with that astounding energy which has characterized the whole of her family. Gradually she took to drifting down to the workshop, watching John and finally picking up bits of material, saying thoughtfully :

" Y'know, John, I could make those. There's nothing in it."

" You've got plenty to do with the house," he returned.

" Plenty ! Not half enough. Push some of those leaves over here, and let me see what I can do."

John stopped his own work to watch her. The woman was

astonishing, there was nothing she couldn't do, nothing was
difficult to her. In half an hour she could turn out leaves which
were a credit to anyone. John mentioned the fact to Signor
Corti with pride. Corti, sensing that for the second time in his
life he was going to get skilled labour at a low rate, smiled,
praised Mrs. Wood and declared that he was always delighted
to see her in the workroom. It was, however, her suggestion
that she might be paid a small weekly wage.

" You needn't have sprung it on him so quickly," John said
mildly. " He'd have given it to you all right. There's not a
more generous chap in the City of London than Corti."

His wife continued her leaf-making, saying, without raising
her eyes :

" The wage he's paying me won't strain his generosity
much."

" Oh, come——" John admired his employer whole-
heartedly, and it was almost painful to hear him criticized.
" He's not so bad."

John's wage at that time was thirty shillings a week, and her's
considerably less. Still, that was enough for the two of them,
they even managed to put a little bit away and still live com-
fortably and well. The house was spotless, the meals well
cooked ; John was as ready to congratulate himself on his luck
as he was to praise his employer's kindness—and with considerably more reason.

They had been married a year when they moved to Thirty-
three Peerless Street—now known as Provost Street—Hoxton.
The original house was big enough for two but not large enough
for three, and the third member of the trio arrived on February
12th, 1870. The baby was christened Matilda Alice Victoria
and she was known later as Marie. Not, mark you, Marie as
people pronounce the name when they refer to Marie Stuart,
but a pleasant, broad, comfortable manner of saying the name
—Mar-ee. At this time and during her childhood she was
called—Tilly. She was a beautiful baby, fair-haired and blue-
eyed, smiling, and healthy. Liable to sudden fits of temper,
even then, when she wanted her own way and discovered that
anyone prevented her getting whatever she wanted.

Things were going well. Money had increased, the joint
earnings were three pounds a week. John continued to expatiate
upon the kindliness and generosity of Signor Corti. Matilda
made her artificial leaves, made them beautifully and—said
nothing.

Again they moved, this time to Number One Pounds Passage, off Lever Street, and again because the house was too small for an additional member of the family, who arrived when his baby sister was a year old—Johnnie. Johnnie was followed by another sister—Alice—who was even prettier than Tilly. Again John smiled, again he decided that no man ever had such children, or such a wife.

"There isn't another home kept like this one—not this side of Aldgate Pump."

Then Grace followed Alice, and he came home one evening to find his wife working. She had before her a tray, divided into sections, small pieces of gauze, thread and needles. John stood watching her fingers moving busily, while with her foot she rocked the cradle in which the newest baby lay asleep— pink and white and golden as they all were except Johnnie.

"Hello!" John said. "What's all this about?"

She looked up and smiled; she had a nice, wide smile, not unlike what Marie's was in years to come.

"This? It's my work. What did you think it was—a game?"

"I thought you were coming back to work with me—after you were up and about again."

She nodded. "I thought so, then I decided that three pounds isn't enough—how could it be for six of us? I went round to Cohen's and got some home work."

John frowned. He had felt a certain pride in the fact that his wife worked with him, that as virtual head of the business he could let her get off home for washing or baking when necessary. This idea of going with a crowd of other women to get work irritated him.

"Since when did you have to go and get home work?" he grumbled.

"Since you gave me four kids to look after." She laughed, but he wouldn't let that end his annoyance.

"I suppose that I can't keep you?"

"Me? Of course you can, but not the four of them as well. Have a heart, old man."

"I could get a rise——" His tone was doubtful.

"Then get one—it's time, Heaven knows."

His temper flared suddenly, and he swung round on little Tilly who was banging a tray with a spoon. "Give over that row!" Then back to his wife: "You're making out that I don't do all I can."

She laid down her work, still smiling, and spoke to him as she might have talked to young Johnnie.

" Look here ! " she said. " Let's be honest. You do all you can. You do a damned sight too much for your old Italian boss ! We've got four of them to keep—and they're going to be kept well, not dragged up anyhow. There's no disgrace in doing an extra bit of work ; why should there be ? I like it—or almost like it. Come on, don't be sulky, Johnnie."

He pursed his lips. " I don't care about it. We've got a nice home, four lovely kids, you've always kept them and the house a proper picture. It 'ul go to rack and ruin if you're going to be poring over those beads all day—ruining your eyesight. Chuck it, mother—I'll get a rise out of Corti, I swear I will. He's not a bad chap."

She looked up at him, then suddenly slapped her hands together with one of those queer dramatic gestures of hers. " I'll make a bargain with you," she cried. " Listen, the day you come home and find any dirt, the day you don't come home to a better dinner than any man in the street, the day you find any of the kids untidy or grubby, or find me ratty or grizzling —take the lot of the beads and bits and fling them onto the street and I'll not say a word ! Take them—like that ! " Again one of those queer, pictorial gestures, a little bit of pantomime which made him feel that he could see the beads, needles, cottons and net all flying through the open door. " Is that a bargain ? "

John stared at her. " Even if I *do* get a rise—you'll still go on ? "

" Even if you do get a rise, I'll still go on."

" I wonder," he said reflectively, " who is the master in this house ? "

" You don't wonder at all ! " she returned. " You know, and you don't need to have me to tell you."

She laughed, and suddenly he was laughing too and the little storm was over. He caught her hands in his, saying : " By God, but you're a grand woman ! "

II

Corti lifted the pink rose on its long graceful stalk and sniffed its perfume delicately, then laid it back on the long table.

"Eet ess moast beautiful, Yonnie. Alvays you 'eve some surprise for me. I em so gled and 'eppy. 'Ave you worked out zee price ? "

John nodded. " Not much more than the ordinary kind. Cost of the perfume won't make a lot of difference. Ought to be able to sell these at very little mor'n the others—the unscented."

The Italian raised his hands in horror. " But, my dear Yonnie, no ! Do you realize zet zeese are vorks of art. One pays for vorks of art."

" Pays, eh ? " John repeated. " Who pays and pays what ? I've made 'em, it's my idea. Do I get paid—I can do with it ! "

Corti's large, rather stupid brown eyes softened, filled with tears, his full mouth trembled. " *Caro mio*, vat do you say to me—your friend, your almost brudder. Vhy do you speak as if I vos a men to drive the slave ? Is dis 'ow you t'ink of me ? Let us sit down and I vill tell you. Ondly dis mornin' my vife, Carlotta, said to me : ' Eet iss time dot our dear friend, Yonnie, get a leetle more every veek.' She says : ' Maybe a shilling.' I grrow very engry. I say : ' For dis fine men— von shilling ! No, neffer. Von shilling end sixpence every veek shell be his.' She say t'at it vill ruin us. I reply, vith my hend on my heart, zat I care not'ing for money, ondly I love vot is rright." He went on to explain that the invention, after all, was nothing. They had always made roses, and to add a little perfume was, after all, not particularly marvellous. Corti had provided the workshop, the light, the materials, the wire—even the few drops of perfume. " Eet is a success, *caro mio*," he continued, " but eef it hed not been a success— tell me, please, 'oo vould 'ave paid ? T'ink of all zee materials, end odder t'ings—for vich I—Luigi Corti—must pay. Let us be fair, Yonnie ; let us be—*amici*, alvays, not try to cutta zee t'roat of each odder, eh ? "

John said, gloomily enough : " God knows I don't want to cut anyone's throat, in business or out of it."

He reflected that it was always like this. Always when he thought out some new idea—like the centres to the daisies, or the violets with leaves that looked real, made into neat little buttonholes and scented—Corti could always prove that whatever he had done was not really very clever and some- how he managed to take away all the joy of attainment and make John feel that he didn't really earn his wages. Yet, Luigi was right, if you looked at it from his point of view, of course he was right. Not such a bad fellow—decent of him to think of that extra eighteen-pence—better than nothing after all.

" Yonni, you look pale this morning. Have you a 'eadache ? "

" I didn't sleep much. New baby at our place."

Corti beamed at him. Like most of his race he was sentimental over children, particularly fair-haired, blue-eyed children with clean pinafores and bright little well-washed faces.

" Anodder ! How many iss ziss ? No, don't tell me—for I know ! Dere is zee leetle blue-eyed girl—'oo sometimes frrown —so ! Tilly—no ? "

John said : " Tilly ! " He laughed because he loved talking about his children. " That's the one who danced a jig with her aunt, Louisa Patti, when she was four years old. Did I tell you about that ? That was funny."

Corti, still beaming, said : " Tell me, Yonnie."

" This aunt was working somewhere—I forget the name of the place—and took Tilly on the stage with her to dance this jig. Everyone was full of this baby—well, that's all she was after all—and threw pennies on the stage for her. Quite a bit of money she got too. Her aunt was delighted, asked if she could take her the next night. Mother didn't mind, so off they go. Tilly picked up a little basket as she was leaving. Her mother called : ' What's that for ? ' Tilly said : ' Pennies —people frow at me when I dance.' However, poor little kid, she was disappointed because that night no one threw anything and she came back with an empty basket. Poor little beggar, she got into a temper about it too. ' I'll not dance for them again ! Not for anyone ! ' And she didn't either."

" Ziss von is ver' cleffer, I t'ink," Corti said.

" Clever ! " John laughed. " I'd say so. She went to Belgium with this same aunt, stayed there a couple of months, came back speaking nothing but the lingo she'd heard out there. French or Dutch or something. Soon forgot it, of course. She quick ? I tell you she's a bloody masterpiece in everything ! "

" And leetle Yonnie, vot about 'im ? "

" Good lad, young Johnnie. Loves school. Thinks nothing of going without his breakfast if he thinks he's going to be late. Loves his books. Often comes round here after school—very useful he is too."

" And zee ozzers ? Elice——"

" She and Gracie are the bonny ones. They are pretty, though I say it."

Corti raised his hands to heaven. " Preetie—— 'Ow preetie !
Like enchels from Paradise. End zee leetle von—Daisy. Zis
is a dear child, no ? "

" That's another good-tempered one," John said. " Like
Annie—well, maybe not quite as good-tempered as Annie, but
she's a good little soul. And Rosie—she's clever. Bit like Tilly
—singing and all that. Now this new one's a boy. Nice little
fair-haired chap——" He sighed suddenly. " But they take
a bit of keeping ! Boots ! Clothes ! Always growing. Mind,
their mother makes every stitch they wear."

Corti wagged his head in sympathy. " Eight of dem, end you
end zee vife ! Ten peoples, end zee Ingleesh eat so very mooch
meat ! But listen, Yonnie ; vonce zee 'eart of me is touched
I care nossing. See, here iss eight sheeling, for zee lettle papies,
end 'ere too iss zee von sheeling end seexpence rrrise in zee
vages. Now, peck me qvickly up zee rrroses, for I veel kerry
zem to see Vest Ent, end ve veel makea mooch money, pronto.
All peoples veel veesh to buy see rrroses of Corti of Chiasso."

John packed the box of samples, saw his employer depart
with the parcel under his arm, then turned and went back to
the work-room. He picked up a rose and sniffed it with
appreciation, then laid it aside with sudden determination.

" Damn it, I made it ! " he thought. " I'll take one home to
show the missus ; why shouldn't I ? There's something wrong
somewhere, say what you like. I make them, and what do I get
out of it ? Eighteen-pence a week. I made a bob a week out of
the centres of the daisies. Corti used to live in Hackney, then
he moved to Bayswater—I'm still stuck down here. Two pound
ten, and when the missus is working that's another eighteen
bob. Three pounds eight, and now this extra—three nine and
six. Whew ! I only hope that my kids 'ul work at something
when they can make their own way, get paid on their merits.
They shall if I've anything to do with it ! "

He moved back to the table where three girls sat working.
A little dark-haired Jewess had just finished a bunch of forget-
me-nots. She was leaning back in her chair watching him
between half-closed lids. Her full lips were twisted into a
smile. John said : " What's the matter with you, young
Leah ? "

" I don't know dot anyt'ings der metter mit me, Mister
Wood."

" What's making you laugh ? "

" T'ings," she said. " My fadder und my brudders play a

game callet poker, it's an American game. It's all played on
vot dey call—pluffing ! I t'ink Mister Corti 'ud play it pretty
vell, ondly 'e'd want you fur a member of der game, not my
fadder nor brudder."

John shrugged his shoulders. " I don't know what you're
gassing about. Get on with your work and don't talk against
Mr. Corti here. He's my boss and a very good friend to me."

The girl stared at him impudently, her lips still smiling.

" If you're setisfied, Mr. Wood—thet's all rite."

" When I'm not," John said briskly, " I'll come and let you
know. Now, come on with those forget-me-nots, they're
wanted for to-night."

" I'm goin' ter vork overtime," she said calmly. " I'm going
ter make a special bunch for you, Mister Wood, fur you ter
wear in yer buttonhole when you're talking wi' Mister Corti.
Maybe they'd speak for you."

The girl who sat next to her laughed shrilly. " Ain't she a
card ! Not 'arf you ain't, Leah Rosenbaum. I never know
what she's leading orf abart ; d'you, Mister Wood ? "

" You all talk too much," he said. " Get on with your work,
you make my head ache."

III

He pushed open the door, scrubbed his feet on the mat and
glanced round the kitchen. Young Johnnie was seated at the
table devouring a piece of bread and jam, a mug of tea at his
elbow. He looked up as his father entered and said : " Hello,
Dad. I got a noo bruvver. He's in bed wiv Mum, upstairs."

Tilly, with a mop of fair hair like spun silk, eyes like corn-
flowers, did not move from where she stood beside the sofa
where Annie lay sound asleep covered with a white woollen
shawl. Her eyes danced, her mouth smiled, she looked the
embodiment of healthy, happy childhood. John watched her,
reflecting how quickly those eyes could darken, how firmly
that baby mouth could set, and how all the serenity could
vanish in a moment, leaving Tilly Wood a small fury while
her temper lasted.

" Where's Gracie and Alice ? " he asked.

" Gone round to grandma's."

" And Daisy and Rosie ? "

" Playin' up in Mum's room."

" An' you're playing at being a little mother, eh ? "

" Just playin' at it ! " she returned. " I don't want to be one really. Mothers have to work all the time, I'd rather be a daddy an' go out."

"But daddys have to work, luvy."

She shook her head with emphasis. "Not ve same way." Then : "Your tea's in the oven. Aunt Louisa put it there. I don't like people in ve house. Not too many—it makes me feel——" She threw out her hands as if something stifled her.

John thought : "That's like her mother. When she can't say what she wants, she acts it. She shows you just what she means. She's a caution, is Tilly."

Young Johnnie finished his bread and jam, drank the last drop of tea, then scrambled down from the table.

"I don't mind Aunt Louisa," he said. "I don't like Mrs. Watson. She's such a big fat woman."

"Don't you be rude," John admonished him. "She's very kind."

"He's not rude," Tilly said. "He just never thinks—that's all."

Johnnie stared at his sister, his expression one of slight surprise, but lacking the faintest hint of annoyance. Rather it seemed that he accepted what she said as a fact. As a matter of fact Johnnie thought quite a lot, but he thought of things which came out of books, not things such as whether Mrs. Watson's kindness atoned for her bulk.

John was busy at the oven, from which he took a really admirable shepherd's pie. He felt it incumbent upon him to say something. Tilly was getting a deal too uppish. She fairly rode rough-shod over her brothers and sisters. If she was like this at ten and a few months, what was she going to be like at thirteen, when she left school ?

"Johnnie might say that about you, maybe, Tilly," he said as he carried the pie dish back to the table and prepared to sit down and enjoy his meal.

It was young Johnnie who answered. "No, I don't say that," he protested. "She can't do sums, an' she don't attend when teacher tells her things—but she thinks a lot. She's clever'n me, so she is."

Tilly said nothing : she rose and straightened the shawl which covered the sleeping Annie, only John watching her face saw that she smiled. He continued to eat his meal, but in the depths of his heart something stirred, something which disturbed him, because it was beyond his comprehension. She was queer, this eldest daughter of his, masterful and self-assured. He knew what would please Johnnie : he could make Alice laugh, he could manage the rest of them, and feel that he made them enjoy themselves ; only Tilly remained different. You never quite knew where you were with her. One day if you shouted at her, she'd cheek you back ; another day if you were only teasing her she might fly into a flaming temper like some young fiend. She was unexpectedly disturbing. Vaguely he puzzled over her and continued to eat his shepherd's pie.

"Aren't you going up to see my mother ? " Her shrill, childish voice made him start. He turned round and stared at her. Why did she always say : " my " mother, and " my " brother ? Kid seemed to think the whole family belonged to her.

"I thought p'raps she'd be sleeping." He flushed as he said it and wondered why on earth he should give reasons to a child.

She shook her head so that the golden hair swung. " No, she isn't. Rosie an' Daisy's there—they talk all the time."

"Why aren't you up there ? "

"Me ? 'Cos I'm lookin' after my baby sister, an' you, an' Johnnie."

He pushed back his chair. " I'll go and have a look at them."

"Your hands is very dirty, Dad."

He felt like a schoolboy, knew that he flushed again, and so acknowledged the rebuke. " I was just goin' to wash them." He said that, but he knew he had forgotten that they were stained with the damp, coloured calico with which he had been making carnations. He did more than wash his hands ; he brushed his hair and set his tie straight, and all the time he knew that the little girl was watching him.

"Almost as if she was ready to shout at me to mind and get my nails clean, or part my hair straight ! She's a caution, that kid."

CHAPTER TWO

" ALL THE WORLD'S A STAGE "
SHAKESPEARE

Her Knowledge of London, like Mr. Weller's, extensive and peculiar
—Melancholy pleasures—Weeping to order—Harry, the waiter
—Mother gives lessons in diction and acting—The Fairy Bell
Minstrels—Alice and Tilly play drama—Tilly at home—and at
work—Entertains the work-girls and gets the sack—" I'm going
on the stage ! "

THREE days later Grandma Wood died, and John,
returning from Bethnal Green, found his wife sitting
up in bed, surrounded by the whole family, all
watching her with round, attentive eyes while she trimmed
their best hats with crape. The infant, Sidney, slept peacefully,
not yet capable of understanding the importance of a funeral
in the family.

Alice says : " I don't know whether we were sorry or not, but
I know that we all went to the funeral and cried bitterly." It
appears that this first funeral gave two of them at least a taste
for that melancholy form of entertainment. Tilly would take
Alice with her on the tram from Bishopsgate to Coborn Road,
a three-halfpenny tram fare. Alice, being still under age, did
not require a ticket and got the ride for nothing. They would
then walk hand in hand to the cemetery and spend hours
watching funerals. Mingling with the crowd, they would stand
quite still and behaving beautifully, until at a given point Tilly
would nudge Alice and whisper : " Now cry ! " And—and
this is the significant thing—cry they did, and real tears.
Then, hurrying away, they would join another procession,
" On a good day we saw as many as seven or eight funerals."

Now, what was that ability to weep " real tears " at a given
signal ? There was nothing essentially melancholy in their
childish make-up, they were far from being thoughtful and
introspective, their minds were not of the type which spends

hours in contemplating another world, and casting themselves for—as poor Walter King used to say—the part of " Baby Angels." They were rank little materialists, and yet they prided themselves upon being able to " cry to order." They were eight or nine when they were one day sent for stout— Tilly and Alice. The stout bought, Tilly discovered that she had twopence in hand, money handed over for the empties. There was a discussion as to what should be done with the unexpected money.

Alice said : " Sweets, eh ? "

Tilly replied : " Sweets—anyone can buy sweets ! Let's buy some gin ! " Accordingly they returned to the bar and demanded two-pennyworth of gin, which they carried outside, retired behind a corner and drank. Their united decision was that they liked it !

At home, money was easier. Both the father and mother were workers ; it was—and is still—his boast that he never lost a day's work except for funerals. He worked all day at his flowers, from seven in the morning until seven at night. When young Johnnie finished school he went down to the workshop and gave a hand. On Saturdays and Mondays, John Wood took himself off, after work hours, to the Falstaff Music-hall, or any other club or place of entertainment where he knew they would take him on for the evening as a waiter. Another of his " stand-bys " was the Green Gate Assembly Rooms. He was remarkably popular, and was—for some unknown reason—always called " Harry, the Waiter." His popularity grew to such an extent that there still remain old " play bills " on which his name appears as an additional attraction.

The result of this overtime—and it must have been something of an effort to a man who had already put in twelve hours to stand on his feet for another four or five—resulted in as much as two pounds a week extra money. That money was always handed over, as soon as he returned, to his wife.

John Wood realised—what the whole family was to realise later—that the strength, the driving ambition, and the force of the family belonged to his wife. Matilda Wood was the Chancellor of the Family Exchequer, and her budget always balanced.

By the time the youngest baby was born—Maudie—the family were sufficiently well off to afford a servant to look after her. The excitement over " new babies " had worn off a little ; the elder children had become *blasé* concerning them,

and paid less attention to the last arrival than they had done
to the previous babies. In addition, they had other things to
occupy their time.

Tilly was never particularly fond of school. She disliked
discipline and spent her time indulging in argument with her
teachers. Recalling the class of woman who was engaged in
those days to impart learning to the young hopefuls of England,
recalling Tilly's ever ready repartee, her quick replies, and her
ability to lose—and regain—her temper quicker than most
people, there seems little doubt that in these verbal duels the
teacher came off distinctly second best.

Then John returned home one evening to find his wife
listening to excited children, chattering one against the
other.

Young Johnnie had discovered that he could get a job after
school hours. " Evenings, Mum, and all day Saturdays. Mr.
Cawthorne, at the grocer's. I can, can't I, Mum. Four shillings
a week, he'll give me. You will let me, won't you? Four
shillings is a lot, isn't it? I'll give it to you every week, like
Dad does, eh, Mum? "

His mother, busy at her bead work, nodded and smiled.

" That's a clever boy. Come and give me a kiss for luck."

" It's what's called a arrand boy ! " Johnnie announced.

" That's right—only it's errand, not arrand."

Tilly stood listening, scuffing the hearth-rug with the toe of
her boot, scowling, her lips pouting. Johnnie, rubbing his
cheek against his mother's, said : " Look, Mum, what's wrong
with our Tilly? "

His mother glanced up and asked : " What's wrong, my
duck? "

Tilly continued to scowl. " Nothing—nothing's wrong."

" There is ! She's jealous of me, Mum. That's what it is ! "
Johnnie cried.

His sister stared at him, insolent and furious. " Jealous of
you ! I'd want something to do to be jealous of your being a
arrand—I mean—errand boy. I can do better'n Johnnie,
Mum. I can sing at a concert—Alice and me. For Doctor
Parker at the City Temple—that big place. We can, can't
we ?—you'd like us to, wouldn't you? "

Johnnie, somewhat subdued by the vision of this glory, said :
" Yes, but they won't get paid, will they? Not like me, eh ? "

" Not yet, we won't ! " Tilly flashed back at him. " But one
day we will. Once they see what we can do, then they'll pay

us. I'm going to be an actress. I can, Mum, can't I be?
Sing and dance. And Alice, and Daisy, and Rosie, and all of
us. Even young Sid and Maudie! Mum, when will you show
us how to say our pieces?"

For once, Matilda Wood's hands lay idle on her lap as she
watched her daughter, saw the rapid gestures, heard the quick
changes of tone.

"She carries you away with her," she thought. "If she can
do that with me—her mother—what will she do with
strangers?"

She picked up her work again and said quietly : "Of course
I'll show you. Learn the words and then come and say them
to me. Only mind, you've both got to do your best. I won't
have you make a poppy show of your father and me. We want
to be proud of you."

That night John listened to his daughters reciting their
"pieces." He was delighted, believing that there had never
been such clever children, never children with such clear young
voices, with such bright hair and such fine sturdy little bodies.
Marvels they were—both of them.

"Throw down the bottle and never drink again——" sang
Tilly.

John applauded and shouted : "Encore—encore.
Splendid!"

His wife glanced at him, smiling, shaking her head.

"What's wrong?" he demanded. "It's lovely. I never
heard anything like them ; they could go anywhere. Marvels
they are!"

"It's not lovely—yet," Matilda corrected. "It may be if
they'll both try a bit harder. Look, Tilly, when you say
'Throw down the bottle—' remember that your arm doesn't
stop short at the elbow. You've got another joint at your
shoulder—use it. Make that movement bigger, more important, as if you were really *throwing* something down, not just
chucking away a cherry-stone. Now, do it again."

Tilly frowned for a second, then her face cleared. "Yes,
that's right. I see, Mum—like this. That's better, isn't it?"

II

The City Temple may have been important, but the real
success was to come. Tilly was bitten with the stage, Alice
followed her sister. The result was a troupe known as the

" Fairy Bell Minstrels." (In those days there were " minstrels "
everywhere—black-faced, white-faced, all kinds. Tilly Wood's
Fairy Bells were little girls.) Their greatest success was at the
Nile Street Mission, a Catholic organization, devised to give
cheap and harmless amusement and entertainment, with a high
moral tone. Johnnie, caught in the vortex of theatrical excitement, was pressed into service and ordered to sell programmes.
He wore a wide paper collar, which cost a halfpenny, his hair
was brushed into a " quiff," and his face scrubbed with hot
water in which a piece of soda had been dissolved to give it the
necessary " shine " which Tilly regarded as the real proof of
cleanliness. Let me add here that this passion for cleanliness
is shared by the whole family. Even now you can hear this
sort of thing :
  " I don't like him much—never have done."
  " Oh, I don't know, he's not so bad, really."
  " Mean as the devil——"
  " Perhaps he hasn't got it to be generous with."
  " Cheeky brute, did you hear what he said the other day
to——"
  " That's because he's only half educated, poor chap."
  " I never think he's particularly straight, either. I heard——"
  " Well, if you believe all you hear, you'll eat all you see."
  " Anyway—he doesn't *wash* ! He's dirty ! "
  " Really ! The disgusting brute. That's finished him ! Not
wash ! "
  That being the attitude of the whole family now, there is no
reason to suppose that it was anything else in those Nile Street
days, and so Johnnie appeared with a " shining morning face "
and a paper collar. The programmes were " whatever you
like to give, but nothing under a penny." Johnnie says :
" They all sold for a penny."
  The names of the other performers have become lost in the
mists of time, but it is on record that the two star artistes were
Tilly and Alice. Alice, looking " just like a doll on a Christmas
tree," recited her famous piece about a kitten. Each gesture
had been taught to her by her mother.

> " I am a kitten, just six months old,
>   A reg-u-lar beauty I've often been told.
>   You may search through all the country round,
>   But a finer kitten will never be found.
>   And true it is as the poets sing,
>   Beauty is not the prin-ci-pal thing."

Then followed the more robust offering from Tilly. The famous " Throw down the bottle and never drink again." It dealt with the joys of temperance, the evils of drink ; it told of children who were run over, burnt to death, who died in hospital, begging their fathers with their last breath to " throw down the bottle." It told of wives beaten by drunken husbands, of ruined homes, and generally appears to have been a most thrilling and touching ballad.

But the real success of the evening was the sketch. In those days no programme was complete without a sketch—and here it was. Two characters—Alice and Tilly. Alice playing the disconsolate, but still strong-minded wife, and Tilly the dissolute but fundamentally admirable husband.

A clock strikes—off. Alice—and remember she was probably eight at the time—starts dramatically. She cries : " Ten o'clock, and he is not yet home. He will be drunk—I am— shewer. He said that if he ever drank again he would—eat his hat. Well—" long and dramatic pause, " I will *make* him eat his hat ! " With that she produced an old straw hat and proceeded to cut it into pieces which were placed in a saucepan.

Steps ! The drama increases ! Tilly Wood enters, wearing her father's coat with the sleeves ten inches too long and trousers billowing round her feet. She shouts, raucously : " Where's my supper ? " The supper is produced, placed before her, and—drunkenly—she begins to eat. Nearly choked by the sodden bits of straw hat. Tense moments, the action is thrilling and arresting. Chokes, coughs, splutters and coughing, turns almost black in the face. The doctor is sent for, backs are slapped and water is administered. Doctor exits, the husband, almost tripped up by his trousers, rendered almost incapable of movement by his long sleeves, weeps and swears never to drink again. The sketch concludes with the final chorus : " Throw down the bottle and never drink again."

Tilly Wood—Marie Lloyd—has scored her first success.

The Fairy Bell Minstrels were sought after, and again and again they " repeated their enormous and unprecedented success." Tilly led them, for Tilly always had to lead everything. It was a physical and mental impossibility for her to play second fiddle. She hated authority, and this may be the explanation why she was never seen at her best in pantomime and why, in spite of many offers, she always refused to play in revue. It is probable that the only producer who was able to work with her was her own mother.

Like most young and successful artistes, even if they are, as she was in those days, only amateurs, success went to her head a little. There was no doubt that she was a "handful." She loathed school, and I can believe that her teachers hailed with something approaching delight those days on which "Tilly Wood" stayed at home because she had a cold or a bilious attack.

She liked working in the house : she loved blackleading and scrubbing, and while she was occupied with violent physical work she sang. It seemed that in working off some of that superabundant vitality she was really happy. The amount of polishing, scrubbing or blackleading she did could be judged by the tempo of the song she sang. If, from an adjoining room, her mother heard the strains of some doleful ditty which told how :

" 'Er pore 'eart was breaking, 'er life it was o'er,"

she would knock on the wall, calling :

"Tilly, change that tune. Let's have something a bit livelier."

Once the tune changed to :

" Where did you get that hat, where did you get that tile ?
    Ain't it a nobby one, just the proper style,
    I should like to have one, just the same as that :
    Where did you get that tile, where did you get that hat ? "

the family knew that the polishing was going forward and being done with "wim and wigor."

She loved bathing the children and, on washing days, invariably the sight of a copper full of good "suddy" water, well impregnated with soda, would be too much for her. The children would be grabbed, undressed and bathed in the copper before Tilly could bear to empty it.

Alice, standing in the copper one evening, conscious that the fire underneath was not yet out, cried : "Oh, Tilly, my feet's burning ! "

Tilly's sympathetic response was : "Well, keep jumpin' about, and—shut up."

With them all, not only with Tilly, there existed a strong strain of the dramatic. It was in their blood, and probably they—in common with more children than one ever realizes—always saw themselves as characters in plays. As noble heroines, magnificent and strong characters, unknown geniuses and so on.

Daisy, on one occasion, managed to set fire to a bedroom curtain. Alice, recalling school stories of heroism and gallantry, dragged all the children out of bed and hurried them downstairs and into the street, first rushing to the window to scream : " Fire, fire, fire ! " The younger children safely in the street, Alice, still filled with the spirit of heroism, went back to the kitchen to fetch the cat and the canary, which she settled safely with her sisters on the pavement. Johnnie was washing in the back kitchen and, hearing the children crying, he emerged and asked what was wrong.

" It's all right," Alice replied proudly, " the house is on fire, but I've saved them all—the cat and the canary—and I've sent for the fire engine."

Johnnie picked up the basin of soapy water in which he had been washing, discovered that the whole fire was only a muslin curtain, emptied the basinful over it—and put it out. By this time the street is filled with people and fire engines, all yelling that : " Wood's house is burning down." Father and mother returned from shopping and had to pay ten shillings to each fire engine !

John Wood's comment was : " Why didn't you let the place burn, you little fool. It 'ud have been far cheaper in the long run."

Young Johnnie never minded work. If one job ended he found another. Tilly was more difficult. She hated school, she wanted to leave and seemed to have no idea as to what she wanted to do, except " go on the stage."

" Don't talk so silly ! " her mother said to her. " Go on the stage ! How are you going to *get* on the stage ? You can't just walk on and say : ' Here I am, pay me for singing to you.' "

There was no mistake about it, she was a handful ! Affectionate, generous to a fault, loving hard work, devoted to her little sisters and her brothers. There was always a tremendous love which existed between them all, a love which had been inculcated by their mother who " created that atmosphere." (The expression is Daisy's.) But washing floors, bathing the children, blackleading grates, even doing the day's wash, wasn't sufficient. Time lay heavy on Tilly's hands, and—the old saying about Satan taking an interest in those people who lack sufficient work began to prove to be correct. Tilly was for ever racing about the streets, always " after the boys," and her mother worried terribly. More than once she said to her

husband : " I tell you what, that kid wants a damned good
hiding ! "

John, watching the vivid face which could change so quickly,
recalling a dozen evidences of sudden unselfishness, of generosity, weighing them against those times when she had been
disobedient, wilful and impudent, had enough good sense to
reply :   " Yes. Knock one devil out of her and knock another
half-dozen in. No, she'll settle down all right."

Matilda deemed that it was time she took matters into her
own hands. She interviewed the manager of a small factory
where babies' boots were made. Those soft, almost shapeless
things which are worn by children still too young to actually
need leather between their feet and Mother Earth. He agreed
to take Tilly, and Tilly's mother returned home and announced
that : " Tilly'd got a job."

Tilly scowled, said that she knew she'd hate it, listened
to her mother recounting the joys of having a " real trade,"
of the pleasure of bringing home money every week and
the benefit of regular hours. Tilly's scowl lifted, the picture
seemed quite passably nice. On Monday she was sent off to
begin work.

She stayed there a week, returned home on Saturday at mid-
day and declared : " Well, I've finished with that place
anyway ! " and nothing could make her promise to return.

Again Matilda sallied out, again she arranged for Tilly to
embark on another trade, this time feather-curling. The
result at the end of a week was the same. Tilly returned,
stated that whatever might be her mission in life, it certainly
was not feather-curling.

For the last time—only she didn't know it—Mrs. Wood
attempted to find a niche for her daughter. She obtained a
promise for her to work in the factory from which the home-
work which Matilda did was issued.   Marie—Tilly as she still
was at this time—was to learn bead trimming. That evening
Tilly's mother sat up making her a black apron which cost
half a crown, the next day she bought her a pair of scissors
also price half a crown. Tilly was equipped.

She stayed four days.

The forewoman, a stern-faced, tight-lipped female, dis-
approved of young Tilly Wood from the first. There was
nothing like unspoken disapproval to spur Tilly on to fresh
demonstrations of independence ! The forewoman was called
away, some of the girls who knew something of the fair-haired

imp's capabilities, cried : " Bet you daren't give us a step-
dance on the table, Tilly, while she's out ! "

Tilly demanded: "Daren't? Who daren't? I'll dance for you."

In an instant she was up on the table, her feet twinkling—no
one ever danced more lightly than Tilly Wood—her hands
moving, her whole face alight with mischief and laughter.
Work was laid aside, the girls sat entranced, watching every
movement, noting each gesture, all the little nods, winks and
smiles which already were part of Tilly's performance.

" She can't 'arf dance, eh ? "

" Light as a feather, ain't she ? "

" See that ? That's saucy, not 'arf."

The door opened, the temperature of the workroom seemed
to drop perceptibly, the forewoman had returned.

" Tilly Wood ! Is this what happens when you're left alone
for a moment ? "

Tilly, shaking the tumbled fair hair out of her eyes, scrambled
down from the table. Her face was flushed, but she was in no
way abashed. She had been asked to dance, she had danced,
her audience had approved of her efforts to amuse them—
that was sufficient for her.

" I couldn't very well do it while you were in the room,
could I ? "

" I don't want impudence ! "

" That's not impudence, that's a straight question."

" You can go—I shan't keep you here."

" That 'ul suit me ! Can I go now ? "

" You *will* go now ! "

" Good morning, everyone."

Tilly Wood, leaving her black apron and her new scissors
behind her, swung out of the workroom and tore out into the
street, singing at the top of her voice.

She opened the door of her father's house, still singing. Her
mother was sitting as usual working. There was a glorious
smell of something cooking. Tilly sniffed with appreciation.

" Oh, Mum, hot-pot ! Grand ! "

Matilda looked up. " Tilly ! What are you doing here, this
time of the morning ? "

" Me ? Oh—I've been sacked, Mum."

" What for ? "

" Dancing on the table to make the girls laugh. It's all right,
Mum, don't worry. I'll get something else. I should never
have been any——"

Matilda sighed. "Where's your black apron and your scissors?" Her daughter threw back her head and laughed. "Lord! I've left them behind! No, it's no use, Mum; I won't go back for them. I can't bear that hard-faced old cat—I'd be rude to her or—something. I tell you what, I'll give you the half-crown for the apron and the half-crown for the scissors out of the first money I earn. Honest I will—only," and the laughter died, leaving her face determined, even a little sulky, "I won't go back for them, now!"

Her mother sighed again. That was Tilly all over. Act first, think afterwards! Impulsive, naughty, determined—and lovable. She held out her hand: "Come here, ducky."

Tilly took the outstretched hand and sidled up to her mother's side.

"Tilly, you can't go on like this. You must make up your mind to settle down to something. It's not as if Dad and I were rich. We can't afford to keep you. Now, come, think what you'd like to do and we'll try and find somewhere for you to work."

"That's all right, Mum," Tilly returned cheerfully. "I've got it all planned out here." She tapped her forehead with her finger. "I want to make money. I'm going to. Don't you worry."

"But what are you going to do?" her mother persisted.

"I'm going on the stage—and I shall call myself"—her voice became almost dreamy—"I shall call myself: Bella Delmare."

CHAPTER THREE

MATTHEW ARNOLD

The beginning—The old music-halls—"Pot-house to palace"—
Dressing-rooms—Audiences—Exit Tilly Wood ; enter Marie
Lloyd—Sings the songs of other artists—The Oxford and the
West End—Criticisms and comments—The family follows in
Marie's footsteps.

TILLY WOOD, when she threw down the gauntlet
and announced that she was " going on the stage,"
was about fourteen. When she said " the stage," she
meant, of course, "Variety," that particularly English
form of entertainment which at the moment is suffering
an eclipse. Other quite remarkably brilliant and lasting things
suffer these temporary black-outs and emerge to shine more
brilliantly than ever. I give it as my firm opinion—for what
that is worth—that a form of entertainment so typically English
will "rise again," we shall find that the eclipse is over, and we
shall enjoy it once more.

But to get back to young Tilly Wood and her story.

First, let me set the stage for you, and for those of you
who have no knowledge of music-hall history explain that
the places where Tilly worked in the early stages of her
career were nothing like the Palladium and the Coliseum of
to-day.

It was H. G. Hibbert who coined the phrase : "From
pot-house to palace," and a very apt phrase it was. The
music-halls passed through a time when they were indeed
nothing more than "pot-houses," where waiters bearing
drinks, pies and other delicacies passed among the audience
even while the acts were in progress. The hall was
frequently attached to a public-house—for example, the
Foresters, and the Grecian where Tilly made one of her first
appearances.

The Grecian was attached to the " Eagle," that famous tavern which is mentioned in the old song :

> " Up and down the City Road, in and out the Eagle,
> That's the way the money goes,
> Pop goes the weasel ! "

Years later General Booth took the Grecian and found to his horror and dismay that, by the terms of the tenancy, he had to actually run the Eagle Tavern as well. The place was famous, it was bound up in music-hall history. It was at the Grecian, where a young man named Henry Pettitt was trying his hand at writing drama—his real profession was that of a schoolmaster—that the Great Macdermott came and wanted a new song. Pettitt produced one : " If ever there was a damned scamp." Macdermott liked it, bought it, produced it at the London Pavilion and sang it for months, the song made such a hit.

Pettitt, returning to his school in the North of England, was " discovered." His headmaster hinted that his school did not wish for junior masters who wrote songs for comedians. Pettitt left and began to write melodramas. He wrote over a hundred—and died worth fifty thousand pounds.

However, to get back to the music-halls when Tilly Wood made her first appearance. They were not luxurious, they were noisy and they were still to earn the right to be considered " respectable places of entertainment." Women who visited them in company with their husbands and brothers usually wore a veil and kept looking round anxiously to make certain that no one recognized them.

The programme was announced by a chairman. This gentleman sat at a table, usually wearing a large single-stone diamond ring, another diamond of equal size and value in his shirt front, and smoked impressive-looking cigars bought for him by the " bloods " who were invited by him to sit at his table.

I still have the chairman's hammer from an old music-hall in Holborn. With this he would rap on the table, announcing : " At great expense Miss So-and-So has been engaged by the management. Miss So-and-So will now oblige."

I have heard that it was the chairman at Barnard's who made this announcement one evening, when his words were greeted by a voice which shouted : " Miss So-and-So ! She's a rotten singer and a . . . old . . . ! " The chairman listened, not a muscle of his face moved ; he replied with dignity :

" Nevertheless—the lady will now oblige."

At the Middlesex, when the Old Middlesex became the New Middlesex under J. L. Graydon, a notice was pasted up to the effect that no person would be admitted unless suitably attired. A sweep, wearing the clothes of his trade, slammed down his money at the pit door and was told by Mrs. Graydon to read the notice. He stared at it, then said : " I carn't read, missis." She read aloud the written word to him. His reply was : " Sootably attired—well, blimy, wot's wrong wiv me, eh ? "

She suggested that he might be improved by wearing a collar.

" Luv us, missus—a collar ! Whatcher tike me for—a ruddy dawg ? "

While I am writing of the Middlesex you will note this date : October 5th, 1885. " The celebrated Irish comic vocalist and clog-dancer—Dan Leno " made his first appearance there. Note too that in that same year Marie Lloyd made her first appearance in the West End of London, at the Oxford Music Hall.

If the music-halls were grimy, the dressing-rooms were considerably worse. What kind of rooms little Tilly Wood found at the Grecian are not difficult to imagine—at least not to anyone who knew the halls even twenty years later. If she had dreamt of splendid apartments, where glorious creatures " quaffed " (that's the proper word !) " bubbly " and were surrounded by magnificent bouquets, lavished upon them by the " swells " of the town, she must have been grievously disappointed.

The rooms were small, badly lit, lacking the smallest degree of comfort, possibly the only concession to the luxury-loving natures of the music-hall artiste was a strip of dirty, threadbare and more than tattered carpet. Running water was " not yet," and you can imagine Tilly—with the family passion for washing —doing what she could to wash in a tin basin half filled with exceedingly cold water.

The audience was drawn from a class which might have excellent critical taste, which might possess those " kind hearts " which are said to take precedence over coronets, but their methods of showing their dislike or appreciation were distinctly crude. After all, when the prices of seats—this is before the days of the Entertainment Tax—ran from tuppence, fourpence, and up to a shilling, when even these low prices might include half a pint of bitter, you could not expect a "dressy" audience.

The artiste who failed to please was given cat-calls and other noises well known to unpopular "pros" even to this day; they might find eggs, and fruit in an advanced state of decay, hurling on to the stage; pennies were less frequent and probably more acceptable.

I can remember a hall in the North of England, not more than thirty years ago, where a "chucker-out" stood at the gallery entrance and confiscated all bottles and "termaters." I have seen on one occasion, when someone managed to smuggle a bag of tomatoes into the hall, a "serio comic" stand with a beautiful white shirt-front plastered with this excellent fruit.

There was something to be said for this training—for the artiste. They knew that from "the word go" they must make good. There was no time for introductory stuff, no "saving yourself for the big number." You entered, began your song, patter, or whatever else you presented, and either you "hit 'em and held 'em" or they told you in no uncertain terms that your turn was not acceptable.

The result was that those artistes who learnt in this school knew their job. They wasted no time, they gave themselves no airs, they had the goods and they delivered them—and delivered them with punch and energy. Only a month or two ago, when I sat in the stalls in one of the big, handsome, modern music-halls, I had this fact brought home to me once again. The house was crowded, the bill was supposed to be an excellent one. I sat back and prepared to enjoy it, every minute of it. I yield to no one in my admiration for Variety. Orchestra—excellent; they played the Overture to Zampa, or a medley of Hermann Finck's; this was right and traditional. The first turn—well, first turns are seldom of a quality to set the Thames on fire, or they wouldn't be first turns. The rest, who followed, did their acts with a microphone on the stage and amplifiers which made their voices sound as if they came from somwhere near the big drum. I watched, I listened, and believe me, I could have wept. "O noble Variety, hast thou sunk so low!" Shades of Marie Loftus, Vesta Victoria, Dan Leno, R. G. Knowles—shades of Our Marie!

A big Cockney, known to me in the old days as a supporter of the Ring, leant forward and whispered to me, hoarsely: "Lumme, none of 'em carn't sell their stuff—they give it away, an' then it ain't worf taking, is it? Mikes—amplifiers—wot nex', I ast yer?"

Then three sisters—the three sisters of little Tilly Wood—Alice, Daisy and Rosie. I looked in vain for the "mikes," and the roar of the amplifiers was still. They didn't need either. They started right away with a bang, they sold their stuff, and it was worth buying. Why? Because they'd learnt how to "deliver the goods," they had studied their work and their audiences, and as my Cockney friend said : "Yer don't mind payin' ter 'ear this, do yer? Damn it, I can 'ear mikes an' radios and whatnots at 'ome for ten and a tanner a year."

I suspect that "Harry, the Waiter" obtained Tilly's first job for her at the Grecian. Her salary was fifteen shillings a week, and her mother made her clothes, as she continued to do for years.

Tilly was under fifteen, and it must have required some pluck to face an audience, hold them, and "deliver the goods" at that age, and with no experience. For, well received, well supported though the "Fairy Bells" may have been, their standard can scarcely have reached that of the Grecian.

I do not know how long she retained the name of "Bella Delmare"—not long, I fancy, for her rise to fame was almost instantaneous. I only know that she was interviewing some manager one morning when he asked her if that was her real name.

"Mine? No, my name's Tilly Wood."

"Well, I might as well tell you, Bella Delmare isn't any use as a name to you. Means nothing—can't you think of a name that will cut some ice?"

Tilly considered. Her face cleared. "I've got it! A real name—on all the hoardings—*Lloyd's Weekly Newspaper*—Lloyd—" again she paused, considered—"Marie Lloyd—that's me from now."

So Tilly Wood disappeared and Marie Lloyd was entered on the salary list at the Star Palace of Varieties, Bermondsey, at fifteen shillings a week, on August 17th, 1885. She was fourth turn, her time was 8.20, and she was given fifteen minutes. She was preceded by a young man called Tom Leamore, whose salary was the same as her own. Leamore, too, later earned big money.

I am indebted to "Billie" Boardman for these particulars, as later I shall be for other particulars of Marie's work and her character. Through the kindness of an old friend of hers I saw

a photograph of her taken at this time. His words were these :
" The prettiest thing you ever saw. Like a beautiful doll, only
when she laughed you realised that the doll had no end of
character."

She knew nothing of " song rights," and whenever she heard
a song which appealed to her she sang it. For a time no one
questioned this ; it was unlikely that anyone paid much
attention to a child of sixteen, singing down in the East End of
London. Probably if anyone except Marie Lloyd had sung
them, they would never have been noticed at all, but being
Marie, people began to hear of this astounding child, and agents,
managers, and others came down to hear her.

One irate lady whose chorus number Marie had been singing,
doing more with it than the original singer had ever accomplished, sent for " Miss Lloyd," and was astonished when,
instead of a woman a very young, very blue-eyed, golden-
haired child entered the room.

Questions were asked ; Marie answered them. Nothing ever
dismayed her, not even in those early days.

" Do you know that the song is mine ? "

Marie stared. " Yours ? How is it yours ? "

" Because I bought and paid for it."

" You did—who did you buy it from ? "

The lady, alternating between extreme irritation and amusement, gave Marie her first lesson on the question of songs and
the rights which are attached to them. Marie listened, frowning
with the effort to concentrate and retain what she was told ;
then she smiled.

" Lord ! I have a nerve, haven't I ? I promise you I didn't
know. What are you going to do about it ? "

" Injunct you, stop you from singing it."

" Me—stop me ? " Then, after a moment's pause : " But
I'm down to sing it to-night, this very evening. I've nothing
else ready."

She ceased to be a self-possessed little music-hall singer ;
she was just a dismayed, rather frightened child ; she was out of
her depth and she knew it.

" When can you get some songs of your own ? "

Marie drew her chair a little nearer, her manner was slightly
confidential. " Will you tell me where to go to get some new
songs ? Let me sing this until Saturday and I promise you when
I open on Monday, I'll have my own songs ready. Will you ?
—I'll be ever so grateful."

Of course, she got her own way. Marie could be irresistible, just as she could be thoughtless and astonishingly bad-tempered if the fit took her. But when she wanted to be charming, I doubt if many people could stand up to her.

From then she sang her own songs, and practically every one was a success, a winner. H. G. Hibbert says : " An audacious essay in mischievousness which never failed to do its work." This, referring to Marie's " The boy I love sits up in the gallery."

Money was increasing, offers were pouring in, and towards the end of 1885 she appeared at the Oxford Music Hall—now one of Messrs. Lyons' restaurants—in Oxford Street. By that time people were talking about her, her songs were quoted, they were reputed to be improper, she was said to be not fifteen, but thirty-five, mutton dressed as lamb ! They said she had been a pupil teacher, that she was a little East End dress-maker, that she was the daughter of a great retired actress who was determined that she should make her own way in the world.

She was appearing for George E. Belmont in his hall at Hackney when he first determined that she must go to the West End—that Mecca of all good artistes.

" Like to appear in the West End, Marie ? " he asked.

Marie returned : " That's where I'm going—and soon."

" I'm going to book you to appear at the Oxford."

She was then doing what was called a " song and dance act." This type of act had been first brought from America by the Hengler Brothers ; it was done—I am quoting now a very old and well-known performer, " Mr. E."—" to perfection by Messrs. Whetley and Traynor, and only petered out after twenty-five years through being overworked. Some artistes tried to freshen it up, but they failed. Marie Lloyd only worked it for a few months." He goes on to tell me that as he watched her on the stage of the Oxford—where he was engaged for a three months' engagement—he " realized the truth of what Mr. Charles Coburn had said once, during a very heated argu-ment with an artiste named Jockey Watson. This was at a time when the neat song and dance was much in vogue. Charles Coburn maintained that this form of singing and dancing was the descendant of the old pastoral poem, in which the artiste —carried away by his or her feelings—broke into an ecstatic dance. He added that those people who were making a freak turn of this dance were individuals who had no real knowledge of the derivation of the work. That it was inartistic to introduce the splits and other acrobatic feats into it, some of them even going so far as to add a few clog steps, until the original dance and the fundamental idea was obliterated."

Now let " Mr. E." go on with the story :

" I stood at the side to watch her, and she made a sensational success. The song which preceded her dance was :

> " ' I hear a voice, I see a face,
> I feel so full of happiness and grace,
> My only joy, my guiding star,
> I wonder, how I wonder where you are.'

Then she broke into a skirt-twirling dance, in one of those pleated dresses which were then so fashionable. I have never seen this dance done with such effect."

Without wishing to offend whoever was the author of that particular ballad, one cannot feel that he had given Marie words which were particularly epoch-making. For sheer banality they would be hard to beat.

There is a sort of tradition that all " pros " are kind-hearted, that jealousy is unknown among them—I fancy that is true enough among the " bill toppers "—after all, your Dan Leno's and Little Tich's can afford to be generous ; their place is secure. Though, heaven knows, poor Harry Relph (Tich) was always inclined to be jealous, right to the time when he was earning the salary of a Prime Minister. As he said to me : " I know I earn more than a Prime Minister, but after all, I do so much less harm, don't I ? " Still, that's by the way.

On the first matinée at the Oxford—this is still the story my friend " Mr. E." tells me—the music-hall profession had gathered in full force to watch this " new find " and to criticise her. The men stood round the bar, their wives and partners sat in the stalls, ready to pick holes. (Here is the truth of the old saying that the " dead head "—the man or woman who " goes in on their Wilkie," otherwise their card, is proverbially the most difficult to please, and nine times out of ten hasn't got a good word to say about the bill.)

It was Marie's first experience of a matinée : the hall was packed and as she sang and danced there probably reached her ears the clink of glasses and the low hum of conversation. Well, she'd got used to that at the Grecian, the Star Palace, and Collins'. The crowd round the bar watched her intently, making various remarks concerning the act she was doing.

" Self-taught, no master would have allowed her to do that——"

" Her voice won't last, she can't use it properly——"

" Candidly, what's the fuss about—the girl can't dance——"

" She certainly can't sing—— She'll be back at her bench in the factory before long."

The turn was over and the criticisms broke out again. Suddenly Lieutenant Albini stepped forward. Albini was a well-known conjurer, a handsome, well-educated man. People listened to Albini.

" Listen, you fellows," he said. " I've not only been watching that girl, I've been listening to you. I tell you now that you're poor judges. I'll admit that she's got a long way to go—that's evident. But she's going to cover that ' long way ' pretty quickly, mark my words."

Albini was right—only as " Mr. E." adds : " Marie got there even more quickly than Albini expected. In a few months she had some of her biggest hits, songs which made music-hall history."

Early the following year she went to Ireland, where her salary was ten pounds. She had a return date—for the winter of the same year—when her salary was one hundred pounds a week.

By that time she was singing : " When you wink the other eye." That was one of her earliest " naughty " songs. It was a silly sort of expression which meant nothing in particular. I suppose that " naughty " was as good as any other word— though when you come to read through her songs you find it difficult to say what was so naughty about them. Admittedly, Marie knew how to " tickle the fancy " of the public and she knew, too, the exact value of her winks and nods, her funny little movements and her variations of tempo.

I have heard people recount supposed lyrics of hers which no manager dared have allowed on a stage ; when I have asked where this particular bit of pure dirt might be heard I always got the same answer : " Well, I didn't actually hear it, but someone told me who said that it had been told to them——" Oh, yes, we know ; the same old story ! On a par with the story that Marie was a grandmother before she was, in reality, old enough to have a daughter. I heard practically all her songs—after these very early ones—for I didn't meet her until 1910, and I can say with truth that I never heard her sing " dirt." Vulgarity, certainly ; more than a hint of

impropriety, but never that unpleasant sort of song which was
so prevalent in the early days of the American invasion. I
have listened to beautifully gowned young women from the
other side of the Atlantic sing stuff which they " got over " by
sheer brassy impudence. I have heard Marie's comments on
them and their songs and, believe me, they were distinctly
terse and to the point. So here is Marie Lloyd in the early
days of 1886, taking her hundred pounds a week, spending it
and giving it away. The family moved. They moved to the
suburbs, kept a pony and trap, a governess was engaged to
teach the younger members of the family and Marie, discover-
ing that her sister Rosie had a gift for the piano, suggested that
this might well be encouraged.

Rosie asked why and was told : " So that you can play my
songs over for me when I'm learning them."

Rosie's comment is that she took every precaution never to
learn sufficiently well for that to be possible.

In addition, while Marie is soaring as a star, and remember
she is only about seventeen at this time, the rest of the family
have their own plans.

Again it is the women who make the headway on the stage.
Admittedly there were more of them, that Johnnie's talents did
not lie in the direction of the music-halls, though at a later date
he managed Marie's affairs very successfully. Sidney danced
well, but left the stage before he gained the top rungs of the
ladder. Sidney remains what he always was, a kindly, decent
fellow, with all the family charm ; and after having had various
" hard deals "—which he has taken like the man he is—is now
married and manages a big cinema. But the women—taking
after their mother—had and still have that boundless energy
and, what is more, real artistry at the back of it.

First Gracie and Alice joined up as a double turn, singing and
dancing. They appeared at the Foresters' Music Hall, in Cambridge Road, where their salary was thirty-five shillings a week.
They were no older than their sister had been when she
began her career, and Alice was to prove—in another
continent—just as successful. Then Gracie married and
Alice continued as a single turn. By this time Rosie had
decided that the stage was her vocation as well and, joining
forces with Bella Orchard—later to be Mrs. Dick Burge—
they appeared as The Sisters Lloyd. The time came when
Bella deserted the stage for matrimony, and Rosie continued
as a single turn.

" You keep the name," Marie said. " Call yourself Rosie
Lloyd, it's lucky ! "

And lastly Daisy followed the rest. She hesitated ; should
she, too, become one of the famous " family of Lloyd sisters " ?
Her mother intervened.

" There are plenty of Lloyds, you stick to your own name,
my girl, and stay what you are—Daisy Wood."

Her first appearance was when she deputized for Gracie who
was to have appeared with Alice at the Palace. Daisy was so
tiny, looked such a child, that the gallery kept calling at her :
" Go it, little 'un ; stick it, baby ! "

Even Annie went on once, when Marie put on a musical
sketch called : " The Bond Street Tea Walk." Marie pushed
her on, they tell me, as a waitress, and declared that she was
the cleverest of the lot of them. Even now they declare that
Annie " at parties is far the best."

And lastly, when Sid and Maudie were old enough, they
went on as a double turn. " Sid and Maudie " singing and
dancing.

That is " merely to introduce them "—all of them will be
dealt with in their proper place and their successes duly
recorded. They made their positions on their own merits,
there was nothing of that lamentable family feeling which makes
the " family star " wish to foist the rest of her brothers and sisters
on to the public. They got there by hard work and real
talent, not through Marie's efforts.

CHAPTER FOUR

"A BRIGHT, PARTICULAR STAR. . . ."
TROILUS AND CRESSIDA

Earning money to give away—Faith in other people's philanthropy
— Marriage — Difficulties — Mistaken kindness — The real
Bohemian—" Little Marie "—Sunday parties—" His name's
—Alec Hurley."

IT was good to be a star in those days. More, it was good
to be young and energetic and popular. Good to have
money to spend, to give away—and at this last Marie
Lloyd was always a " past-mistress." Mòney, literally, burnt
a hole in her pocket, and it was utterly impossible for her
to listen to " hard luck " stories and not wish to do something to
help. Looking back, remembering a dozen incidents, I feel that
she had a rooted horror of pain or unhappiness. It frightened
her, she never wanted to hear the whole miserable story, all she
wanted to do was—end it as quickly as possible, and offer
practical help.

I have heard this sort of thing, not once, but many times.
Marie entering the stage door, inside there is a shabby
little woman crying. Immediately the Queen of Comedy
would stop and ask in a voice which was not particularly
gentle—because I always felt that she hated to listen to stories
of bad times and lack of money. She could not bear it, they
upset her and worried her, so she adopted this rather hectoring
style :

" What's the matter with you ? That's a nice face to see
when you're just coming in to work—and coming in late too ! "

" Oh, Marie ! " That expression always meant the same :
" Thank Heaven, here's a little practical kindness coming " ;
and the story would be poured out. Bad times, illness, no
money coming in, the children at home crying because there
was no fire for them to sit by, and——

That was where Marie always put an end to it. " All right—

all right. I don't want to hear any more—here you are, now get off home to the kids."

I recall one Saturday—no, Friday—night at the Oxford when this sort of thing happened. Marie arrived with half her family behind her, for she hated to be alone, and always travelled with a crowd of friends and relations, and there was poor little K—— L——, who had been " almost a star," standing crying.

Marie stopped, listened, then broke in with : " Here, damn it, I can't wait. Here you are ! " Taking her purse she emptied the whole of its contents into the crying woman's hands.

" Oh, Marie, whatever can I do to thank you ? "

Marie considered, then burst into a laugh : " Do for me ? Buy me a drink, I haven't got a penny until they pay up from the front."

(Artists were—probably are still—paid on Friday nights.)

When she was eighteen she was working at the Oxford, and old James Kirk, in a burst of generosity, suggested that she ought to have a benefit, on a basis that she received a third of all the money taken. Marie was delighted and told everyone about the " decency " of James Kirk.

That was Marie all over : let anyone do anything or appear to do anything for her, she always accepted it on its face value and believed that they were philanthropists. Even at that early age she ought to have known that philanthropists " in the business " are rather more rare than the Dodo.

There was a bumper house, every seat sold, and Marie working harder than anyone to make the benefit a success, introducing new songs, wearing new clothes and generally carrying the weight of the whole show on her shoulders. Kirk " benefited " ; so in a lesser degree did Marie, who took the money she had earned and went to a bootmaker friend of her father's, placing an order with him for eighty pairs of boots, half for girls and half for boys, which were destined for the children at her old school.

Consider that at this time she was only eighteen, when it might have been likely that her head would have been filled with many other things, certainly not with thoughts of boots for poor little children down in Hoxton.

She had her own house by now, in Lewisham ; very handsome, perfectly kept and a source of great pride to her. She had been married a year—at seventeen. When she was eighteen her daughter was born. Her husband was Percy

Courtney and she met him first at the Foresters' Music Hall when she was only sixteen.

He followed no particular business, except that of a " racing punter " ; he has left no particular record—his claim to fame is that he was Marie Lloyd's first husband.

He was a " good talker " ; apparently he amused Marie, who loved to laugh and allow her interest to be held and she became infatuated with him. The marriage lasted about three years, and their only child was Marie Courtney, who was later to appear as " Little Marie," and later as " Marie Lloyd, Junior."

Here we are faced with one of the problems of Marie's character, her inability to choose men who were her equal in mentality, wit or refinement. That word—refinement—has nothing to do with her ability to indulge in vulgar stories, to sing songs which were improper : it was something essential in her, something which exists in the whole family, which prevents them ever appearing in dingy or soiled stage clothes, which makes their houses unbelievably clean and prevents any of them being lacking in that characteristic which may belong to dukes or dustmen—good taste.

Admittedly, Marie was headstrong and, admittedly, she was a law unto herself. She liked admiration, she loved popularity, and she enjoyed the consciousness that men admired her and wished to tell her so. Only, whatever may have been her faults, she never, as her sisters say, " cheated." Marie Lloyd stuck to her men, behaved with decency and honesty until something—snapped. When that happened, it was all over and done with : she " rang down the curtain " and made no bones about having done so. That accomplished she went her own way, and put her former obligations behind her.

In her own fashion, she was strict about such things. I have heard her use particularly hard words with reference to women who tried to get other women's husbands from them. Her belief was that so long as you were married—that was that ! Only when you severed that bond, you were at liberty to go your own way and allow the other person to go theirs.

Whatever may have been her faults, then or later; her first marriage did nothing to deter their development. Look at the position. Here is a girl of eighteen, young, particularly attractive, sought after and flattered. She is earning a tremendous salary, spending it, longing to get the best out of life as she saw life at that time. She marries a man many years her senior, of no settled occupation, on whom therefore no profession is making any demands. She is a star—and stars are expected to always be in form. Otherwise they soon cease to be stars. Remember, too, that Marie had, then as always, an almost fanatical sense of duty to her management and her public. She very rarely gave a show which was not up to standard. I have seen her in later years, when troubles and worries, physical distress, were all weighing heavily on her, when she sat in her dressing-room crying.

"Miss Lloyd—five minutes!" The call boy was at the door. She dried her tears, made some remark about "looking a sight," pulled herself together and was ready, at the side, to go on and earn her money as if she had not a care in the world.

It is not easy, particularly at eighteen, to forget troubles at home and go on the stage "merry and bright." At eighteen one's troubles are dreadful, weighty things, which seem to have come to stay for ever, which can black out the sunshine and leave the skies one dreary sheet of grey.

Among the letters which I have received from people who want to share in this book, who are proud and glad to have their names associated with Our Marie, there are some which are so pathetic that it would be almost indecent to publish them. There are others which my publishers would not allow me to publish, but I can tell you one fact, for fact it is, not one of those letters reflect anything but credit on Marie.

At this time she was scarcely more than a child; her baby, to whom she was devoted, was carried round each evening to the hall where she was working, so that Marie might give it that care which many mothers, who don't work "two houses a night," are often willing to deny their children. That in itself was no small thing when you remember how young Marie was, how hard she worked and how much she was earning. That last because—as I have said before—your star must be on the top of his or her form, and there is no consideration given to artistes because they are mothers, or because they prefer to feed their child and not leave it entirely to the charge of an expensive nurse.

Even in those days Marie had difficulties to face, and often those difficulties rose from her own character. Marie never stopped to think. If she met anyone, and liked them, then in five minutes they were old friends, and she laughed and talked with them as if she had known them for years. To have been restrained, to have been slightly aloof, to have behaved

as so many of the stars did—and with considerably less excuse—
was impossible for Marie.

I cannot say too often that Marie was always essentially
decent ; I doubt very much if she ever " flirted " as so many
women do ; she was only friendly, ready to exchange a volley
of words, anxious to laugh and have a " good time." She was
very attractive, she loved admiration, and—she got it.

Five minutes later she'd have forgotten the name of the man
who had talked to her. She would have asked : " Tell me,
what's the name of that bloke who was talking to me just now ?
Not half a bad fellow, made me laugh ! His story about the
old apple woman ! What a scream ! "

Only everyone didn't see it that way when she stood laughing
and talking, those very bright blue eyes dancing, her whole
trim little figure alive with vitality, her laugh ringing out at
every fresh witticism ; there were people who frowned and
scowled. Marie never brooked questioning, she was a law unto
herself, she had a quick tongue and an even quicker temper.

Marie's replies were always very much to the point, and when
she chose she could rap out some astonishingly keen remarks.
Well, it didn't always answer too well, and there were scenes and
recriminations and people lost their tempers rather badly.

Then little Marie Lloyd would protest and speak the sincere
truth when she asked : " Yes, but what have I done ? That's
what I don't understand. I didn't *do* anything."

That is something perilously near tragedy, particularly when
you remember that the nerves of a girl of eighteen, with a very
young baby, are not the most steady things in the world. To
have to go on the stage after a day of scenes and disturbances,
conscious that you are " topping the bill " and that you must
keep your audience amused, interested for twenty-five to thirty
minutes, demands, not only strong nerves, but considerable
physical strength.

That, believe me, is when friends often become a real danger.
When some kindly soul says : " You're not looking terribly
well to-night."

" I'm not feeling quite up to the mark—headache, feel
tired."

" You want something to pull you together." And it is said
in all kindness. " Have a little brandy-and-soda."

" Will that do me good, d'you think ? "

" My dear—put you right in no time."

And it does—the first time. Just a small brandy-and-soda.

Sends you on, feeling that you are on top of your troubles, that you can face the chilly stalls and a noisy gallery. There is nothing like it as a " pick-me-up." Only one drawback, that in a few days the small one becomes a large one, because the effect wears off, and that large one several large ones and—that's the beginning of the end.

Remember, when you think of this fact, that the performers who couldn't " stay the course " without something to steady them, who let stimulants master them, did not, and do not, drink because they want to drink for pleasure. They drink because they want to be able to " deliver the goods " to the audience who have paid for them in advance. It may result in something pathetic, lamentable, dreadful—but the original idea sprang from that loyalty to the public who are their masters.

Still, that's looking on the darker side, and for those first few years life must have held more than a few tolerably pleasant moments for Marie. She had her house and, then and later, she loved cleaning it. It was an axiom of hers : " Look after the corners and the middle will take care of itself." She cooked well, though never liked it as much as she did cleaning.

I believe that it always gave her a real thrill of satisfaction to swill a bucket of dirty water down a drain and exclaim as she did so : " More dirt on its way to the sea—good for the fishes, let's hope." She had a passionate love of order and her home. Nothing was too good. Admittedly she was extravagant. Her mother's motto had always been : " Never buy anything until you know that you can pay for it." Marie's motto was : " If you want it—get it, and see about paying for it afterwards."

Mrs. John Lawson tells me that one evening they went to the Shaftesbury to see a play called *The Du Barry*—at least, Cissie Lawson thinks that was the name ; she is as hazy over names and dates as most artistes. One of the scenes was a magnificent bedroom with a huge four-poster bed, covered with a magnificent red silk spread, edged with gold *galon* and finished off with an immense gold tassel at each corner.

Marie's comment when the curtain fell was : " I can tell you one thing, Cissie ; when I get home my bedspread goes into the attic. I'll have one like that to-morrow."

The next time they met, Marie greeted her with : " Got the bedspread. I told you that I should ! "

From this it would be quite erroneous to believe that her

house was in bad taste. Admittedly, many variety artistes had a marked lack of taste ; they had money and spent it wildly on furniture which was utterly unsuitable. I have seen a gilt piano, I have seen satin-covered chairs which made your eyes ache with their brilliance, and carved furniture which made you giddy with its convolutions and dreadful lack of outline. While I don't doubt that in those early days Marie's knowledge of furniture was not what it was later, I cannot believe that she was ever guilty of abominations such as these.

After her death I saw a notice in a shop window to this effect :
" All the goods in this window were bought at the sale of the late Miss Marie Lloyd's effects."

I went in and looked them over. A travelling clock, I recognized that ; it's ticking away in my bedroom now ; some little bits of silver, ash trays and so forth. They were right enough, but when I turned to find myself confronted by a huge piece of pottery in the shape of a nigger boy, smoking a cigarette and holding a china basket, I knew that it had never seen the inside of Marie's home—and said so.

Some time ago I read a book in which the author told how he entered the house of a friend, well versed in old furniture and its value. He noticed a particularly dreadful " occasional table " and protested ! His hostess replied : " It belonged to Marie Lloyd," implying both explanation and rebuke.

Well, well ! There is only one explanation, that the table had been given to Marie by some old friend, that it was probably the only thing they had to give to her, and that she accepted it as it was given, regarding it with eyes which saw beneath the actual ugliness and bad taste finding something which she rated very highly.

I know that her house was better run than most women's houses, and that never have I seen cupboards, drawers, and so forth in such a state of exquisite neatness.

My very old and kind friend, Mrs. Mary Reynolds, who lived next to me when I lived in a block of workmen's dwellings off Edgware Road, in the early days of the war, wrote to me her recollection of Marie Lloyd. Marie came to see me—Marie didn't care where you lived, and I remember that her car could scarcely get into the street. She climbed the stairs and came in. Immediately saying to me : " Now, where's this ' Ma ' who looks after you when you're ill ? Let's see her."

I called Mrs. Reynolds, and this is what she tells me she remembers.

"She said : ' Hello, so this is Ma, is it ? ' and gave me a *good* smile. I don't mean a lot of it, but it made you feel that she was good. She said to me : ' Have a little drop of what you fancy with Marie Lloyd ' and gave me two half-crowns. Then she looked round and said what a nice little place you'd got, and : ' Nice cupboards—let's see how you keep them.' Threw open the cupboard doors and laughed and said : ' Not too badly. Still, you'd better come up and let me give you a lesson ! ' I knew that she thought a lot of you because whenever she looked at you she smiled so nicely. She had on a lovely pair of blue ear-rings, and I thought they just matched her eyes. Another time I took a message up for you to her house in Golders Green. I was shown up into her bedroom—what a lovely room. She remembered me and told her maid to bring up a bottle of beer, then laughed and said : ' Or are you a tea-punisher like Micky ? ' I can't remember a great deal how she looked, but I'm certain that she looked grand—she always did."

I might explain here that a " tea-punisher " is a person who drinks tea to excess—I do. She never liked to see me drink much alcoholic drink. I don't know why—as a matter of fact she didn't care to see youngish people drinking intoxicants. Bransby Williams tells me of an occasion when he appeared at a benefit given at the Star Music-Hall for Alice and Gracie. Marie drove him down in her brougham. " She knew how to do things," Bransby says, " and did them well. It was a lovely two-horse affair, with a coachman and footman. On the way she talked of my show and said that I was the best mimic she had ever seen. She asked how old I was ? Did I drink—no ? " Oh, well, you're just as well without it, only one now and again won't hurt you. You're a nice quiet chap. Do you ever swear ? No ? Oh, well, I do—once now and again ; it relieves your feelings."

George Graves wrote to me in that neat handwriting of his, which always runs sideways across the page :

" Now for dear Marie Lloyd. I was dining with her in dear old Romanos ; during dinner, in her adorable, husky voice, she said : ' Listen, young cocky, you've made a big name—keep it, hold it. *Work for it*, and keep away from cards and racing and the Boys of the Village.' Wonderful advice, too. I did a mental *verb. sap.* on the spot."

There was a time when she fancied—not without foundation —that I drank too many whiskies and sodas. I had been very ill, and at that time life didn't seem to hold very much that mattered. I was in her dressing-room, and had a whisky and soda in my glass. Marie " cocked an eye " at me and said in that offensive tone which she could use on occasion, and did, when it suited her :

" How many's that, eh ? "

I said : " Two, and *I've* paid for them ! "

" Have you ?—nothing to what you *will* pay for them if you go on ! "

" Oh, come, two whiskies and soda—what's that ? "

She came over to me, took the glass out of my hand and threw the contents into the wash basin. I lost my temper and said several things which didn't reflect much to my credit. " I'm not going to be treated like a child ; I suppose other people can drink as much as they like," and so forth. All very stupid and not particularly clever. She screwed up her eyes until they were like blue slits in her face ; I thought for a minute I was going to be thrown out.

" Listen," she said, " you poor, silly little fool. You ought to thank God someone does treat you like a child ! Because other people make damned fools of themselves, is that any reason why you should ? "

For the minutes which followed I listened to someone talking who was not the Marie Lloyd the public knew. I listened to the kindest, most motherly soul in the world, talking real wisdom. It ended with Marie's own smile, breaking through all the seriousness like sunshine through a cloud, and : " There, that's all over. Kiss Marie ! "

I knew, and knew very well indeed, three women on the music-halls, each one of them a star, and each one reputed—by people who didn't know them—to have ruined their lives and their health through drinking too much. I have known other women who managed to achieve a reputation for " always keeping themselves right," who, whenever you went into their dressing-rooms you were pretty certain to find some young man or woman being encouraged to drink. It was regarded as a joke ; it was amusing to watch some raw young-ster slowly losing his head and his sense. A joke ! And yet the instigators of that joke retained their " spotless reputation."

The three women to whom I refer, who I am proud to remember as my friends, who—I think—liked me and felt kindly towards me, were every one of them weighed down with troubles which were not of their own seeking. They loved their work, they tried against frightful odds to do their duty to the public, and if sometimes life was too much for them, and they took a course which, in reality, hurt no one except themselves —well, they paid the penalty. I only know that in their houses, in their dressing-rooms, I never saw any young person, man or woman, encouraged to drink.

Remember when you hear people wag their heads—oh, those clever people who know nothing of the business, nothing of the artistes—and remind you that " Miss So-and-So was a brilliant artiste and killed herself with drink," that a star has only to be seen *once* in a public place, a restaurant, a night club, anywhere where people congregate, not quite themselves, just a little bit elated, noisy, excited—and their doom is sealed. They automatically become not only drinkers, but " hopeless drunkards."

I know that in these days Mel B. Spur is old-fashioned, out of date, sentimental, and all the rest of it, but some lines of his come back to me here :

> " O God, that men would see a little clearer,
> Or judge less harshly where they cannot see——"

I'm not trying to. tell you that music-hall artistes are white-washed, that they are angels ; nothing like it. I am only trying to show you that a reputation may be gained or lost upon very little solid foundation. When, as I have done, you have seen men and women fighting against ill health and worry, when you have known that they laughed and sang with something as near a broken heart as the human body can achieve, then it does make you understand some of the difficulties. It's not a question of " hating the sin, but loving the sinner," because both sins and sinners are words which very few of us are qualified to use. It's just weighing everything up in the balance and coming to the conclusion that it's not the people of this world who thank their God they are not as other men—who are justified.

To get back to Marie Lloyd, of nearly nineteen—Mrs. Percy Courtney, the mother of " Little Marie," living in her house at Lewisham, with a pony and trap of which she was inordinately proud.

Money was going up steadily, the music-halls were booming and work was plentiful. It was before the days of " twice nightly " and it was no uncommon thing to work more than one hall a night. This meant driving quickly from—let's say— the London Pavilion to the Empress, Brixton, and possibly after that on to the Grand, Clapham. Hard work, and no wonder the Sundays were looked forward to with pleasant expectation.

Marie kept open house, and her idea of open house was magnificent. Each Sunday you might have met a crowd of people at her house whose combined salaries would have reached many thousands of pounds. She was the best hostess in the world : what her guests wanted it was her pride to obtain for them. Little Dan Leno, with his thin, sensitive face and great melancholy dark eyes ; Lottie Collins, vivacious and lively ; Marie Kendal, who was making such a success everywhere ; the whole family of Woods, including father and mother ; R. G. Knowles, witty, and cultured ; Joe Elvin, Harry Randall, Gus Elen—the whole profession seemed drawn to Lewisham to attend Marie's Sunday parties. The table laid early in the morning—when you arrived, if you " felt like a snack," you went in and cut yourself whatever you fancied. Luncheon, a huge meal ; everyone laughing and talking, trying out new gags, recounting amusing things which had happened during the week, stories of provincial landladies and grumbles concerning the rooms in Wigan and Oldham. And later, tea, only one degree less elaborate than luncheon— because some of the crowd might not have arrived in time for luncheon and might want something more substantial than sandwiches and cake.

One Sunday, down the road, came the cry of a man selling winkles. Marie had a passion for winkles and made no bones about it either.

" I'll go—let me just get some jugs or basins——"

She ran off, returning, her arms full of receptacles in which to put the winkles. " Here—you—take these two." She handed them to a good-looking young fellow who had drifted in with half a dozen people from Brixton way. She looked at him, stared, then smiled.

" Hello—I didn't know that you were here ! "

" I came over after luncheon with Jimmy."

" I haven't seen you for ages—it's nice to see you again."

Dan Leno, watching them run down the road together, asked someone who stood near him : " Who is the young fellow with Marie ? "

" That—a coster comedian—got a lovely voice—his name's Alec Hurley."

CHAPTER FIVE

"A LITTLE SEASON OF LOVE AND LAUGHTER"

A. LINDSAY GORDON

Marie never "cheated"—A second venture—Another Marie—
—Good times—The coster and the millionaire—Saloon and
steerage—Offer for "the Lane"—Her love for Dan Leno
—Opinion of herself in pantomime.

ONE thing is certain as a result of that Sunday party at
Marie's : she couldn't forget the young man who sang
coster songs, and sang them so very well. He amused
her, he knew how to praise her work and pay her all the
deference due to a great artiste—for even at twenty she was
that—without smothering her with that fulsome flattery which
so many of her so-called admirers relied upon later.

Alec was a clever fellow, he knew how to " deliver the goods "
to the public, and the public loved him. He had met Marie
when they were both beginning, when she was playing the old
Foresters' at a weekly salary of something like eight pounds, and
he was probably drawing rather less. I remember, years ago,
reading a book by Hitchens called *Felix*. It was a melancholy
book and the only character which made the slightest appeal to
me was a " coster singing comedian." I always felt—though
probably I am wrong—that the author painted that character
with Alec Hurley as a " verbal " sitter.

He was popular, his work lay in the same profession as
Marie's own, which meant that they had mutual friends and
mutual interests. He met her in London when they were
working the same halls, he met her in the provinces when they
were on the same " tours," and they realized that each made a
tremendous appeal to the other.

Now remember what I said before : Marie never cheated ;
and she went on working as usual, living the same life—only
she knew that if she was to find happiness she would ultimately
find it with Alec Hurley.

When you are a star—in fact, if you are on any stage, music-hall or legitimate—you might as well live in a glass house, because the whole world can watch your life as it goes on. Marie, young, eminently successful, attractive and sought after, was watched by everyone. Everyone knew if she and Alec were working in the same hall that she had been seen standing at the side listening to his singing ; everyone knew that Alec had watched her, that he had laughed when she sang " When I wink the other eye " or some other number. In fact, everyone knew everything long before there was very much to know, perhaps long before little Marie Lloyd understood herself exactly what had happened.

Now all her life one of Marie's favourite sayings was :
" Once you've got the name you might as well have the game." And I imagine that it was due to these people who knew so little and assumed so much that she finally came to a decision. She was earning a big salary, she was the mistress of her own home, she had her own position, won on her own merits—and she was barely twenty-one. At twenty-one when the world is indeed your oyster, when nothing seems impossible except the prospect of continued unhappiness, you make up your mind pretty quickly. She knew that if, after three years of marriage, things were not particularly happy, they were not likely to improve. She mentally compared her husband with young Hurley and young Hurley got the better of the comparison. Marie admitted to herself that she was in love with him, and he —he had never made any bones about it. He once told me, years afterwards : " I loved her the first time I saw her. I loved her just as much the last time I saw her ; only I was a . . . fool, and didn't understand it."

There was trouble at home, scenes—as there always are when a man understands that he has lost something and lost it through his own fault—and Marie separated from her husband, Percy Courtney.

I have heard the most fantastic stories about Marie's love affairs, always retailed to me by two classes of people : (a) those who had never had any of their own ; and (b) those who had never known her and whom she would have automatically hated on sight.

Remember these fantastic stories followed Marie all her life. This is one of the penalties of being a star—and an attractive woman at the same time. Even when she died these fables continued. One man had the bad taste to write—at a time when Marie could no longer come round to his office and demand an explanation, at a time when her family, when her audiences, mourned for her—" She had five men in her life." I mentioned this to her sisters and they were as much at a loss as I was. Percy Courtney, Alec Hurley and her last husband, Mr. Dillon. The others—if there were others—are a matter of absolute speculation. Not even her sisters—who have never attempted to be anything but frank concerning Marie—could decide on the names of the other—*imaginary*—two.

Mind, if there had been fifty men, five hundred, it was not the business of anyone except Marie—but I repeat this because these imputations are so foreign to the nature of the woman we knew—she was essentially decent. To attempt to stick labels on various people, declaring them to have been " Marie's lovers," is pure rubbish. Again, this only bears out the truth of what I said : Your star lives in a house of glass. One supper, one conversation at the side of the stage, one visit to Epsom, and a certain class of person will immediately whisper, and whisper pretty loudly too : " My dear, I *know*. Why, they are always together. Everyone knows ! " And what " everyone knows " is generally a first-class lie !

It has always been my contention, and this belief is backed by her sisters and those who knew her best, that Marie was always essentially " decent." She was headstrong, as she used to sing in one of her most successful songs : " If you like a thing, you like it—that's enough." She hated discipline, loathed being dominated ; but she had no time for anyone who lived a life of sheer selfish immorality.

Because Marie was married three times many people seem to think that constituted a record, that no woman had ever been divorced, had ever sued for divorce except Marie Lloyd. One thing is certain : that she never had a train of lovers, to be encouraged, discarded, kept in luxury, or thrown out as her fancy dictated.

When John Drinkwater wrote *Mary Stuart* and said of that unhappy queen : " She was unlucky in her men," he might have written that line about Marie Lloyd ; in fact, I can read that play and find line after line which might be applied to Marie. Take this passage : " All the witnesses lied, and nearly all who have considered it (the case of Mary Stuart particularly in reference to her alleged indiscretions. N. J.) have been absorbed in confirming this word, refuting that. And at the centre of it, obscured by our arguments, is the one glowing

reality, a passionate woman." Here, again, " A woman
of great wit. And nothing better coming to her than——"
Well, Heaven knows, nothing very much came to Marie except
that which she attained by her own efforts and the lasting and
unwavering love of her brothers and sisters. As I turn the pages
I find other lines, all applicable to Our Marie. Here is one :
" Such as these do not love unworthily." That's true of her,
too. When she loved she loved with that generosity, the
selflessness which was typical of her in all things. " Her love
was magnificent." And last of all, Mary Stuart's own song, so
the play tells us, might in its extent, its meaning, have been
applied to Our Marie.

> " Not Riccio nor Darnley knew,
> Nor Bothwell how to find,
> This Mary's best magnificence
> Of the great lover's mind."

One more queer little twist which, when you have read this
book, you will find bears out what Mrs. Reynolds noticed when
Marie came to see me in a little flat off Edgware Road. Mary
says : " No—the blue pin, so ! Hugo Dubois, in an elaborate
treatise on the coiffure, says : ' Women of a fair complexion . . .
so much affect azure or lazuline for the hair, as it were corn-
flowers in sunny corn.' "

If you have sufficient interest read that first part of John
Drinkwater's *Mary Stuart*, and it will surprise you how many of
the lines applied to Marie Lloyd.

I doubt if it would ever have occurred to her to ask Percy
Courtney to " provide her with grounds for a divorce." I don't
believe that Marie would have thought it fair ; she called the
tune and she paid the piper ; she was divorced, but she had the
custody of the child, remember that. True, there were various
troubles over this child ; Courtney, like most fathers who have
not evinced any great affection for their children or the mother
of those children, had sudden, and it would seem, quite
inexplicable urges to recover it.

However, that came later ; the divorce went through and
Marie Lloyd began life again with Alec Hurley.

I imagine the years that followed were the happiest of her
life. Success was hers, money came easily, and she had a
husband who adored her. The only fly in the ointment was
when he or she had to go on tour without the other. They were
inclined to be sentimental, no doubt ; but sentimentality

isn't too bad a thing between two young people very much
in love.

Mrs. John Lawson says in a long letter about Marie :
". . . When I was shown in to the drawing-room she was
standing behind him (Alec) as he sat in a low chair with her
hands on his shoulders. Once, as we were talking, she laid her
cheek against his and I thought that I had never seen two people
look so completely happy, or seen such a handsome couple."

Both Marie and Alec were engaged by Harry Rickards to
appear in Australia, and after a good deal of persuasion—for
Marie hated to leave London—they departed for the Anti-
podes. I am deeply indebted to Mr. Fred Paley, of Melbourne,
for the following recollections of Marie's visit. Mr. Paley, a
brilliant comedian and a lover of the stage and music-hall, is at
present engaged on his own book of theatrical memories,
which makes his kindness in sending the following words to me
all the more marked.

He says :

" MARIE LLOYD IN AUSTRALIA

Marie Lloyd visited Australia in 1901. She and her husband,
Alec Hurley, who was famous for his coster impersonations,
were the ' star turns ' at the opening of Harry Rickards' New
Opera House, Melbourne, on May 18th of that year. If there is
any truth that folks turn in their graves I am sure the late
Rickards would become very restive in his if he knew that
Marie's engagement in Australia was credited to any other
manager for he never tired of relating to his friends the difficulty
he had in persuading her to leave her beloved London.

As a counterblast to the music-hall craze, The Cake Walk,
Alec Hurley's opening number was entitled The Lambeth
Walk, which had the chorus :

' You may talk abart your " Cake Walk,"
" The Lambeth Walk " it knocks 'em all to smithereens ;
It ain't no bloomin' fake walk,
It's the same as we do when we're out a sellin' greens.
For we don't want no banjoes, burnt cork or any fake :
The Lambeth Walk—there ain't no talk,
For that walk takes the cake.'

At the conclusion of the ditty a number of 'Arrys and 'Lizas—
pearlies, feathers and all—executed a kind of exaggerated walking dance and there was one 'Liza who got well-deserved and

separate applause ; but the audience was unaware it was
Marie Lloyd in an unrecognizable ' make-up.'

Later in the evening when she bounded on the stage—yes
' bounded ' is the word—Marie had a sustained and flattering
reception and it was quite a time before she could get on with
the work in hand. The success of this Queen of Vaudeville, or
Variety as it was then called, was electrical.

If a fading memory does not play tricks her opening numbers
were : ' The Barmaid—The idol of the Rose and Crown,'
' Folkestone for the Day,' ' Everything in the Garden's Lovely '
and ' Milly from Piccadilly.'

> ' Milly from Piccadilly—Milly was adored,
> A rare high stepper and they called her " extra pepper,"
> And they said 'Er 'Er whene'er she walked abroad :
> Milly she isn't silly (ahem) Milly (saucy wink) she's all right.'

Sydney and the other capital cities greeted her with no less
spontaneity and enthusiasm than did Melbourne.

Marie's sojourn in Australia was happy, but not exactly
devoid of anxiety and undue excitement. Hubby Alec became
the owner of a string of racehorses. One of his fillies he christened Marie Lloyd ; but, alas ! she was not nearly as fast as
some of her namesake's songs, and proved a bookmaker's joy
and a punter's lost hope !

Marie—she was seldom called Marie Lloyd or Mrs. Hurley,
but just Marie—scattered many seeds of kindness and charity in
Australia, and garnered a bounteous harvest of well-wishers and
sincere friends, who to this day (after the waning of so many
moons) revere her memory."

Even tours were fun sometimes. They might be working the
same town or even on the same bill. Leslie Reed, who was
working at Yarmouth with James Chappell's concert party,
tells of one week when Marie and Alec drove down there. It
seems from the rest of the story that they could not have been
working themselves that week—they went at once on their
arrival to see Chappell's show, where Leslie Reed was playing.
Later everyone was invited round to the hotel—supper, drinks,
as Leslie says : " Believe me, drinks galore."

" All of a sudden Alec looked round and said : ' Good Lord,
where's Marie ? ' There was a general hue and cry, and finally
we found Marie outside having a second supper of whelks off a
stall which stood there. Nothing would satisfy her, but everyone must taste them ; and she bought up the whole barrow-

load. The owner had never had such an order. He felt that his fortune was made."

The same week I heard this from the same source : Alec and Marie invited Reed to have luncheon with them. A cold collation. However, Marie demanded fish.

" Sorry, Madam, we have no fish on this morning."

" No fish—and you tell me this is Yarmouth, where the bloaters come from ! "

" We have no fresh fish, Madam. There are kippers, of course. They were on for breakfast."

Marie said : " What's this—luncheon ? Right—call it breakfast and serve some kippers—and serve them quickly. I don't care what you call the meal ! "

In all the towns the arrangements were the same. Marie never really cared for hotels ; she liked to keep open house, and the restrictions of an hotel bored her. The standing dishes were a huge cold ham, cold chickens, tongue, and so forth. The table was kept laid the whole day. Marie always took practically the whole house, and old pro's who were hard up would walk for miles if they heard the news that Marie was in a town anywhere near. Everyone got the same welcome !

" Come in—haven't seen you for years. Come a long way ? Slip into the dining-room and cut yourself something and get a drink." Some poor old down-at-heel comedian meant as much to Marie as a successful comedienne who topped bills and wore Paris clothes. Position never mattered to her. In that she never changed.

I remember once in her dressing-room an elderly man was shown in. Marie greeted him as " Uncle Someone "—I fancy the title was affectionate rather than real. He was a stout party, with a spotted muffler round his neck and an accent you could have cut with a knife.

She was entranced to have him there. He could have drunk champagne by the bucket, only he stated that he preferred " draught bitter." Adding in a hoarse whisper : " An', Mar-ee, not in a glarse, ducks. I 'ate 'em. I like mine outer a jug—thet possible ? "

Possible ! Anything was possible for Marie when she entertained. The jug, filled with draught bitter, was procured ; Uncle drank, noisily and with appreciation. Marie talked, her eyes dancing, ready to laugh at everything he said.

" Remember Mrs. Barker, Mar-ee ? "

" No, uncle, tell us about her——"

"You don't remember Mrs. Barker—well, you remember George Billings—— ? "

" No, uncle—what about him ? "

There were others she didn't remember, people I can only suppose who loomed large on uncle's horizon and had long been forgotten in Marie's life. He was in the middle of recounting some magnificent exploit in which George Billings and Mrs. Barker figured largely, when Marie's maid entered, announcing that Mr. J—— wished to see Miss Lloyd. Now Mr. J—— was a person of considerable importance ; he was more than rich, he was astonishingly wealthy.

Marie scowled. " Oh ! . . . Mr. J—— ! Look here, tell him that I can't give him more than a minute ; tell him that I've got my uncle 'here." And during the next few moments I watched the pleasing sight of a millionaire being " pushed out " so that Marie could listen to the stories of an elderly coster from the East End of London. When he left, having had the jug replenished several times, Marie was on the stage. He glanced round as if to make certain that no one could overhear him, then said to me : " That girl's workin' too 'ard. She'll do 'erself a injury, mark my words."

I expressed surprise, adding that I thought she was very fit.

He tapped his forehead with his finger. " It's 'ere, that's w'ere the trouble is. Mem'ry goin', due to too much 'ard work. Fancy 'er not rememberin' Mrs. Barker and George Billings ! "

But that was years later, and at the time when she and Alec first toured together she probably might have remembered those two celebrities.

In 1896 she had an offer for Africa, to work for Morris Hyman and Alexander. This was her first venture outside England, and she determined to take her small daughter with her. At the moment Percy Courtney was making one of his periodic fatherly demonstrations, and refused to allow the child to travel ! Refuse ! That was enough for Marie. If anything could have settled definitely whether Little Marie went or stayed, that would have done. Their passages were booked on S.S. *The Moor*, and Marie, never able to face being alone, took with her Mrs. Dick Burge and another woman friend. Johnnie Wood was ordered to take the child down to Southampton with Marie's maid, and smuggle her on board *The Moor*, which he did. Marie arrived later and faced the photographers— without her child.

Her success in Africa was astonishing. She had a tremendous

number of good songs, her dresses were magnificent, and every-one was prepared to make a fuss of her. She sang : " Wink the other eye," " Mr. Porter," " Whacky, whack, whack," " Keep off the grass," and " Twiggy Vous "—also " There they are, the two of them on their own "—set to a well-known waltz tune called " Narcissus," " Among my knick-knacks," and " Hello, hello, hello."

How many of us can remember that " Hello " song, with its imputation of " naughtiness " ?

" Do you take milk and sugar, dear," asks the lady break-fasting at the Metropole or some other famous hostelry, of the gentleman who is escorting her for the week-end, and then came Marie's stupendous bit of acting, of wonderful inflection, when she ejaculated :

" Hello, HELLO, HELLO ! "

Not only was Marie a success, but her little daughter, Marie Courtney, scored a hit on her own. The child, who was about eight years old, had a real talent for imitations—which she still possesses in a very marked degree—and gave imitations of the whole company, including her mother. The management, seeing these done in private at the hotel, offered Little Marie Courtney £150 a week to appear on the stage and do this turn. Her success was enormous ! " Following in mother's foot-steps " with a vengeance !

If South Africa took her to its heart, it was more than the first-class passengers did on the way home. They were what Marie used to call in after years : " Public school !—yes, Public *house !* " Poor limited souls, whose mentality was not attuned as hers was to welcome everyone, no matter from what walk of life they sprang. They lacked her generosity, and probably never knew what they were losing in missing the opportunity to get to know Marie Lloyd. For, remember, though Marie loved to laugh, there was a side to her nature which was deeper and more thoughtful ; in addition, she could give voice to some pretty sound axioms, phrases which were worth noting and remembering. However, they cold-shouldered Marie, and Marie, who was really childish about such things, though she pretended not to care and swanked a good deal and carried off everything with a tremendous show of bravado, was hurt and disappointed. She was twenty-six—and she wanted a good time ! The time came when concerts were arranged.

One of the first-class passengers approached Marie Lloyd.

He was effusive, he had heard so much about her ; it would be such a help if she would appear and so on, " for charity."

I can imagine Marie's face, a set smile, and her brows drawn down, what I always called " shutting out her face." I can hear her voice as she answered him, not a bit the " dear old husky voice " that George Graves speak of, but a queer, clipped, almost over-refined enunciation. " Oh, yes, I'll appear."

The night came—Marie had not appeared for a rehearsal and the committee were a little anxious. Again the gentleman came up to her and reminded her of her promise.

" But," Marie protested, her eyes very wide and innocent, " I have appeared—four times. Twice in the steerage and twice for the second-class. They were lovely to me."

" But—er—this concert is for the—er—first-class."

" Oh, I see " and the smile died and the wide open blue eyes narrowed, " but the first class don't recognize me—and I'm *damned* if I'll recognize them ! "

Before the African tour—and here I have to admit that I am bad at dates and can never get anything in a chronological order—Marie had fulfilled one of the ambitions of all right-minded Variety artistes. She had played in the pantomime at Drury Lane.

Augustus Harris, " Drurylanus," saw her at a charity dinner, where she sang " Wink the other eye," and on the principle of never losing a chance, he asked her if she would like to appear at Drury Lane. Marie said : " Yes—only I can't see the Syndicate Halls letting me work the Middlesex."

Referring to the " barring clause "—one of those elaborate and difficult clauses in Variety contracts, by which certain halls could " bar " an artist from appearing at other halls in the immediate vicinity.

Harris said with some coldness, for he was immensely proud of " the Lane," " Middlesex ! I mean Drury Lane Theatre—The Royal Theatre."

" Oh, where's that ? " Marie asked in all innocence.

He told her, adding : " But, my dear young lady, you must have seen the sentries on duty outside ! "

Her face cleared. " That ! Oh, I thought that was a barracks."

She appeared twice at the Lane—once in 1891 and again the year following. I don't think—judging from what she and others told me—that she was a great success. The first pantomime was *Humpty-Dumpty*, and the second *Bo Peep*. Now we have it on the authority of the late Julian Wylie—one of the greatest pantomime producers who ever lived—that no pantomime which has a "manufactured" story is ever a real success. He gave it as his opinion that the two best pantomimes were *Dick Whittington* and *Alladin*, with *Robinson Crusoe* as a runner-up.

In the caste of the first pantomime were Little Tich, Fanny Leslie, Marie, Mabel Love—doing speciality dancing—Herbert Campbell and Dan Leno. In the second, the caste varied very little—Ada Blanche, Marie, Marie Loftus—a great principal boy, badly miscast as a principal girl—Tich, Campbell and Leno.

Marie had always a great admiration and deep affection for Dan Leno. She had always a very warm corner in her heart for people who were simple. Dan was essentially that. She loved his work, as she loved the work of any great artiste, always believing them to be far more clever than she was herself. Marie was not a particularly modest person, but in the presence of "greatness" (and no one will deny that quality to Leno) she became almost shy.

They had met at a benefit given at the Star Music Hall for Gracie and Alice, who were appearing there in pantomime. Then later at a show at the Tivoli, when Dan was "off" for one evening, and young Bransby Williams deputized for him. On Dan's return Marie hurried to tell him how well this practically unknown young man had done.

Dan repeated this to Bransby, adding : " I'm glad that I was off, my boy—*glad*. Gave you your chance, eh ? "

" Gave him ! " Marie repeated. " He *took* it." Then to Bransby, quite a lad and blushing terribly at this praise from two great artistes, " Now stick to it, and show them what you can do—every time."

They all three met again at the Manager's Benefit at the Tivoli. An all-star sketch was produced. Leno, the Brothers Griffiths, James Fawn (the forerunner of Harry Lauder) Vesta Victoria, Gene Stratton, and Bransby. Bransby made up as a " Hal Ludlow " hero. (Let me remind those of you who have forgotten that excellent artist Ludlow, that he drew exquisite young women, and scarcely less beautiful young men.) Gene Stratton appeared as a " pretty girl "—without his usual " nigger " make-up. Marie, standing in the wings, watching the two " good lookers," shouted " Blimy, what's this ? A beauty show ! "

Leno loved to listen to her, to encourage her to say the most reckless things, and shout with laughter at her turns of phrase.

I once said to her—and here is a little proof of Marie's deep understanding—" Why do we all laugh at Leno ? More than at other people ? "

She looked at me, her face suddenly quite grave, and said : " Ever looked at his eyes ? They're the saddest eyes in the world. If we didn't all kill ourselves laughing at Dan, we'd cry our hearts out."

I have often wondered if, knowing him, loving him as she did, she sensed even that cloud which hung over him, and which was in time to dull his brightness and his wit.

She did not like the pantomime, and I imagine that the air of dignity and " pride of place " in the Lane disturbed her. She was so essentially a " one man " show, and though she always gave unstinted praise to other artistes, though she always recognized talent, she was never a team worker. Her art was spontaneous. I heard her sing some hundreds of songs ; I heard her sing the same song a dozen times, but she never sang *exactly* the same song. Pantomime cramped her, made her more than a little self-conscious, and dimmed her brilliance.

Marie's light didn't shine at its brightest at the historic Lane ; in fact, at one moment, she came perilously near " getting the sack." It was Dan Leno's fault. Dan who knew that she was capable of endowing the smallest, most ordinary incident with humour. Dan knew that whatever Marie did would be funny —it might be vulgar, but the humour always remained.

Little Red Riding Hood and Marie in the name-part. For some reason she was in her " grandmother's cottage," alone and going to bed. 'Gus Harris, thinking, no doubt, to " point a moral and adorn a tale " decided that " Little Red Riding Hood " should say her prayers. Obediently, Marie knelt by the bedside, hands clasped and her eyes closed ; the prayers over, she opened them and looked round. Dan, in the O.P. corner, whispered— a loud stage whisper :

" Marie, look under the bed ! "

That was enough for Marie, she looked under the bed ; there was, of course, nothing there ; and rising, Marie—who had to follow everything to its logical conclusion—paraded round the room looking for—well, for what she had expected to find under the bed.

The audience roared, Leno was delighted, Marie chuckled—

and Harris was furious. There were lectures, admonitions, and
Marie promised never to do it again.

Now that was Marie's sense of humour. Nothing mattered—
if it was " in the picture," and—mark that word " and "—if
she felt that in some incident was a smack of humour.

Years later, when she was singing "A little of what you
fancy," she used to carry a small handbag. Nothing magnificent, the sort of bag that some simple old body might have
carried with her full of used tram tickets and possibly a pawn
ticket or two. It was rubbed and looked well used. One night
at the Oxford the bag had been left in the dressing-room.
Marie was furious, it was not her first song, the audience were
waiting for her, her " *ad lib* " was playing. Someone offered
her their own bag, a splendid crocodile thing with plated
fittings, looking—as it was—expensive. Marie, in the middle
of one of those tempers which made her for the time being
like a small thunderstorm, glanced at it.

" You silly fool—look at me ! "   Pointing to her shabby
clothes and general make-up : " *Would* I have a bag like that ?
What's the matter with you, for God's sake ? "

And the curtain was kept down, the orchestra went on
playing until the real bag was found, and Marie went on,
content.

No, brilliant artiste though she was, pantomime was not in
her line ; and though she appeared once with considerable
success, at Peckham, she never really enjoyed it. Later she was
asked to play " Marie Lloyd, herself " in a Drury Lane drama
with—I think—Albert Chevalier, as " himself," playing opposite her. She refused, as she refused many other offers to
appear in revue. The only time she ever attempted anything
in the nature of a " part " was when she went on tour with a
musical play, by Chance Newton, called *The A.B.C. Shop Girl
or Flossie the Frivolous*. I believe this was founded on a musical
scene, which she devised, called " The Bond Street Tea Shop
Walk."

Edith Karno, herself a great " mime " artiste, used to say
that once, when Marie was appearing at the Lane, she went
round to her dressing-room and prepared to say all the right
things.

Marie turned from where she was removing grease paint
and said :

" Hello, Edie, what was I like ? "

" Very good, Marie—that dance you do is——"

" Yes, well, cut out the dance.   What about the rest ? "

" I thought that song about the——"

" Yes, yes ! " impatiently.   " Never mind about the songs and the dances and all the rest of it—what was *I* like ? "

Edith Karno, the kindest soul in the world, and one of Marie's most devoted friends, " hummed and hawed."

" Well, to tell you the truth, I don't think perhaps—what I mean is—you see, Marie, dear, one's so used to—you know, it's difficult to——"

Marie grinned her adorable " street-urchin " grin.   " That's all right.   I was b—— awful, eh ? That just what *I* think ! "

CHAPTER SIX

" MEANWHILE, WE'LL DRINK YOUR HEALTH—QUEEN ALICE ! "
THROUGH THE LOOKING GLASS

Where Alice obtained her training—The McNaughtons—Their practical jokes—American offers—" Queen Alice " among the stars—Pantomime—Sidney Wood—Alice and her " fans."

I HAVE said that the whole family were brilliant. There were at least four of them who were stars and, by the time the chronicle of Marie's life reaches this stage, those stars had twinkled for some time and with considerable success.

The first was Alice, who had been one of the Fairy Bells—the minstrels of whom Marie had styled herself manageress. Marie once referred to them thus (this is taken from a newspaper interview. The opening sentence doesn't sound like Marie's phrasing to me, somehow !) :

" The theatre of my maiden effort was the schoolroom of the Fairbank Church, New North Road, in the fashionable end of Hoxton—where the hooligans come from. We—friends and I—called ourselves the Fairy Bell Minstrels, which was a lie. We set teetotalism to music. I sang ' Throw down the bottle and never drink again.' There was a man in the audience with a bottle of whisky and his wife, and in response to my appeal he threw it at her and said he wouldn't touch another drop as long as he lived."

That was where Alice got her training, from Marie and her mother. She made her first public appearance, as I have said, with Gracie, at the Foresters', where they were on the salary sheet for thirty-five shillings a week. After a month they were working four different halls a night. The act was very successful, though I can get no very clear statement on what lines they worked. Then Gracie married George Hyams, the well-known jockey, and the partnership ended.

Alice continued to work a single turn, she was popular and made a considerable success, particularly as a principal boy.

She was working at the Pavilion, Whitechapel, playing "Sinbad" in the pantomime, when she married Tom McNaughton. They were married on January 16th, 1905.

Now Tom McNaughton was a particularly clever young comedian. He, with his brother Fred, had worked as a double turn ; first as knock-about comedians, then as comedy boxers and finally in the act which was to become famous, as cross-talk comedians.

Acts of this character were very popular in those days. There were many who were really clever ; others, who seem to have survived and do a good deal of broadcasting, who were merely boring. I listen—I listened only last night—to a pair of cross-talk comedians who were still " handing over " the same gags that turns like the McNaughtons, Dale and O'Malley, the Poluskis and others were discarding as too threadbare thirty years ago.

The cross-talk act consisted of two artists ; one the real comedian, the other the " feed." One was usually dressed in the style of a " dude," the other in some costume which without being too wildly improbable, was distinctly eccentric. They were really a development of the old "minstrel" troupes, where the comedy was all " questions and answers."

" Mr. Bones, did you see my bruvver this marnin' ? "

" No, I didn't see your bruvver this marnin' ? Warrerbout your bruvver this marnin'," and so on—*ad lib* and often *ad nauseam*. Only the feed in a " cross-talk " act was a much more brilliant fellow, and he and his comic partner divided the laughs pretty equally. The art of " feeding " is a delicate one and a really good feed can do as much to make or mar an act as his more active partner.

The McNaughtons—Tom and Fred—were working at Sea-bright's when they were noticed by that astute agent George Ware, who was, incidentally, Marie Lloyd's agent for many years and also wrote several of her best songs. He noticed these two young men, saw that they were good, and moved them very quickly to the West End.

Later, when Tom McNaughton went to America, and stayed there, the turn became " Gus and Fred " ; though I have an idea that the new importation was not a brother at all. I may be wrong there and am open to correction.

They were great practical jokers, and though many of their jokes do not lend themselves to print there is at least one which is amusing and repeatable. They were the originators of the

" taking the cruet " ; though many other people have claimed it and certainly hundreds have " worked it." (I have myself, in Darlington, I remember.)

The landlady produced the weekly bill. Landladies used to do this on a Sunday morning because you usually had an early train to catch and never sufficient time to look over the items, which, believe me, were many and varied, not to say strange.

" Cruet, half a crown."

The usual cruet, very large, with the silver-plate wearing off in patches, making it appear to be some kind of slightly anæmic gold. Eight bottles and a salt cellar. Salt usually well mixed with dust, the top of the pepper-pot inclined to hurl itself into the soup whenever you used it and smother you with pepper, the rest of the bottles distinctly " has beens." True, there might be about half a teaspoonful of vinegar in the bottle, but the rest were merely stained with the sauces of " yesteryear."

" Cruet, half a crown."

The McNaughtons paid the bill and then asked for a sheet of brown paper and some string. Enquiries as to what they wanted to pack. The reply was : " The cruet—half a crown's more than it's worth, but still—let's have the paper and get the thing packed up." That half-crown came off the bill a good deal more quickly than it went on !

There were, and are, landladies who are distinctly trials. Just as there are others who are splendid, kindly women, who make it their work to make the professionals who stay with them comfortable. The McNaughtons had a method of dealing with ladies who had made the week's stay a burden.

They went out and bought a quarter of some really pungent cheese, the more advanced in age the better. This was carried home and cut into small pieces which were deposited behind the pictures on the wall. (Landladies invariably have a large selection of most hideous pictures—photographic enlargements of deceased members of the family are the most popular.) Or a kipper was lightly tacked to the underside of the table and left there.

Given a few reasonably fine days, or one or two good fires if it was winter time, and the room began to be filled with a fine, full odour. The landlady might clean it—probably did—but you don't always remove the pictures from the walls, neither do you turn the table upside down when cleaning a room.

There are other stories—stories which are magnificent in their robust humour and which still " go the rounds " ; but they need the right atmosphere, and print is a cold medium. There is the story of the Superior Actor on Derby Day; there is a story of old Mrs. Brown, the dresser at the Cambridge; there are others—but they won't bear writing down.

So Tom McNaughton married Alice Lloyd in 1905; and they were very much in love, very happy, and it is pleasant to be able to put on record that they were, as Alice said only the other day: "Always very, very happy."

They had two children—Alice and Gracie. I can remember Gracie coming round to the side of the stage at the Pavilion to watch Marie work, the prettiest little thing you ever saw, with golden hair and blue eyes. "Just like a doll on a Christmas tree."

And if she is as clever as she is pretty—and there seems no reason to suppose that she is not—she ought to do well in the dress shop which she and her sister Alice have just opened at Epsom. Her sister, who is the elder of the two, is clever—I state that, as Bransby Williams used to say in the Penny Showman, "without fear of con-tra-dic-shun"—for she admitted to me not long ago that she liked my books and always read them as soon as they were published! Incidentally, her comments on my novels and a good many more struck me as quite remarkably to the point.

But let's get back to the days when these two children, who are devoted to their mother in the truly characteristic Lloyd fashion, were undreamed of.

Tom McNaughton, who had by this time transferred his business to Richard Warner—known to everyone as "Dick" Warner and one of the best and most successful agents who ever lived—was booked for America. He was to appear at the Colonial Theatre, New York. He refused to go unless his wife Alice Lloyd (who was also a client of Warner's) accompanied him. Accordingly, she was booked as a good, but not outstanding turn at a salary of 250 dollars a week.

They arrived in New York. The bills were "topped" at the Colonial by a celebrated American artiste; the McNaughtons "bottomed" and Alice Lloyd was, as the saying goes, among the "wines and spirits." Which, being interpreted, means that she was billed in small letters as having no particular claim to fame.

New York saw her, heard her, and raved about her. They could not have enough of her singing. Alice Lloyd "stopped the bill." The next day the bills were simply plastered over with huge slips bearing two words—"Alice Lloyd." Later she was called : "The Little Lady who made New York sit up and take notice."

She played out her six weeks' engagement, when her contract was renewed—only this time her salary was 1500 dollars a week. She remained in America, a star with a star's salary, for twenty-five years, only visiting England at intervals. At one time she played both the Colonial and the Orpheum at Brooklyn. Percy Williams, who owned the Orpheum, had Harry Lauder against him at the other Brooklyn theatre. He persuaded Alice Lloyd to work as a counter-attraction. That week she earned £300 at the Colonial, the same amount at the Orpheum, and another £300 making records for His Master's Voice.

In 1918 she came to England with her husband and played "Dandini" at the Lyceum in the Melville's pantomime of *Cinderella.* I fancy that Tom McNaughton played the "Baron," and poor George Bass "Choddles." The Prince—I forget who played it—was good, had an admirable voice ; but Alice Lloyd walked away with the honours. Admittedly, "Dandini" is a far better part than the Prince ; though nine times out of ten the Prince—who is playing a most thankless part—gets the money.

Old John Tiller of Manchester, the founder of the famous Tiller troupes, used to say that two pantomimes always ended in trouble, because there were virtually two "principal boys" in each—one was *Cinderella* with its Prince and "Dandini," the other was *The Forty Thieves* with the Captain of the Forty and "Ganem."

Alice's songs were many and varied, she was never so "provocative" as Marie, but her individual style has always been admirable.

"Who're you getting at ? " " Never introduce your bloke to your lady friend," " Stockings on the line," and " Splash me " have been her greatest winners. In the pantomime at the Lyceum she sang a number called : " Many happy returns of the day." I had never seen her working before and the sheer artistry with which she " worked " and sang that number still remains with me as a delightful memory.

She went to Australia in 1924, and later to Canada. It is worthy of note that, though Marie had not appeared in either Australia or Canada for twenty-two years, when Alice appeared the applause which she received was invariably punctuated with cries of : " Good Old Marie ! "

Poor Tom McNaughton died in November, 1923 ; and later,
after her Australian tour, Alice Lloyd joined forces with her
two sisters, Daisy and Rosie, and worked—with considerable
success—a three-handed turn.

She is very like—sometimes quite startlingly like—Marie ;
though she must always have possessed a greater claim to
strictly good looks. Her voice is better and always has been
than Marie's ever was. But there is the same quality, which
they all possess, in inspiring something which is almost a
personal affection between themselves and their audiences.
They are more than merely " Alice, Daisy, and Rosie." They
are definite personalities and occupy a real place in the hearts
of their audiences. That quality is something which the whole
family possess. They have an astounding capacity for meeting
you again after ten, fifteen, twenty years, and making you feel
that the gap of years is automatically bridged. You begin again
just where you left off ! I met Sidney the other day. In twenty
years I had only seen him once since the days when we all lived
at Brixton. In a moment I felt that it was only yesterday since
he came and offered to clean the long flight of steps which led
up to our house, because our servant had " walked out on us " ;
times were bad and it was doubtful, in my mind at least, if we
could afford a new one—and Sid didn't like to see me doing it.
He was inclined to be an " exquisite " in those days, but he
took off his really admirable coat and washed those steps in a
way that would have done credit to any housewife.

We agreed that I had gained weight and he had lost a good
deal of hair since those days—and the gulf was bridged. But
that's just what this astonishing family can do quite easily.

Sidney, the younger brother, married when he was quite
young, perhaps too young. The lady was beautiful and well
known, coming as she did from a theatrical family of considerable standing. The marriage was not a success and was
eventually dissolved. Sidney married again ; and when I saw
him this summer and met his wife they both seemed perfectly
happy, as he deserves to be.

Flo Hastings wrote telling me of an incident in which both
Alice and Marie played a part—probably Daisy and Rosie as
well. It is valuable in that it shows the spirit which existed in
those days in the music-halls. Mr. Graydon had a benefit at
Brighton, and Marie, " her three beautiful sisters, George
Robey and Eugene Stratton, with many others, went down to
appear." This is, of course, at a big benefit matinée. Everyone

had to rush back to London to work that night, and they all pushed into the train—without waiting to take off any make-up. The train slid into Victoria and everyone tumbled out of the carriage, when Marie saw a porter with long bushy whiskers of the type used by " hayseed " comedians in cheap films.

The sight was too much for Marie, and making everyone join hands, they danced round the unfortunate porter in their full stage make-up, singing, at Marie's instigation, " Here we go round the mulberry bush."

That sort of thing couldn't happen now. Scarcely anyone who is a " pro " wants to look like one or be thought one. They prefer to be taken for golfers, or ladies and gentlemen of leisure. It's only of recent years that this terrible " spewdo accent " has come in among the profession. A sort of bastard Oxford accent—Mile End Road, out of Swank, by Conçeit.

Bransby Williams, who has won sufficient success himself, and possesses a sufficiently generous heart to be able to spare a little praise and heartfelt admiration for other people, says :

" I have known the Lloyds for over thirty years—and loved them all. I toured America and Australia and New Zealand with Alice, and Africa with Rosie. I spent many wonderful hours with dear Daisy—but there was only one Marie."

To bear out my contention that there is a personal affection between these artistes and their public, here is an extract from a letter received by Alice only last year when she was playing in Leeds.

" You do not know me, but I have never missed an opportunity of going to see you, and I saw both performances on Tuesday, and only wish that the modern artistes had a suspicion of your talent and versatility. How many ' stockings are hanging on that dear old clothes line ' ? I loved your rendering of that song—alas, how many years ago."

Alice adds : " I answered his letter and said that there were still three pairs " (referring to herself and Daisy and Rosie), " but that the largest and best pair had gone—more's the pity."

And again : " To Mrs. McNaughton, Miss Alice Lloyd, with love from an unknown Yorkshire admirer whom you dared refer to during the first house as ' an old man.' (I suppose that, by chance, she pointed to him in her song ' I can't get up the stairs like I used to do,' in which the lines occur : ' Although I'm not a chicken, I'm pretty good at clicking, when I see a nice old man—like you.') With what joy I recall your singing ' One pair of stockings on the line ' at the Bradford

Empire, pre-war. Bless those days—and all the talented
Wood family."

It's sufficiently easy for young and attractive actresses to get
" fan letters " and chocolates and flowers, but when people take
the trouble to sit through two houses, when they go back to
" pre-war " days—then you are getting a real tribute.

I travelled up from Chichester this summer, where I had been
spending a week-end with Winnie Corin (who was once upon a
time Winnie Bransby Williams). It was Bank Holiday, and in
the same carriage was a little man who confided to me that he
was a " billing inspector."

He had been in " theatre business " ever since he was a boy,
and all his jokes had a distinctly " professional flavour."

He was talking of bad houses, empty seats, what is technically
called " having the Wood Family in front "—which means just
what it says, wood instead of flesh and blood—and money.

" I made a good riddle the other day," he said. " When
doesn't a manager mind having the Wood fam'ly in the 'ouse ?
I'll tell you the answer—when it's Alice, an' Daisy, an' Rosie !
'Cos theer naime's Wood, reely, did yer know that ? Yerse—
thet's the naime—Wood."

It is not easy to have made a fortune—and a big one at that—
as Alice Lloyd and her sisters have done, not easy to have been
starred and fêted, made much of, and travelled everywhere in
the greatest luxury, and then to start again under very different
conditions as Alice and Rosie Lloyd and Daisy Wood have done.
Not easy to keep up your vitality, your pride in your work,
to play halls up and down the country where the type of
entertainment has changed entirely, to stick to your own
style and make something very good out of it.

You can " get there " by your talent, your youth, your looks,
and all the admirable qualities which nature gives you before
forty, and begins to take away from you after your forty-first
birthday. But to make a " come back," to resist the temptation
of singing cheap syncopated numbers in a " modern " style,
and to still keep your position and your popularity, that takes
—it's a good old word—GUTS.

Someone wrote to me the other day : " I went round to see
the Lloyds after their turn in the first house. Do they never
have an empty dressing-room ? It was packed—Fred Barnes—
looking so thin, poor fellow, Gus Dale—who used to be ' Dale
and O'Malley,' a double turn whose names I never caught,
though Alice told me their first song was ' perfectly brilliant '—

Johnnie's daughter and her husband, and what appeared to me to be dozens of other people who drifted in and out perpetually."

And why? Well, the answer isn't difficult. Unless you happen to be that sort of fool who buys your popularity with unlimited drinks and cigarettes, which means that your visitors will all be " second raters," the man or woman who has a dressing-room which is always full of their fellow-artistes is someone who is really and deservedly popular.

CHAPTER SEVEN

"THERE ARE MORE STARS THAN A PAIR"
CHAUCER

The "Little Lady"—Marie's hints—A soldier's letter—The
Poluskis—The first Poluski and Sir Henry Irving—Bella Burge
and Rosie Lloyd—Marie's ambition—Where the mayor had
gone.

ROSIE and Daisy. Daisy, who at her mother's suggestion
stuck to the family name, as did Sid and Maudie
when they joined in a double turn. Daisy, as we
have seen, began by deputizing for Gracie when she was so
tiny that the audience shouted : " Go it, little 'un." Daisy has
always been rather a " little 'un," not in her measure of success,
but in her type of work. She adopted a boyish style, wore
knickerbockers and " coon clothes," and generally left the
" character " songs to her sisters.

That's a silly expression—" character songs," " character
actress," because all songs ought to be " character songs " and
all parts character parts. However, it is the accepted
expression, so let it go.

Daisy has always had the reputation for being a " little lady."
That is another expression which takes some explaining. It
sounds as if it might mean " stand-offish," and in one case,
where a well-known star was always referred to in those terms
—it did ! Daisy Wood wasn't that ; she has as much genial love
of her fellow men and women as the rest of her family ; she
loves a joke, likes to laugh—nothing prudish about her, only
just—well, she has always been—a " little lady." And if that
conveys nothing to you, go and see her, meet her if you can,
and you'll probably see what I mean.

She married " out of the business." Donald Munro was the
owner of the freehold of the Pavilion, Whitechapel, and the
Crown, Peckham (where Marie played pantomime and—I
think—so did both Daisy and Alice, but I am not certain of

94

that). He was also director of both these companies, and a man of considerable wealth. Later he became a successful stockbroker, which profession his son, Donald, now follows.

Daisy had two children, this boy Donald, and a daughter, Dorothy. She, too, has toured Africa, Australia and America with her mother. Daisy made a huge hit in Africa some years ago when she toured there accompanied by her daughter. But her greatest successes were in pantomime, where it is not too much to say that she attained a position in the very front ranks of " principal boys."

She was billed as " Daisy Wood, on her way to the top," or as " Lancashire's own principal boy." Her work was essentially neat, vivid, and done with that economy of movement which is one of the tests of a good artiste.

One of her first appearances in London was with the late Charles Godfrey, at the South London, where she played in *My Willie* at the age of thirteen. Later she sang a song—a winner—called : " Mary, my Mary," and later " Splash me," " Hurry up, there," " My Diamond Queen," " Saturday afternoon 'til Monday morning," and " Cupid."

Like all the others, her diction was admirable, for Marie liked to give an eye to their work because she regarded herself —and rightly—as the final court of appeal.

Alice used to sing a child's song, of the sympathetic variety, in which the line occurred : " There was a cry, a scream, a horse." Marie listened to it, then said to her after the show : " Gor' blimy, what the devil do you want to say it like that for—' acryascreamanorse ? ' Listen, a cry—stop !—a scream—stop a bit longer—a HORSE ! " Alice says that the song was a different thing altogether after that. Marie was always putting them right on little points of that kind, giving them " tips " as to business, and generally helping them to make their acts reach that standard which she regarded as necessary.

Make no mistake about this ; they all—every one of them —took their work seriously. They realized that they were " servants of the public," and it was part of their mentality to give good and faithful service.

Daisy was almost idolized in the North whenever she appeared in pantomime. The following letter will give some idea of what the " Lads in the Broad Acres " thought of her. In parenthesis, I'm not sure that it was entirely due to her work. That, admittedly, was excellent, but there was a youthful cleanliness about her, a bright humanity, which delighted the men who came to listen to her and remembered her.

This letter was written after she had appeared in pantomime for Wylie and Tate, when she drew £150 a week, and almost immediately afterwards she announced that she was going to leave the stage. She played her last week at the Hippodrome, Manchester, under the management of Sir Oswald Stoll, and her salary was £175. She retired when she was still on the "crest of the wave."

Here is the letter and, personally, I regarded it as one of the most touching I have ever read.

"DEAR MISS WOOD,

Ever since the news of your intended retirement was published I have been burdened with a desire to write to you, to tell you how I regret your passing from stage to retirement, but mainly to tell you that your art, your personality, will always be remembered by one who during the past fifteen years has followed your career with interest and admiration."

And at that juncture you put down the book and say : "Just an ordinary letter from a very ordinary young man." Wait ! Let me add the date of this letter : October, 1928.

To continue : "It is not, however, only my appreciation for your work which prompted my letter. It is something deeper, a sort of duty that I cannot shirk without giving offence to a grand old lad who, posted as ' missing ' in 1916, has never returned.

Does that startle you, Miss Wood ? Please let me explain. For several years prior to the outbreak of war my brother and I numbered ourselves amongst your followers. We both joined up at the outbreak of war and on our last leave before going to France we were happy to see and hear you in pantomime at the Manchester Palace.

You sang ' Michigan ' (' Down on the Farm ') and danced. Do you remember ? I don't think you ever danced better, and how Harry and I enjoyed it. We cheered and clapped. Oh, it was a splendid night.

Then we went to France and being in the same regiment saw each other occasionally and coined a sort of ' password.' ' If you get home first, book seats for Daisy Wood.'

June, 1916, we were resting at Montauban, Somme, aware that the British were to attack in a few days. The tension was horrible and along with some others I was lounging outside

our billet when my brother and his bombing squad passed on
their way to the line. He was cheery, as usual ; and, strangely
enough, the squad were whistling ' Michigan.' Harry saw me
and shouted :

' Cheer up, kid. You'll soon be home, and don't forget to
book seats for Daisy Wood ! '

That was the last time I saw him, for his words came true.
I was soon home ; but he, brave lad, lies—posted as missing
—in a grave outside Delville Wood.

Can you wonder that each time you appear in Manchester
I pay a pleasurable pilgrimage ? Can't you understand that
on the eve of your retirement I am forced to write and tell you
the part you—all unwittingly—have played in our lives.

For Harry and myself I pray that you may have long and
happy years to enjoy your retirement.

On Saturday I make my last pilgrimage to Harry's memory
of you.

With affection,

Yours sincerely ——"

And whoever can read that letter without being conscious
that their eyes smart and their throat aches—well, they lack
something that goes to make up that quality which we call
" humanity."

It gives me a sense of pleasure to remember that the writer of
that letter can—and probably has—seen her again, and if he
heard her sing that song : " An old pair of shoes," as I did a
few months ago, he won't notice much difference between the
Daisy Wood of 1928 and the Daisy Wood of 1935.

That letter bears out what I have contended, that these
Lloyds have the ability to become something more than names
on the weekly music-hall bills. They can, every one of them,
project their personality so that it reaches individual members
of their audience.

At one of the big pantomime suppers at The Midland,
Manchester, Marie was one of the party. She made the speech
of her life—and when Marie wanted to make a speech no one
could make a better. It was filled with allusions to the various
people who had appeared in the show. And every allusion
fitting, neat, and amusing.

" Dear Dorothy Ward," said Marie, " with her beautiful
voice, beautiful form and still more beautiful face ; my sister
Daisy, with her hop, skip and a jump "—at which everyone

laughed, for it somehow describes Daisy's work admirably. Marie looked round and smiled at them all, then said : " Well, I seem to have clicked with that remark ; but there's another b—— thing clicking, and that's my taxi ! Good night all ! "

There is another example of your good artiste who knows when to leave " on the crest of the wave." That was one of Marie's axioms : " Always leave them wanting a little bit more."

It was one of Marie's funny little foibles to resent anyone seeming to assume a greater sense of refinement or control than she herself felt at the moment. She was once driving with Daisy (" The Little Lady ") through some village when a child ran across the road and was almost knocked down by their car. Marie, white with fear, shouted : " You bad little b—— ! You want a damned good hiding ! "

Daisy leant out of the car, shook her finger at the child, saying : " Oh, you naughty, naughty little boy ! "

Marie turned on her a look of righteous indignation and demanded : " And what the hell's the matter with you, Mrs. Bloody Munro ? "

There, then, is the second of the three Lloyd sisters who made a fortune and, through no fault of their own, lost it. Daisy and Alice both, at one time, not only rich but very rich women, taking up their work once more and cheerfully " starting all over again."

Lastly Rosie, who married Will Poluski, a member of that famous family which included at least two very fine comedians. I imagined that the family were of Polish extraction.

Rosie Lloyd (Mrs. Will Poluski, junior) put me right on this point. She sent me the following note on the origin of the Poluski family. She says :

" Will Poluski was not a Jew, but when young he was apprenticed to a foreigner who ran a troupe of acrobats ; this accounted for his foreign accent which clung to him all his life. His mother was a Jewess and his father a Christian named Govett."

At all events I know that in the great days of the Lyceum, when Henry Irving was electrifying all London with his " Matthias " in the *Bells*, the old father of the Poluskis expressed a wish to see him. His sons booked stalls with a gangway seat for the old man who, wearing evening clothes and full of dignified excitement, took his place and prepared to enjoy the evening.

The play began, old Poluski gripped the arms of his stall in an agony of excitement, excitement which gradually changed to indignation when he realized the plot to murder the Jew. At last he could stand it no longer and, leaping to his feet, dashed down to the orchestra rails, shouting to Henry Irving.

" You devil ! That's what you are—a devil ! But the police shall know of it ! Mark my words—you shan't escape."

The late James Lindsey used to say that Henry Irving loved to tell that story, adding at its conclusion :

" But what a tribute—and unsolicited ! I was delighted ! "

One of the brothers, a son of this old gentleman who was carried away by the acting of Henry Irving, went into the circus business ; the other, Will, remained on the halls and worked with a partner as " The Poluskis." The son of this Will Poluski, who was always known as Will Poluski, Junior, married Rosie Lloyd.

He died in South Africa—which has been the last stage of so many actors' life journey—when on tour there with his wife. She refused to leave his body there and brought home his ashes, which were placed at Golders Green.

Rosie began her career as " duettist and dancer " with Bella Orchard, who was afterwards Bella Burge, and they appeared as The Sisters Lloyd. After Bella married Dick Burge—that fine sportsman who had such a varied career, who was implicated in the famous Goudie Bank Scandal and who refused to turn " Queen's Evidence " and clear himself at the expense of his friends. He served his sentence, came out of prison and set to work to live down his mistake, which he did with such success that, when he died, one of the first telegrams of condolence sent to his wife was from King George V.

After Bella's marriage Rosie worked alone. I fancy that of all the family she possessed the best voice and certainly the best stage presence. I heard her sing a ballad a few months ago and I thought that her voice had changed remarkably little since the days when she used to sing : " Charlie met his Poppy in the cornfield and said : ' What will the harvest be ? ' " Believe me, to sing a ballad well is something of an achievement. Anyone can bawl a good deal of sickly sentiment, set to a " spewdo " waltz tune, dressed in an evening dress, and with the " limes " arranged to " pick them up." Those singers were known as the " Thirty-bob a dozen " and usually occupied the same place on every bill—first turn—and if they had gone on after the " bioscope " not one would have missed them.

The sort of turn that was good for the bars ! A ballad " worked properly " and a ballad just sung are as different as chalk from cheese.

Rosie Lloyd can work a ballad, as she can work any other song she handles ; as she sang " Will you remember me," and another, the name of which has escaped me. Something to do with a " flip-flap "—a " swing-boat "—I don't remember.

What she ought to have been is a raconteur, for she can tell a story into which she can compress more real wit, more characterization, than anyone I ever heard. That should have been her line and she would have been unique at it.

She is taller, thinner than Marie ; dark-haired, as unlike as she well could be ; her voice is different and yet, at the end of their act, when they each sing an extract from one of Marie's songs, you can hear " bits of Marie " in all their voices. Alice —is almost Marie with : " My ole man said foller the van——", the good old " cock linnet." Daisy sings—and personally it's a song I can never listen to with equanimity—" One of the ruins." And Rosie, the chorus of one which was called, I think, " My Directoire gown."

" Do you think my dress is a little bit—eh ? "

" Not too much of it—— "

It's that half-articulated " eh " which is so like Marie that it seems impossible that it can be anyone else. Probably nothing more than a bit of good technique, but—it's Marie's own technique.

Gracie I have already mentioned. She married and left the stage very early ; Annie only " trod " the boards once, in Marie's sketch ; and Maudie, when she married " Whip " Wheatley, left the stage and for the past eleven years has lived —and lived very happily—in Egypt with her husband.

So there is " the Family " for you—and there is a photograph of them all taken together, which will prove how much alike in feature they were, and are. I had considerable difficulty in tracing that picture, for it was taken many years ago, and they tell me that it was only after hours that the photographer managed to take it at all. Marie, who looks as if butter wouldn't melt in her mouth, was in one of her " good moods " ; she was astonishingly funny, and each time they were all " posed," and the photographer retired under his black cloth, she uttered some remark which ruined the gravity of everyone and necessitated the whole thing being started all over again.

At the time at which we have arrived in this chronicle they

were almost all working. The house at Lewisham—you see, they always liked to be within hailing distance of each other, and when Marie went to Lewisham, the rest of the family moved there too. There never was a family so devoted, so full of wholehearted admiration for each other. One of them might be difficult, but that never prevented the same real unity existing among them all.

Rosie tells how once she lost her temper with Marie. Marie, the great star, the sought-after and—let's admit it—spoiled pet of London, was inclined, or so Rosie thought, to " throw her weight about."

Rosie's remark was : " You think you're everybody because you're Marie Lloyd ! "

She says that Marie's expression of utter, blank astonishment was wonderful. It had probably never actually occurred to her that she was either " coming the heavy " or that being Marie Lloyd might have been a certain excuse for doing so.

She stared, open-mouthed, then said, as if dismissing something too ridiculous for serious comment : " Don't be so damned silly ! "

The house at Lewisham was given up when the family began to scatter and Mrs. Wood—full of energy as ever—took the Prince's Tavern in Wardour Street. Many people believed that the place was Marie's because her photograph hung in the window. Many years afterwards when Marie was working one of the big provincial towns and getting her full measure of applause a certain artiste who always did pretty well herself and certainly need not have grudged Marie her success, sniffed audibly as Marie left the stage.

" When you see her work," she said to a companion, " you realize why she must have been a success—behind the bar of a public-house ! "

A remark just about as sensible as saying : " When you watch him eating bread and cheese you understand why he was such a good chimney-sweep." Marie had never been a barmaid in her life.

As always when a person is famous all kinds of strange, utterly untrue and intensely silly stories were told of Marie in those days. Not only of Marie, but of the whole family. I have heard Mrs. Wood, when she stood at the side of the stage watching Marie's turn, pointed out as " Marie's elder sister." I have heard these " knowing people " state that Daisy was Marie's daughter ; and not long ago George Wood, who was then a little boy billed as " Wee Georgie Wood," told me that many people believed him to be Marie's youngest brother.

I remember one time practically every week in the " Answers to Correspondents " column in the *Referee* you could find replies to some question regarding Marie's age, family or marriage. People were continually writing to ask what was the " real name of Marie Lloyd," when she was born, and how many sisters and brothers she had.

No statements were too fantastic when they concerned Marie Lloyd and some of them were so preposterous that you wondered how people could be such crass idiots as to even credit them for a moment. The only story you never heard was that Marie was the eldest daughter of John and Matilda Wood, that she had a large family of brothers and sisters, one daughter, and that she was devoted to them all.

I once told her some of these stories ; she laughed, then said :

" I must seem to have had a busy life, eh ? Wonderful constitution they must think I have ! "

Marie herself, at this time, had left Lewisham and was installed in a beautiful house in King Henry's Road, Hampstead, on the way to that last house of hers at Golders Green. Marie always boasted that she found Golders Green and made it popular.

She said once : " They tell me that Gerald du Maurier's going to be Mayor of Hampstead—well, they damned well ought to make me Mayoress of Golders Green. I should look all right in a chain and cocked hat."

On one occasion in the provinces she was attending a function at which the Mayor was much in evidence. He was a stout, fussy little man, and her comment was :

" Tell me—who exactly is the little fellow with the pear-drop tummy ? "

Again, at an even more important function where, not only was a very important Mayor to be present, but councillors and aldermen were there in full force, Marie was invited, a guest of honour. The Mayor was detained and Marie was growing restive ; she might not be particularly punctual herself, but she disliked being kept waiting.

An alderman tried to explain : " I cannot think what has become of the Mayor. He ought to be here any moment."

Marie said : " Oh, damn the Mayor—gone off to run in the Oaks, I suppose ! "

The house in King Henry's Road was to be the scene of one of music-hall history's greatest events. It was from there that the famous music-hall strike originated. An event of sufficient importance to demand another chapter.

CHAPTER EIGHT

" IF SO IT SEEMS GOOD TO THE REPUBLIC, DO IT AND STRIKE "

TACITUS

The music-hall strike—How it happened—Marie on " picket
duty "—Belle Elmore—Crippen—The King's birthday—Berlin
—Paris—Marie and the old pro—" 'E'll allus be Seymour
'Icks ter me ! "

FEW artistes are good business men or women, and the
artistes of the Variety stage were no exception to the
rule.

They accepted their contracts, usually long and complicated
documents, from the hands of managers or agents, and wrote
their names at the bottom of the sheet, only asking what
salary they were to expect at Manchester, Leeds Glasgow or
wherever the contract stated.

They knew that there were various matters in connection with
these contracts which needed attention, they knew that certain
abuses were creeping in, and yet for years they continued, more
or less happily, to " sign along the dotted line."

In the latter days of 1906 matters had reached a head and
the grumbles and dissatisfaction took concrete shape. The
trouble was over the matinées.

The usual contract—for there was no real standard music-
hall contract in those days—was for so many evening performances and one matinée. Mark what really happened.

The agent accepted the contract for the artiste, for the man
who did the work and paid the money—to the agent. Agents
liked to keep on the right side of managers for obvious reasons.
When, therefore, Mr. Bazooker announced to the agent that at
his theatre he found that he could run three matinées a week
and make money on every one of them, the obliging agent
merely added an " s " to the end of the word " matinée,"
and when the artiste came to sign, said as usual :

" Sign there, old boy—nice date for you, eh ? "

The careless " pro " signed, and found himself committed to work three matinées in addition to the usual evening shows and the one matinée.

This went on until in many cases artistes were playing as many as four matinées a week, in fact, giving ten performances a week for the price of seven. Very good business for the manager, not too bad for the agent, but distinctly not so good for the wretched performer—the man who made the money for the other two.

It was legal enough. If a contract specifies " evening performances and matinées," the manager was legally entitled to have a matinée every day if he wished to do so.

Now there are two classes of funny people in " the business." One is the performer who employs—just notice that word—an agent, and the other is the agent himself. It would seem probable that if you pay a man to work for you, he is your servant, and treats you with respect and civility. Not in this case. I have no doubt that there do exist agents who are polite and respectful to their clients, but I know that there are dozens who treat them and talk to them as I should hate to speak to my dog. I have been in an agent's office, an office handsomely furnished with the latest type of desk, a heavy pile carpet, silver inkstand (a Christmas present from a client), a huge silver cigarette box (a present, last New Year's Day, from another client), where the agent has produced a heavy gold cigarette case (another present), flashed splendid cuff links (they, too, a present from a client), looked at the time on a very fine " thin " gold watch which hung at the end of a platinum and gold watch chain (more presents), and talked to a client like this :

" Whatcher want ? I'm busy—cantyer see that ? Brixton—well, what about Brixton ? Didn't yer sign the contract—very well, yer can read, can't yer ? And I'll tell yer another thing—I saw yer last week at Finsbury Park—HORRIBLE; my boy. Horrible ! Can't yer get some new stuff ? What ? That song of yours about—I've forgotten what it *was* about and I don't wanter remember, neither ! It's got whiskers on it, whiskers ! Yer've not been so well—I can't help that, can I ? Doctor says—I don't want to hear what the doctor says. If you can't do the work—lay off ! No, that's all—I've nothing else ter say."

And that from Mr. A——, the man who is being paid—to Mr. B——, the man who is employing him !

Now, tell me that music-hall artistes are not funny people to have ever stood that kind of stuff. To have stood in awe of some half-educated, Ghetto Jew, who generally denied his origin. That was why he was usually such an unpleasant customer, for the Jew who is ashamed of his race—well, it's about the only thing he is ever capable of being ashamed of!

So the matinée racket went on. Managers rubbed their hands and the agents rubbed theirs, because they were both making money, and the man who earned it for them paid for working. The stars, the big people like Marie Lloyd, Harry Randall, Bransby Williams, Marie Loftus, Tich, Cinquevalli, and Harry Tate, were not materially affected. They were the people who didn't really need an agent at all, because they didn't have to " find work " ; on the contrary, " work found them." It was the rank and file, the little people, who were fighting their way up the ladder, painfully, rung by rung, on whom this pressed hardest. They dared not offend their powerful agent, they needed work badly and so they took whatever offered. Two, three, four matinées for nothing— they worked them and kept their mouths shut. The stars, when they found that they were expected to work more than one matinée, simply refused, and demanded " No pay, no work."

Marie Lloyd coined a phrase : " If they play me—they pay me ! When the managers take it, I want it ! "

Even a manger, even an agent, dared not offend these powerful stars who could make or mar a bill by appearing or not appearing. This explanation is necessary to show that the " Big People " had nothing to gain through protesting against this " matinée habit " ; they were immune, and the fact that they did protest only goes to prove what a fine, selfless, splendid-spirited, human lot of people they were. They prepared to fight for the under-dog, and were prepared to lose several hundreds of pounds each in order to do so.

So meetings were held, deputations were sent to managers and agents and other " powers that were," demanding that this grievance should be put right. The reply was " in the negative," the managers cast themselves for the role of " Shylock " and the Variety artistes for that of " Antonio."

Then the heavy guns spoke, and those all-powerful stars announced that they were on the side of the " small people," and that unless this abuse was ended they were prepared to call a music-hall strike. They added that they did not stand alone, the musicians—on whom this matinée business pressed heavily—had declared that they too would join the ranks of the strikers.

The threat was regarded as a huge joke. Managers and agents roared with laughter, daily papers got quite humorous over the idea of music-hall artistes going on strike.

A meeting was held—because again the managers treated the artistes with contempt—at Marie Lloyd's house in King Henry's Road. Plans were discussed, ways and means arranged. An ultimatum was issued, causing more laughter in managerial circles.

But on the evening of January 1st, 1907, the London Pavilion, the Holborn Empire, the Oxford, and other London halls found that they were without an orchestra and without artistes. The strike had begun. There was a good deal of frantic telephoning ; turns who had been treated with scorn, talked to like dogs and generally bullied, found themselves suddenly hailed as saviours of West End entertainments. Elderly artistes who had long ago retired from " active service," were persuaded to return and " give us that song of yours, old boy, that they liked so in '62."

One young woman—an agent's wife, if I am not mistaken—tore round from hall to hall, playing as many as eight halls nightly. But the majority stood firm and the strike went on for many weeks. The big stars, not content with losing their own salaries of anything from £90 to £150 a week as long as the strike lasted, gave lavishly and with open-handed generosity to the " strike funds," and the small artiste suffered very little.

And the public ! They supported the strike. They delighted in visiting the stage doors where the pickets stood. And what pickets, what sallies of wit, what amusing remarks, what real comedy could be heard from these " strikers " ! Imagine Charles Austin and Joe Elvin together outside the Holborn stage door—on picket duty. Think what a crowd must have gathered at the stage door of the Euston, where Marie Lloyd, the late Gladys ffolliott, and Millie Payne were begging the British Public to " support the strike."

That was when poor Belle Elmore—with her nasty little husband, Dr. Crippen, in attendance as " music carrier "—hurried to appear. She had possibly once topped the bill in some small provincial hall, but—kindly woman though she was

—Belle Elmore was no great artiste, and she was weak enough to let herself be persuaded to be a " blackleg." As she entered the stage door, Millie Payne called :

" Belle—don't be a blackleg, support your own people. Stay out and help the strike."

Marie cried : " Go on, let her work. She'll do the strike a lot more good by going on and singing than by stopping out ! You go and work, Belle ! "

The word had only to go round that Marie was picketing, and the hall emptied, all the audience came out to hear what " Our Marie " had to say—and I don't blame them, either.

Managers realized that they were playing a losing game, they had not understood that the artistes had such backbone, that they would stand shoulder to shoulder. Matters were discussed, men and women sat round long tables and talked, new agreements were drawn up, and the " matinée bogey " was laid. As Harry Randall says : " We all went back to work— Pro bono—' Pro.' "

Dr. Hawley Hervey Crippen was an unpleasant little man, blinked at you from behind very thick-lensed spectacles and wore red waistcoats with brass buttons. He was fond of asking people to have a drink with him, and invariably the same monologue followed :

" Yours ? Whisky-and-soda ?—I'll have the same. Two whiskies and a split, miss." Then the " fumbling " began. His hands dived into every pocket and each time drew a blank. Finally, he would giggle nervously, and say : " I'm afraid that I've—stupidly—come out without any money. Could you lend me half a crown ? "

Marie said of him : " When Crippen asks you to have a drink—pay for your own, it's a damn sight cheaper."

Marie's visit to America must have taken place about this time. Alec Hurley went with her, probably appearing— though I cannot be certain of this. She was a great success, though Bransby Williams tells me : " In many places she was never able to touch the success of her sister Alice, who was one of the greatest and most popular stars in America. I fancy that—though they would never admit it—the Americans were disappointed in Marie, because she was not as ' blue ' as they had hoped and expected. I admit that she was a singing Sunday-school teacher compared with some of the people who have hurled dirt over the footlights since that time. Marie put everything over so cleverly that she never offended anyone

unless they possessed a prurient mind. There was nothing of
' filth for filth's sake ' about her."

While she was on this American tour she gave a huge party.
It was King Edward's birthday, and Marie was determined to
show the affection Britishers had for their king. Every English
artiste in New York was invited. The table-cloth was a Union
Jack and there were floral decorations in red, white, and blue.
This took place at the Astor—Marie liked the best, and always
saw that she and her guests got it. Again I refer to Bransby
who writes :

" There was a certain comedian's wife present, looking very
grim and austere, disapproving of the laughter and fun. Marie
watched her for a few moments, then said : ' Smile, for Gawd's
sake ! You look like a blinking wardress come to tie us all up !
Damn it, it's the King's birthday—now then, everyone—God
Save the King.' She had paid the band to play it, and the
room—in fact most of the hotel—re-echoed with the British
National Anthem, led by Marie Lloyd."

And Bransby adds a little footnote, which is worth recording
here because this man is not only a great artiste, he is a man of
wide sympathies, warm affections, and possesses a capacity of
knowing and understanding human nature.

" Alec was there that night, I remember. She loved Alec,
and I am sure that he loved her. I always felt that during the
later years of her life she was heart-broken, but that was long
after that memorable supper-party, when she was the life and
soul of the party."

Returning to England, she was booked for Berlin and Paris.
She went, appeared with considerable success, but never really
cared a great deal for playing out of England. Her art was
essentially English and her sense of humour appealed particularly to English people. Curiously enough there were other
artistes whose art was definitely international. Tich was a
positive idol in Paris, and the Parisians made his life a burden
to him, because they recognized him in the street and used to
follow him, crying their admiration. Tich, who was almost
morbidly sensitive, who hated to be noticed and made con-
spicuous, rarely went out in Paris except after dark, and if he
had to sally forth in the day-time, hid in the recesses of a cab,
cowering in a corner as if he was " wanted by the police," and
not a great star appearing in a foreign capital where he was
admired.

Marie, after this Paris visit, had a song written for her called

"The Coster Girl in Paris." She appeared, magnificent in "fevvers" and a striped red, white and blue satin dress. I still have a gramophone record of her singing this number; it is nearly twenty years old, and still Marie's voice and that famous "family" diction is as clear and good as ever. Not long ago I was offered five pounds apiece for my three, small, double-sided records of Marie Lloyd singing various songs. I did not accept the offer.

I shall deal with her songs later, but here is an impression of her at that time, written by J. B. Booth, author of *Master and Men* and *Pink 'Un Yesterdays*.

He writes of the Pavilion when it was the "Centre of the Universe," when they gave you twenty-four turns on one bill, which might include the following stars: Marie Lloyd, Dan Leno, Vesta Tilley, Cinquevalli, T. E. Dunville, Gene Stratton and Maggie Duggan. And now—Marie enters—and listen to what he says of her:

"A dainty little figure, Parisienne in its *chic*, its clothes, and its manner, steps out, and again the cheers ring out. It is Marie Lloyd, the greatest artiste of her type and day, the spirit of London and of the old music-hall, incarnate. The tune of her song has a certain sparkle, the words have a certain point, but it is the curiously attractive, husky voice, the flash of the eyes, the wonderful, restrained gesture, the marvellous play of the hands that betrays the great artiste. The ditty has something to do with the adventures of a simple London girl in 'gay Paree'—'Paree' is always gay in music-hall land—and is sufficiently banal; it is the personality of the singer that counts, and again the cheers ring out as with a final mischievous wink and nod the singer darts off to change.

"The orchestra repeats the chorus a trifle perfunctorily, a bell rings, the chorus is abruptly abandoned, and a new tune is struck up. From the thunderous welcome it receives it is a favourite, and again the singer twinkles on to the stage.

"This time she is London, the incarnate cockney, the 'gamine' of the greatest city in the world. Gone is the *chic* Parisienne, with her demure naughtiness, her piquant point, and in her place is all Mile End, Whitechapel and Covent Garden. The song itself is little or nothing, the air has the usual catchiness, but the art of the singer epitomises and embalms a type—a type known to every member of the audience. Every gesture, every intonation, every 'aside' is utterly and absolutely right; there is a polish, a finality, that stamps the work as that of a consummate artiste. And a consummate artiste is ' Our Marie,' as the gallery boys call her."

Then follows a further comment on her and her life and work which has no place at this juncture, and J. B. Booth ends his eulogy :

" But the future is as yet hidden from us, so as the curtain falls on ' Our Marie ' we turn towards the crowded bar, for the inevitable acrobat turn seems in the nature of an anti-climax, and we are holding ourselves in reserve for ' the incomparable Mr. Leno,' as Sir Henry Irving invariably styles him."

That, ladies and gentlemen, is Mr. J. B. Booth, a man who " was " London. Nothing of the enthusiastic provincial about him, and that is how he wrote of " Our Marie." A man who had seen all that was best on the stage and the music-halls and still gives Marie " pride of place."

Sarah Bernhardt once said : " We are both great artistes— she was stating no more than the truth. Mrs. Patrick Campbell, who, I suppose, may justly claim to be the greatest English tragedienne since Sarah Siddons, said to me once, of Marie :

" I shall always regret that among all the people—interesting people—I have known, I never met Marie Lloyd. I always felt that we should have had a great deal in common. What an artiste ! "

I didn't say so, but I felt certain that if they had met, Marie would have shown up at her very worst. She was like that, and deep in her heart had, I believe, what we call now an inferiority complex. The existence of that made her, when she felt insecure or not at her best, assume a queer truculent air, a kind of rather childish pose of " I'm as good as you are, and a damn' sight better." Rather like a child who has been adorable in the nursery, who has been sweet and affectionate, amusing and utterly charming, then bring it down to the drawing-room, hope that it will " show off " just sufficiently to prove to everyone what a darling it is—and it stands near the door muttering : " I don't want to talk to these horrible people, so there ! "

The trouble with Marie was that she was always nice to people who didn't matter a hoot one way or the other. People who just lived to " sponge " on her, who made use of her in every possible way, always got a welcome from her. She had devoted friends, people who would have spent their last farthing on her, who might be poor, who might lack education, but who possessed hearts as clean and generous as her own.

Those people would have loved Marie had she been "first turn" or "on a line with the bioscope." But the others, the hangers-on, the blood-suckers, who never came to her without some hard-luck story, and who never went away empty-handed, those were the people who "talked her over," who tore her reputation to shreds, who scandalised her, and who were always ready to repeat—with glorious additions—her smallest indiscretions, and who magnified every one of her poor little failings. Those are the people who make a remark I heard the other day so tragically true : "If only Marie had not stooped so often to find her friends—or the people she believed to be her friends."

Those years at King Henry's Road were, as I have said, probably the happiest of her life. Open house, as always wonderful parties every Sunday, life was a good business.

"Billie" Boardman, in his admirable book, tells an amusing story of an old "pro." arriving one morning to visit Marie and Alec Hurley. (And now, when I want to verify this story and take down the book—I can't find it anywhere, so must record it from memory.) Open house as usual. The old pro. told the story like this :

"In comes Marie, merry and bright, asks me if I could do with a little something to eat. I said that not 'arf I couldn't. She said : ' I thought so ! What about a nice little steak eh ? ' I didn't say no, and off she went. Came back after a time with a steak—piping 'ot, I'd swear it weighed a pound. Blimy, Alec ain't 'arf making a lady outer ' Our Marie ! ' " I may be wrong, but that story sounds to me as if it came from Ted Hanley, Alec's brother. The same man who told Arthur Stratton, when he had a bad cold, to "get fre'pennorth of Friar's Balsam, an' ignore it !"

But Marie didn't need marriage with Alec Hurley or anyone else to develop her generosity. She passed through the saloon bar of a well-known "Pro. House of Call" one evening, and there sat an old music-hall artiste sipping—very slowly to make it "spin out" as long as possible—a small whisky to which had been added a very large soda. Marie nodded and smiled. "Hello—what are you drinking?"

The old pro., delighted to be recognized by the Queen of Comedy, sprang to his feet and said : "Oh, just a little—whisky, Miss Lloyd."

"Whisky?" Marie eyed the glass doubtfully. "Looks more like gin to me !" Then, with that wonderful smile, she passed on, stopping the waiter on her way, ordering a " double Scotch," and, slipping back, did a little bit of " palming "— the old pro. found himself with a sovereign in his hand.

Think of it, down and out, then suddenly in front of you a double Scotch, and in your hand what you hadn't seen for months—a real bright " Jimmy." Do you wonder that when I asked that the old pros. at Brinsworth would be so kind as to send me their recollections of Marie, their letters make such reading that brings tears to one's eyes ?

Sir Seymour Hicks—and I shall interpolate a story about this brilliant actor later, although it has nothing to do with Marie Lloyd—sent me the following story about her :

He says : " She appeared Sunday after Sunday for me at the Prince's Theatre during the war, at the concerts I used to give for the soldiers. She used to sing as many songs as they liked. She was—wonderful ! " He continued : " Years ago, I was talking to her and enquiring after Alec Hurley, I said : ' How's your husband ? ' She said : ' I don't know—he's gone all " racing." He's bought a race-horse. We keep it in the garden. Up to now all it's done is to walk about and eat the geraniums. He says that he's going to back it each way, which means, I suppose, that it won't bother about the other horses, eh ? ' "

To me the idea of that horse—probably entirely mythical— walking about eating the geraniums, conjured up a picture which is not unlike a Bateman drawing.

The story about Sir Seymour after all *has* a place here, because it goes to show the type of affection which real artistes, kindly, human people, inspire in the hearts of the poorest of their audience.

I was walking up Grosvenor Street the day before the Derby last year. That morning I had read that Seymour Hicks had been honoured by His Majesty. A flower-woman stopped me. " 'Ave a butting-'ole, I taken scercely anythink all day." I pulled up and allowed her to fix a slightly damaged carnation in my coat. I asked if she knew what was going to win ? She replied in the manner of London flower-women that she did. " This is a cert, ducky," then gave me the name of a horse which I fancy is still running. She said :

" You in the business, dear ? "

" I was—once upon a time."

" 'Fought so ! So was I. Panto—me ! Was you West End ? "

" More or less—yes."

" Whatcher think of Seymour 'Icks gettin' knighted, eh ? Nice, ain't it ? Not that I shall ever think of him as *Sir* Seymour, any more than I'll ever think of 'er as *Lidy* 'Icks. 'E'll allus be Seymour 'Icks to me, saime as she'll allus be Dere Little Ella Terriss."

That's how real artistes are regarded by their public, that's how Marie's public regarded her.

BOOK TWO

CHAPTER ONE

" . . . ARE LIKE STARS—THEY RISE, THEY SET, THEY HAVE
THE WORSHIP OF THE WORLD, BUT NO REPOSE"

SHELLEY

The pity of it !—Encouragement to young writers—Her practical
jokes—The house-boat—The sinking of the *Moonbeam*—The
fiasco which was a success—Marie goes fishing.

A HOUSE in London, a house-boat on the river,
plenty of friends—and what more could anyone
want ? Work, admittedly, but work which was a
delight, work which brought in hundreds of pounds,
all ready to be scattered to the winds—or rather for the benefit
of those people whose hands were always outstretched.

Yet there was a " little cloud no bigger than a man's hand "
on the horizon, and, try as you would, there it stayed, and
Marie Lloyd realized its existence and hated it. Nothing very
much, just a matter of a man becoming " used " to his brilliant
wife, taking their magnificent home for granted, and even—
maybe—grudging her that measure of popularity which was
hers.

Now it is a maxim of the Variety Stage that no home can
support two stars—if they happen to be husband and wife. One
or the other is certain to resent the fact that he or she shines
with a lesser radiance. At first when life is " love and the world
well lost," then it's easy to swear that nothing matters, that no
pride can equal that which they feel for each other's success.

That doesn't last, and that little sense of jealousy creeps in
and stays there, souring everything.

That was what was happening to Marie Lloyd and Alec
Hurley. Everywhere she went she was hailed as the Crowned
Head of Variety. Every night she held court in her dressing-
room and distributed largess. Her house was crowded with
people who came to laugh, to beg, to eat, and drink, while a few
came because they loved her. The position of Prince Consort is

not easy, as more important people than Alec Hurley have
discovered. It is a position needing tact, backed by very real
affection and devotion, and only bearable to a man who can
actually take pleasure in his wife's success.

Now Marie loved admiration, she loved praise, and she loved
—let's be honest—flattery. With all her cleverness, her ability
and her undoubted intelligence she could never distinguish the
real from the counterfeit, could never differentiate between
honest admiration and self-seeking flattery.

There was a childish quality in her mental make-up which left
her vulnerable to everyone who could offer her " lip service." I
shall always feel that this lack of discernment went hand in hand
with that strange inferiority complex of hers. She was intensely
nervous, she never appeared without a certain amount of—oh,
controlled, certainly—stage fright, and this blatant admiration,
this fulsome flattery, in some strange way, stabilised her.

Time and time again I have heard her say, when she left the
stage, while the applause was still shaking the house : " How
was I ? All right ? "   And, mark this, she would put the
question not only to brother and sister artistes, not only to
people whose opinion might be worth listening to, but to people
who were obviously " hangers-on," who replied : " Marie—
you were—*lovely !* I never heard you go so well ! You worked
beautifully—you'll never work as you did to-night, if you live
to be a hundred ! Never ! "

Those remarks pleased her, she accepted them as worth
listening to, whereas half the time the person had scarcely
watched her turn, but had been sniggering and laughing,
swopping stories with some comedian !

Marie, like many another successful person, like many another
great artiste, had her little army of " Yes-men " and " Yes-
women," who would have praised anything she did, because it
paid them to do so. The trouble was that where she might
have bought their praise, for what it was worth, with the price
of " small gins " and " pints of bitter," Marie, being Marie,
had to pay for this worthless lip-service with vintage wine and
bottles of champagne !

She never gave this fulsome praise herself. If she liked your
work, admired it, she said so briefly and sincerely. If she
didn't, she said nothing at all. I noticed how often she was
always ready to give hints to artistes who were beginning.
Hints which might seem unimportant, but which in reality had
great value.

She used to say to Bransby Williams, who still has wonderful black hair with a natural wave : " Go on, take off your hat whenever you're working. Never mind if the character demands it, take it off for a minute. Show the gals that natural wave of yours—we poor mutts have to pay for ours ! "

I once asked her what she thought of a certain actress. Marie said : " Nothing much—she doesn't *mean* anything." Then a long pause : " Wonder if she's any good at dressmaking or trimming hats ? She might open a shop and do quite well."

It was her great joy to encourage the struggling artiste. " Plenty of room at the top of the ladder," she used to say, " it's only the middle rungs that are crowded." She had very little time for the " average " performer, who lacked real originality, and who cared little or nothing about their work. Another dictum of hers was : " Be civil to everyone—no matter what their place is on the bill. The first turn of to-day is the top of the bill to-morrow." She once said that to me, after she had indulged in a splendid exhibition of temper with another performer. I grinned, she scowled at me for a moment, then said : " Oh, well, we don't all practise what we preach do we ? "

" Mr. E "—who I have mentioned before—tells me that he was once on the bill with her at the Palace, Manchester, and one night he showed her a song which he had written. She read it through, nodded, and said : " That's the kind of stuff I want." Then handing him a sovereign, she said : " You see, I always make it a rule to buy the first song that any author submits to me, just to encourage them. This is the first I've ever had from you, and it's very good. I'll send it to George le Brun to-night and tell him to write a melody to it."

On the other hand, nothing infuriated her more than people who " tried to get to know her," and pestered her to " tell them how to get on the stage," and so forth. There is a classical story of her reply to the young " man about town " who wanted her to tell him what dress to wear at one of the Fancy Dress Balls at Covent Garden. Unfortunately, like so many of Marie's sallies, it can't be written down ! There was one young fool who met her somewhere or other and insisted on talking about " his girl." Marie was bored, she cared neither for him nor his young woman, and showed it pretty plainly.

" Marvellous girl, Miss Lloyd, nothing she can't do— wonderful at everything—plays the piano divinely, sings beautifully——"

Marie interpolated : " Very nice ! "

" That's not all—she rides, drives a car, plays tennis like a professional——"

" Splendid ! Interesting girl ! "

" Does wonderful needlework, knits jumpers, knitted me the pair of golf stockings I'm wearing at this moment, very clever at gardening——"

Marie, by this time hating the young man intensely, said : " Well, provided you can cook and do a bit of housework you ought to make a very good pair. Good night."

I wonder if Rosie Lloyd remembers one night at the Canterbury, when Marie played one of her most elaborate practical jokes on a young man with more money than sense (and even then, believe me, he needn't have been particularly wealthy), who had pestered her all the week before, when she was working Brighton. He could sing comic songs—" they assur-ah me that I'm wasted—that I ought to be on the halls. My friends tell me that I'm really bett-ah than any of these fellers—Robey or Champion, or Randall." On and on—*ad lib.* and then some.

Marie, in desperation, said : " Look, I'm working the Canterbury next week. Come along one evening after the show and I'll get the manager to hear you. Bring a song. What's your best number ? "

They were all good, he told her, but his masterpiece was one called " The Man behind the Gun."

He arrived, the show was over, and Marie was ready for him. She glanced over the song, told him that it demanded a " property gun " to give it the right " point," provided him with someone's umbrella, paid the pianist to remain and accompany him, found the manager, Ernie Lepard, and—fixed up the " part two " of the joke. The young man sang his song with all that " swank " and self-assurance which can damn any amateur, particularly in the eyes of a great artiste. Marie applauded wildly, then cried : " Ernie, there's Dick Warner and ' Spot ' Oliver—there in the bar—make them come and listen to this—they'll never forgive you if they miss him." Two rather bored barmen were dragged out to play the parts of " two important agents." Again the young man bawled his silly song, again Marie applauded. At the end of the song she again found other people—a scene-shifter, whom she hailed with " If it's not Mr. Oswald Stoll ! " ; a check-taker who was given the character of " Frank Allan," and so forth. Fifteen times he sang that song, and by the end of the fifteenth time

Marie had the stalls half-full of the most extraordinary crowd of people, all of whom bore names—for this performance only— of the " Big Noises in Variety." Then Marie's amusement began to pall, and she went home and left someone else to get rid of the young man from Brighton.

She had no use for "swankers," for people who tried to force their way into her circle, but for the others—that was another story.

Here is the other side of the medal.

Flo Hastings says : " The dearest and best friend I ever had in my life was Marie Lloyd. When I first came to London she gave me some beautiful stage dresses, and as the years went by we became firm friends. One afternoon I was standing in the Holborn, very sad, with no work in view. Marie came up to me and wanted to know why I was not working. She said that she had heard I had turned down two weeks' work—and wanted to know why ? I explained that work was impossible unless you had the clothes to wear. Marie stared, then said in that impetuous fashion of hers : ' Lord ! Is that all ! Give me your address.'

" The next day a trunk arrived filled with most beautiful clothes, and a note saying that if ever I needed money I knew where I could get it. I shall never cease to regret that kind heart, that dear face—another Marie Dressler ! "

Mrs. John Lawson, who was a great actress and a generous friend, told me that she was putting on one of her famous sketches at the Camberwell Music Hall, which she owned at that time. I think that the sketch must have been the famous *Devil's Sunday*. Mrs. Lawson—Cissie Lawson—was worried as to what shade of dress she should wear. She talked this over with Marie, who said promptly : " Don't you buy a thing ! I've got the very dress and cloak for you ! Green. I'll send it round and come and see you wear it." Although she was working, she rushed to Camberwell to see Cissie appear in this sketch, wearing the cloak and dress. Then tore round to the dressing-room, saying :

" Cissie, old darling, you're wonderful ! Don't let anything worry you, you'll get right to the top, nothing can stop you."
" She helped me by saying that with such conviction," Mrs. Lawson adds, " it made me try all the harder. If only people would be as generous as she was, not only in material things, but ready with a kind word, the world would be such a much nicer, happier place."

H. A. Kennedy, who is "Ken," and was known to every patron of the halls when he appeared for so long with Harry Tate in *Motoring*, tells me a story of the famous house-boat. It was his first meeting with Marie, and he was taken over by Harry Tate to Staines, where the boat was moored. After tea —and be sure there was the usual crowd—Marie suggested going on the river. She had a punt, and "Ken" says he was very struck with the admirable way this attractive woman handled her punt-pole. Things have changed now, but in those days very few women were adept at any sort of sport.

"I sat watching her, all admiration, when suddenly her pole seemed to slip and she went into the river—in all her beautiful clothes, just as she was. There was great consternation, until someone whispered to me that ' Marie did it for a joke.' The whisper went round, and no one laughed louder than Marie Lloyd herself."

But I wondered. It would have been just like Marie to turn a slightly undignified catastrophe into an accident to make everyone laugh.

Alice Lloyd tells me the following : " Marie was a leader of fashion and was always first with everything, whether it was hats, horses, or house-boats. She was living on one of the latter, near Staines, when she was nearly drowned. She had been working very hard all day, rehearsing for the New Tivoli Revue, and arrived back very late at night, ladened with boxes which held her new clothes for Ascot. The hat, which was part of the costume, she was wearing to save carrying a huge hat-box. It was a large hat, covered with a mass of red and black cherries, and *très chic*. As she got into the punt which was to take her over to the house-boat, instead of sitting down in the punt, she sat down quietly just ' out ' of the punt." Alice adds : " Only because we suddenly saw that hat, with its bright cherries shining, as it floated on the water, we should never have found her."

Here is another river story which Johnnie Wood tells me. It is called : " The Sinking of the *Moonbeam*." (Carry on Johnnie, you tell them the story !)

" Marie was very fond of the river, and bought a house-boat —in fact, two house-boats, from Mr. Vernon Dowsett, who was manager of the Tivoli in 1900. This ' boat ' was composed of a day and night boat, and Marie named them the *Sunbeam* and the *Moonbeam*. They were large and comfortable, and as many as seven people could sleep on board. Marie had possessed these boats for several years, and at the end of the winter gave me the job of renovating them for the coming season.

" I went down to find that the Thames Conservancy had given orders that all owners were to cut off waste water pipes, to prevent the pollution of the river waters. These pipes were attached to the wash-basins in the several bedrooms, and whoever had done the work of cutting off the pipes had neglected to seal the openings. Instead of being outlets, they became—inlets.

" There is a phrase applied to boats, ' between wind and water,' and, as the *Moonbeam* was riding high, these ' inlets ' were well out of the water and all was well. The fun began when Marie arrived to spend Whit-Sunday on the river. She got down at midnight and chartered the station 'bus to bring her and her friends down to the boat.

" They arrived, and Marie was loud in her praises of my work. ' You really have made her look a treat, Johnnie. That's what I call a real good job ! Good for you ! ' and so on. I was frightfully bucked, but when the luggage began to come on board—oh, dear. Nothing but box after box, all to be stacked on the *Moonbeam* and unpacked when they all had time. On went the boxes, I should think that Marie and her friends had ransacked every shop in the West End for ' river clothes.'

" I left them unpacking, talking and laughing, all excited over the prospect of staying on a house-boat, and went back to my digs in the village, and—so to bed. Alec was ' alone in his glory,' being the only man of that party, the rest being Marie, Bella Burge and several of my sisters.

" Quite early next morning I was awakened by a banging on my door and heard a voice shouting : ' Johnnie, you're wanted at once ! ' I rushed down to find Alec in his pyjamas, calling : ' Hurry up, the *Moonbeam's* sunk !' Then he began : ' What the so-and-so have you done to the so-and-so boat ? ' I ' told him the time ' and then hurried down to the river.

" I realized what had happened. The *Moonbeam* had been ' riding high ' in the water, the weight of seven people plus boxes and bags, provisions, hat-boxes and all the rest of it, had lowered her into the water. The waste pipes were open—and in had rushed the water !

" There was Marie and there was Bella Burge, there, too, were my sisters, all flying about in their nighties. Marie was full of the story. She had gone to bed : ' And I had the most

horrible dream, Johnnie. I thought someone was drowning
in the river, I could hear the poor devil splashing about in the
water. I jumped out of bed, and there I was—pretty well
drowning myself!' There had been about three feet of water
in the boat. She rushed into the next room, and as she opened
the door, in rushed more water. In a few moments down the
Moonbeam went, she was securely moored and so only sank in
about three feet of water, and there was comparatively little
damage done—except for the ladies' 'pretties' and their
tempers. Then—believe me, when it was over and all the
clothes that had been saved were drying on the bushes on the
bank, we heard all about it from Marie! The beauties of the
river, the joys of having house-boats, she had it all ready, I can
tell you! They all transported themselves to the village inn,
where Marie stayed for the rest of the summer. Her doctor told
her that the river was not good for her health, and finally she
sold the boats. But she always loved it, and I think those days
were the happiest of her life. This story became one of her
favourite and best 'flavoured' yarns—' This is a good one,'
she'd say, ' thrilling, too! It's called, "How Johnnie sunk
the *Moonbeam!*"'"

The Adelphi Revue, the first revue ever produced in London,
was a great success. It was when she was appearing in this
that Marie met one of her greatest admirers, Sarah Bernhardt.
Marie was doing an imitation of her in the revue, and the late
Willie Clarkson sat with Bernhardt in a box and watched the
show. The French artiste was delighted with Marie's impersonation and begged Willie Clarkson to persuade Marie to come
and meet her. Marie came, was amusing and delightful.
Bernhardt told her how she admired her work, gave her a
signed photograph, and asked for one in return. Marie had
one taken in her "Bernhardt make-up" and sent it, signed
"Sarah Bernhardt." The great tragedienne christened Marie
Lloyd "The Bernhardt of the Halls."

That must have been one of their "good days" when they
met at the Adelphi, under the auspices of funny little Willie
Clarkson, for Bernhardt, like Marie, was a temperamental soul,
and liable to have moods as stormy as Marie's own.

That these great artistes are temperamental is not surprising.
They literally carry the weight and obligations laid on them by
huge salaries and tremendous reputations. If your little first
turn is not particularly brilliant, not "right on his toes," well,
after all, we don't expect a great deal from a first turn. They

are drawing their five or six pounds a week, they sing what is probably a "free song," they do a little dance, which is quite pleasant, but doesn't mean anything much. They get a spatter of applause—and it's over.

But consider your star, the bill topper. The moment they enter a town they are faced on every side with posters : "Special engagement of So-and-so," possibly even the prices of the seats have been raised, everyone is expecting something very much worth seeing. The salary sheet carries £250 for Miss "So-and-So"—and she has got to earn it.

The public—the British public—are faithful to their favourites, but any audience is a hard taskmaster. They have paid 5s., 2s. 6d., 1s. or 6d. towards the star's salary, and they want value for money. They are not there to accept anything but the best. They make no excuses : "Poor soul, perhaps she's got a cold," or "a headache," or "Maybe her mother's very ill," or "She's lost everything she's got in the X.Y.Z. crash"—no, they must have a performance which gives them their money's worth.

The strain on the performer is enormous. Twice nightly, remember, several changes of clothes in each house, noise, the blare of the band, people coming to the dressing-room asking for help, claiming acquaintance, obviously expecting to get a small "free entertainment" and to find the star as scintillating in the dressing-room as on the stage. More noise, drinks to be offered, the place misty with smoke, the manager coming round : "Could I just have a word with you? That new number, don't you think that it might be better if you— etc. etc."

Home very late, to eat a meal when everyone else is thinking of going to bed. Can't go to bed immediately afterwards, talking, playing patience to pass the time, or "some of the crowd" drop in. Bed, at one or two !

Next day, requests. "Will Miss So-and-so give a donation to the Mothers' Knitting School," or "provide half a dozen pairs of boots for the Fund for Shoeing the Local Newsboys." Will she "kick off" for the football team on Saturday, will she give away the prizes at the local Flower-show, will she—will she— will she—— ?

Headaches, physical weariness, personal worries, griefs, must all be left in the dressing-room, they must never be allowed to intrude on the stage.

Not the easiest of lives, not conducive to iron nerves and a sunny temper, not liable to improve a character already highly strung and ultra sensitive.

Small wonder that Marie Lloyd's nerves got out of hand sometimes—for £250 to £300 is a heavy load to carry.

New songs were always a bugbear of hers. She liked to know that someone stood at the side with the words written out on a piece of paper, ready to prompt her if she "fluffed." Had she done so, it is unlikely that she could have taken a prompt, for many stage people go stone deaf with this particular type of nerves. You might shout a line at the top of your voice, and they would never hear it.

Mrs. Dick Burge—Bella Burge—was always a close friend of the whole family's, and very often she would go with Marie to a hall and stand at the side to watch her work. One evening Marie had a new song, smart, up-to-date, amusing. For some reason she was terribly nervous of this song, and demanded that Mrs. Burge should stand in the Prompt Corner and " hold the book," ready to prompt if necessary. They were a little late coming down from the dressing-room. The call-boy was shouting : " Come along, Miss Lloyd, please ! " " Miss Lloyd, your music's playing ! " and when they finally dashed down, Bella realized that she had left the precious paper on which the words were written in the dressing-room. Marie was ready to go on. Bella Burge looked round wildly and saw, lying on the floor at the side of the stage, a dirty bit of paper. She pounced on it, and held it in her hand.

" Ready, Miss Lloyd ? "

" Ready. Got the words, Bella ? "

" Yes, I've got them—here."

" Right, watch me ! "

On Marie went, confident that if she " fluffed " Bella had the words ready. She didn't, she went through without a hitch, and came off smiling and delighted—she had broken in a new number.

" Thank God, I got through all right, Bella," she said. " I never should have done if I hadn't known you'd got the words ready to give me." Bella, wise woman, said nothing.

Tom Fancourt reminds me of an incident which happened when he and Marie were playing in pantomime at the Crown, Peckham. She played the principal boy, in *Dick Whittington* (a part which Julian Wylie used to say was the best " boy " part ever written), and Fancourt played the " dame." He and Marie used to sing a topical number, and Tom—who liked composing

new lyrics—used to produce new verses almost every evening·
The song was one of those " back-chat " numbers, with the
refrain :

    " Don't say I told you ? " . . . " Certainly not ! "

He produced a new verse—and offered this to Marie. She
said : " Oh, damn it, I can't spend my life studying new verses.
I'll tell you what—you sing it, and I'll put in the ' twiddly
bits.' " Tom agreed, and off they went. Half-way through the
new verse he forgot his lines and stood there—dumb. Marie
glared at him, and he says : " Bless her, I knew Our Marie.
I tell you, hot and cold water ran down my back with fright."
Pulling his scattered wits together, he said—sufficiently
loudly for the audience to hear : " Go on, it's your turn now ! "
To which she replied—with equal distinctness : " You dirty
little dog, you ! You said you'd sing it." Marie's temper was
rising rapidly. They continued to blame each other, the
audience thinking that it was " part of the game," and shrieking
with laughter. Now it's all very well to " gag " and create a
situation of this kind, but it has to end somewhere, and the
difficulty is to " make a getaway." Fancourt turned and
blamed the conductor !
Neither he nor Marie were to blame—the conductor had
made a hash of the whole song. The conductor promptly left
the chair and walked out. Tom took a flying leap into the
vacant chair and embarked on a little comic conducting.
Marie's scowls vanished, she laughed, her eyes twinkled, and
she broke into a dance—and there was no one who could dance
more neatly, believe me. Tom, seeing that the barometer
was now at " set fair," left the orchestra, came back and
joined her in her dance. The house was delighted, and the
improvised turn was kept in the pantomime for the rest of the
run.
He told me of another occasion when they were both appearing at the Derby Castle, in the Isle of Man. Marie was filled
with the bright idea that they should all go fishing.
" What for ? " Tom asked.
" Mackerel, you fool ! " she replied. " There's tons of it.
We'll get enough to have fresh mackerel—really fresh, not that
tired-looking stuff out of shops and off barrows—for supper."
It sounded splendid and off they went. The catch was considerable. Tom says : " We kept pulling them up, and pulling
them up in dozens., I said ' They didn't look like mackerel to

me.' But Marie said : ' Get along, you've never seen a live one in your life—they always look different.' "

They returned, carried the catch, positively staggering along with them. They stopped at Tom's lodgings to leave some, and the landlady stared at the pile of fish.

" What d'you want me to do with these ? "

" Cook them for supper ! "

" But they're pollack—uneatable, Mr. Fancourt."

So much for Marie's mackerel. I don't mind wagering that—for that evening the whole of the party dined with her !

For Marie loved giving dinner parties and supper parties, and Mrs. James—where she used so often to stay at Bristol—says : " She always took the whole house and brought a troop of people with her and dozens of other people used to pour into the house all day long. Marie liked nothing so much as to order wonderful meals for the whole party. Although when she began to grow so ill—she ate scarcely enough to keep a bird alive—the meals went on just the same. Invariably, just as they sat down, someone else would turn up ; and then the bell would ring and it would be : " Another knife and fork, another plate——"

I first met Marie at Bristol. Marguerite Broadfoote was playing at Bedminster Hippodrome and we went into the matinée at Bristol. When we went round Marie had just got some " eye-black " in her eye, I remember, and was fairly dancing with the pain. If you have never experienced this particular form of torture, " eye-black " is a kind of soapy grease and if you get it in your eye the pain is quite unbearable. In addition it makes the eye water and the tears spoil the rest of your make-up. Marguerite always used a special kind made by Thomas's in St. Martin's Lane. She said, in that accent which was always fairly reminiscent of Edinburgh : " Why don't you use the kind that doesn't smart, Marie ? "

Marie snapped back that she didn't know *why* she didn't, but she could only suppose it was because she was a (something) fool, and, anyway, she'd use the other kind now and that was that !

I slipped out, got a taxi, drove over the bridge to Bedminster and came back with a spare box of the stuff.

Marie had recovered slightly, her temper was less uncertain (and, mind, it would take a saint to keep her temper with a good piece of " eye-black " in her eye !), and she took the box.

" Where did you get this ? Do they sell it here ? "

" No, I nipped back to Bedminster."

She stared. " You did ! Well, I call that damned good of you." When we left she said, in her very nicest voice—the kindest, dearest, huskiest voice : " You can come again any time you like, young—what's-yer-name."

CHAPTER TWO

" REPUTATION IS OFTEN GOT WITHOUT MERIT, AND LOST
WITHOUT CRIME "

OLD PROVERB

Marie in Edinburgh—Harry Claff, representing the people of Sheffield—" So this is Ardwick ! "—Nell Gwynn—H. B. Irving and Marie—Impersonators—The L.C.C. objects ; and so does Marie—The American invasion—The Duchess of Hoxton—" God save the Queen ! "

THIS success of Marie's was not by any means universal. In spite of her art there remained towns in the provinces where she was never particularly popular. The reasons were various : they might be due to a puritanical narrow-mindedness which could not see further than that " naughtiness " in Marie's songs, and credited them with being considerably worse than they ever were. It might be that there were towns where the audiences disliked her personality, her style of work, a dozen reasons, but the fact remained.

She had gained a reputation for being far more risqué than she ever was in point of fact, and I can only repeat Bransby Williams' assertion that her songs, her methods of work, were never anything approaching the " dirt for dirt's sake " merchants who were unloaded upon the British public later.

James Adair, for many years theatrical critic for the *Stage* in Edinburgh, told me that on one occasion, years ago, he asked Sir Edward Moss why he never engaged Marie Lloyd for his Edinburgh hall. Sir Edward—he was Mr. Moss then—replied that he didn't think his audience would care for her, that the capital of Scotland disliked vulgarity and that he preferred not to risk an engagement.

This only goes to prove that even an authority, a man who has his finger on the pulse of public taste, can make grave mistakes. He reconsidered his verdict and Marie Lloyd appeared in September, 1900, on the same bill as Lottie Collins, the mother of José Collins and the creator of that famous song " Ta-ra-ra-boom-de-aye." She appeared again in December, 1901, when James Adair adds a note to this effect : " Huge reception, in new songs and old favourites." Again, September, 1902, he notes : " She added to her turn a sketch called ' The Bathing Parade,' supported by Charles McNaughton and a bevy of appropriately attired bathing girls, with Marie herself in an engaging bathing ' get up.' The sketch was bright and most entertaining and had a great reception." Continuing, for James Adair is methodical, keeps his " date book " in strict order and has far too great a respect for real artistes to be anything but exact concerning them : " November, 1903, Marie Lloyd in magnificent form and rapturously received."

So much for Sir Edward Moss's, fears that Marie might not be to the taste of " Auld Reekie."

James Adair adds that this music-hall magnate admitted to him that, by not engaging her sooner, he had made one of the few mistakes of his life in matters connected with Variety. He stated that he had never admired an artiste more.

On the other hand, Harry Claff (chairman of the Variety Artistes' Federation) tells me of an occasion at Sheffield where the audience did not care for her at all. He says : " They were decidedly hard and refused to accept Marie at any price." When she came off she flew into one of those celebrated tempers of hers and made remarks about the inhabitants of Sheffield, their knives and razors, scissors and circular saws ! " Damn the whole lot ! " and other less-restrained epithets. With that she went into her dressing-room and banged the door. Johnnie Wood, who was her manager, was dreadfully upset and told Harry Claff that he believed she was capable of " packing up " and not appearing again.

" Go and talk to her, Harry. Smooth her down a bit. You can, you know—you know how to talk to her."

Harry, one of the kindest and most charming fellows in the business, waited until Marie had cooled down a little, then knocked on her door. He was told to come in and found Marie looking like a small thunder-cloud.

" What do you want ? Don't come here trying to smarm me down ! "

Harry said : " Marie, just listen to me, will you. Try to be civil, because I've not come as myself at all, not as Harry Claff ; I've come representing the populace of Sheffield ; I'm—well, I'm a deputation."

Marie said : " I know one thing you are and that's a liar !
Well, go on—what else ? "

" They wish me to tell you that they are perfectly obedient to
your commands, that their one wish is to do all you ask. They
will take their knives and razors and scissors—and take them
where you suggest, and use them exactly *as* you suggest, *but*
they want to know if you'll let them off taking the circular
saws ! "

Marie threw back her head and shouted with laughter, made
him have a drink, forgot all her bad temper, " went on," Harry
says, " for the second house and—worked like a Trojan, with
the most marvellous results."

Only this morning comes a letter from Wilkie Warren, the
manager of the New Palace Pier at Hastings. Wilkie Warren
has been performer, composer, lyric writer, and has written
sketches. He says :

" I won't say the usual things about her great heart—everyone knows that ! I'll tell you instead something which I once
saw when she appeared at Ardwick Empire. She hadn't gone
well ; in fact, at the second house on the Saturday the audience
were noisy and restless and obviously did not care much for her
work. By the time that the second house was over and she
was dressed ready to go home, probably feeling a little des-
pondent—and who does not on such occasions—she sauntered
down on to the stage. You know what a stage looks like, late
on a Saturday ; surely one of the gloomiest places on earth.
No one about, stage empty except for a few baskets standing
about, ready packed, waiting for the baggage man. The
curtain was up, lights lowered. Marie walked down stage
towards the footlights and stared at the empty auditorium,
then said aloud : ' So this is Ardwick, eh ? Well—to hell with
the lot of you ! ' I shall never forget the tone of satisfaction
in her voice and, being a ' pro ' myself, I knew just how she
felt."

It's not such a far cry from Manchester to Birmingham and
this is what Jules de Block says of her visits there :

" Whenever Marie Lloyd came to Birmingham she always
had the reception of a queen. Two weeks before she was to
open in this city every ticket would be sold. For hours crowds
would wait outside the Empire to see her arrive at the stage
door, all saying : ' We've come to see Our Marie.' Even the
cabmen on the ranks would shout as she passed : ' Theer she
goes. Hurrah for our Marie ! ' "

The Colonies adored her. When she opened in Melbourne[1] there was not a seat in the house, a horse running in the Melbourne Cup was called after her, she went everywhere and her progress was—royal.

Alec Hurley went with her and, as ever, Marie had to trail other people with her to give them a good time, and this trip was an opportunity for a distant relative of Alec's to see the world.

They'd been at sea about a week when this gentleman went to see the Captain. " Got a complaint, Mr. X. ? "

" Well," X. admitted, " I 'ave a bit of a complaint as a matter of fact. It's the food ! "

The Captain bristled. The liner was a first-class boat, he was very proud of her and the cooking was admirable. He said, a trifle stiffly : " Oh, and what is wrong with the food ? "

Mr. X. said : " No suety pudden ! Been out a week and never once 'ave we 'ad suety pudden."

" I see—the omission will be rectified. Good morning ! "

Every day, whatever else was on the menu, the gentleman got a small " suety pudden " all to himself, until he loathed the sight of it. This was the same gentleman who went into a chemist's shop and, handing a prescription to the chemist, said : " Make up that subscription, will yer, an' look lively."

The chemist read it, then asked : " Will you have it effervescent or otherwise ? "

" Come again ! "

" Effervescent or otherwise, sir ? "

The Londoner was stumped. What the devil did the fellow mean ? He considered a moment, then said with great gravity : " As regards to which ? "

Marie loved the " hail-fellow-well-met " attitude of the Colonials ; she hated " side," and hated it still more when there was nothing " behind it." Yet her admiration for anyone who could do something which she didn't happen to be able to do herself was unbounded. When I had my first book accepted, I told her, rather bucked about it. She said : " A book—you've written a book ? What for ? Your job's acting ; what do you want to write a book for ? "

[1] After all these years, Australia still remembers Marie with affection. Thanks to my friend, Miss Shain of Melbourne, who has " broadcast " my request for recollections of Marie, letters reach me by every mail, unfortunately too late to be included in this book. Still, it's good to know that Marie is remembered so vividly and with typical Australian whole-hearted admiration.—N.J.

I told her, explaining that it was possible to do the two things.
She said : " Well, perhaps you can, perhaps you can't. Don't
go and spoil both by dabbling about writing." Then later :
" Mind, I don't know how you can do it ? What do you write
about ? how the devil do you know what to *say* ?—it beats me.
I suppose you're clever, that's what it is." I naturally said :
" Oh, I don't think I'm clever."

" Of course, you *must* be clever, or you couldn't write
books ! "

I suggested once that she should let me write her life ; she
stared at me, open-eyed.

" My life ! Don't be silly ; who'd want to read my life—even
supposing you could tell 'em the truth—which you can't ! I
don't believe that anyone ever tells all the truth in those books,
do you ? "

I once told her that I believed, if there was anything in
reincarnation, that she was, or had been at one time, Nell
Gwynn.

Marie said : " Who d'you mean ? Sweet Nell of Old
Drury ? "

" That's the lady."

She looked a little doubtful, then said : " Mistress of the
King, wasn't she ? You're shoving me into high society, aren't
you ? Why d'you think I'm Nell Gwynn or she's me, or
whatever do you think ? "

I told her, recounting various episodes of Nell's career,
including a practical joke once played on Moll Davis. Marie
roared and said :

" History, all that, eh ? Well—if all of it's like that, it might
be worth doing a bit of studying. It beats me where you learn
all that stuff ! I never learnt any of those funny things when
I was at school—they taught us all about Alfred and his rotten
old cakes, and King Charles getting his head chopped off ! "

Often, when she was in a good mood, she'd make me a kind
of " show piece " and say : " Go on, Micky, tell us some of
that history of yours," which usually ended by Marie telling of
Nell's naughty escapade with Mistress Davis—with additions.
That story became a sort of " standing dish " with Marie and
gradually attained proportions and embellishments which were
pure " Marie Lloyd," and terribly funny.

When Harry Claff put on his *Henry VIII*, about twelve years
ago, he was " working turns " and was just coming off the stage
at the London Pavilion when Marie rushed in. She took one

look at his very elaborate make-up, then said—(Harry adds :
" as only Marie could say anything ") " Blimy, there's Queen
Elizabeth ! "

At one time H. B. Irving toured the halls with his father's
great success—*Waterloo*, by Sir Arthur Conan Doyle. He was
on the same bill as Marie and Gus Elen. The late James
Lindsey was appearing in the play, and was in " H. B.'s "
dressing-room one evening when word came, asking if " Mr.
Irving would please go and speak to Miss Lloyd."

Irving said : " Miss Lloyd—Miss Lloyd—do I know the
lady, Jimmy ? "

James Lindsey replied : " Well, if you don't know her,
Harry, it's time you did. She's well worth cultivating."

Irving disappeared, and returned only just in time to make
his entrance for the second house. Later, Jimmy asked what
Marie had wanted him for.

" I don't really know," Irving said. " She seemed a little
surprised to see me, but she was most amusing and very kind.
She has a great fund of entertaining stories—most entertaining."

Later, Jimmy asked Marie why she wanted to see H. B.
Irving.

Marie said : " I didn't want to see him. I'd never met him
before. He just drifted in and sat down and talked—all rather
dreamy, and had a drink. I told him a few stories and he
laughed and then he drifted out again. Funny fellow. Not
unlike Sam Mayo's style of working, that kind of almost
miserable way of talking, isn't it ? "

" But," Jimmy persisted, " why did you send for him ? "

" I didn't," Marie said. " I told the damn' fool of a dresser
to go and tell Gus Elen I wanted to see him, and she mixed the
names ; didn't listen—thought I said—what's his name ?—
Irving."

There was an additional richness in her mental composition,
something that was very spacious, something which prevented
her ever being petty and mean spirited. She ought to have
played in *The Merry Wives of Windsor*—what a Mistress Ford,
what would Marie have done with the " buck basket scene " !
What a Nurse she would have made in Romeo and Juliet—
and what additions she could have made in the way of looks and
added inflections. If anyone could have written a play round
Nell Gwynn which could have been the real Nell, and not a
whitewashed, over-refined imitation—who could have played
it so well as Marie Lloyd ? How she would have fitted some of

the parts in Restoration Comedy; how rich and varied and full-blooded she would have made her part.

I read somewhere, the other day, an article recalling—what a word to use in connection with Marie—her to the public. In this some wise person stated that if Marie came back now her songs would contain no hint of "naughtiness." Rubbish! Her songs would contain just exactly what she wanted them to convey, no more and no less. I agree that if the average modern music-hall artiste sang her songs they would contain nothing at all, naughty or otherwise. The music, never outstanding, even for a Variety song, the words often smart, but never anything out of the ordinary, with all due respect to Marie's very able song writers.

It has become rather fashionable to give "impressions" of Marie Lloyd. Young women do it fairly frequently on the radio. I doubt if any of them ever heard her—I feel that it's a good thing she can't hear *them*. I long to be able to say to them: "My good young women, a 'stage' Cockney accent, a slight affectation of huskiness in the voice, an added inflection here and there, do not make anything resembling Marie Lloyd."

Clarice Mayne can imitate her, her sisters can—in varying degrees of consistency—and there is no one else.

These horrible imitations—why are they allowed to go on? After listening to them one feels as Nat Goodwin did when he had listened to some Vaudeville imitator giving a "slight imitation of that celebrated actor, Mr. Nat Goodwin." Goodwin leant out of the box to listen closely, and when the dreadful imitation was over, the artiste (save the mark!) called to him: "How's that, Mr. Goodwin?"

"One of us is damned awful!" the actor replied.

There are several victims of this imitation craze. Harry Lauder, and all that is needed for imitation purposes is a Scottish accent and plenty of "Hoch ayes"; there is poor Julian Rose, nothing necessary but a "spewdo" Jewish accent, and taken at a quarter the pace which that fine artiste used to take his stuff; there are several North Country comedians, the Yorkshire ones are made to talk Lancashire, and the Lancashire ones speak Yorkshire; there is Marie—I've described how they "imitate" her, and one or two more equally horrible efforts. It's very painful, and not a bit like it!

At various times there were fusses over her songs—the late Sir Henry Tozer, at the Tivoli, once objected to a song of hers about a young lady who sat in a garden surrounded by various

vegetables. Marie, all obedience, superficially, went home and
promised to make the demanded change. She returned the
next night and sang the new line—it was fifty times as
" naughty " as the original one.

Whenever one of these " storms in a teacup " blew up, Marie
was always ready. She knew that the public had heard all
about it—the stories always went round, and always became
swollen to the most impossible and enormous proportions.
It was after one of these periodic rows that she had a song
written for her : " You can't stop a girl from thinking."

Years ago the Watch Committee, or the Morality Committee,
or the Committee for Public Safety, or some such collection of
prurient-minded old gentlemen, made a fuss about her songs.
London was undergoing one of its periodic moral spring-
cleanings and Marie was a good victim. She was ordered to
appear, complete with all her songs and a pianist, and allow
this committee of old men to decide if those songs were fit for
the ears of London and the provinces.

Marie arrived, furious ! She sang her songs, sang " Wink
the other eye," " Mr. Porter," " There they were, the two of
them on their own," " The Land of King Alphonso," and
many more. She sang without the introduction of a single nod
wink or movement ; the songs—and the singer—were dull.
She might have gone on immediately for some Mothers'
Meeting or Sunday School gathering.

The elderly gentlemen who, I cannot help feeling, had hoped
for something really salacious, something that they could repeat
probably entirely incorrectly, to each other in their stuffy old
clubs, listened—and let's hope they were bored. The Chairman
rose and informed Miss Marie Lloyd that she had their permission to continue to sing her songs, as they had found them
perfectly harmless.

And then the famous Marie Lloyd temper snapped. She
addressed them as follows, and I can imagine how those very
bright blue eyes flashed and how very tight that generous
mouth became at the corners as she did so.

" You've had me here for over an hour. I've had to sing
more than a dozen songs—and now, I can go ! Thank you for
nothing ! It's my turn now. I'm going to sing to you a couple
of songs which your wives sing at home in the drawing-room
after dinner. See what you think of them ! "

She sang : " Come into the garden, Maud," and " Why
should we wait for to-morrow, when you're queen of my heart

to-night." (I give the title of the latter fully, because that will give you some idea of the opportunities which it gave to Marie Lloyd.) She put into those two songs everything she knew : her little twists and turns, her nods and winks, in fact she did everything to make those two respectable songs the most improper, the most impossible musical productions ever offered to an audience.

Then, when every old gentleman was sitting there before her with a scarlet face, she gathered up her gloves, her bag, nodded to her pianist, wished the whole Committee a very good morning—and made her exit.

In the early days of the American invasion, when every second-rate artiste in the United States was dumping inferior rubbish in the music-halls of England, I was at a party where Marie was present. She was in great form and quite ready to sing a song or two. A newly arrived American performer was present, she was to open at the Tivoli the following evening, and her great claim to fame was that she " used a gang plank." Which meant that she walked on a plank which stretched from the stage into the auditorium. No, you might not think that was a particularly clever feat, but it was a novelty. Unfortunately for the audiences of England, it didn't remain so very long.

Marie had promised to sing, and was just finishing a drink when the voice of the Importation cut through the air.

" I'd vurry, vurry much like you to hear one or two li'rrle numbers that I'm goin' to give them at the Tivoli to-morrer. Claud—jest get my moosic, will you ? "

She sang a " li'rrle " number, playing her own accompaniment, then swung round on the piano stool and said : " Now this next is the cutest li'rrle thing you ev-er heard. Just listen !" We did. Again, " An' now, well, I can't help thinkin' you'll all jest go crazy about this one." And again, " Now, George E. Cohen told me that this was the finest—female—number he'd ever heard in his life ; he said : ' My dear, that is goin' ter be a riot.' "

Believe me, that lady sang sixteen songs on end ; she never stopped except to make the " introduction " for every song and give us some reason why we should " go crazy over it." This brilliant effort took an hour and half. When it was obvious that the the lady really had finished, Marie rose and walked over to her.

" That's your act, eh ? "

" Waal—Miss—I didn't catch your name—oh, Lloyd, Miss Lloyd, that is *part* of my act, yes."

" I see—well, you know a lot of songs, don't you ? Good night."

But let her find some wretched little first turn, struggling with a third-rate song, unable to buy any clothes except a few very Wardour Street-ish garments, and those obviously " marked down," with band parts which were inadequate, and see how differently she would behave.

" Let's see that song. This is how you want to sing it—see ? —make a lot more of this—and that. Tell the conductor that he wants to have the drum there—POM !—so ! I believe I've got just the dress for you—I'll send it round to you in the morning. What size shoes d'you take—that's all right ! Mine'll fit you. I'll be down at the side for the first house to-morrow to listen to it. Come and see me afterwards and I'll tell you how it went."

I remember once at the old Canterbury—and it was a dust-hole as far as dressing-rooms were concerned too—a lady appeared who was billed as " Princess ——." Well, I can't give her right name—" Barbarola," let's say. That is as sensible as the name was in reality. Marie asked for further information and discovered that the lady was no princess but a " rejuvenated " turn who, with a particularly " sticky " reputation, had changed her name. Changed it for the same reason that most people change their names : because they want people to forget what they were like before.

This princess never used the dressing-rooms. She had a sort of tent erected at the side of the stage and dressed in there, very aloof and proud, talking fluent and—I imagine—incorrect French to a maid whom she alternately bullied and petted.

Marie, admirably serious, said to the stage manager : " I shall need a dressing-room built for me on the Prompt side of the stage."

He replied : " Quick change, Miss Lloyd ? There's the little room there, the one you had before—that's ready for you. It's right on the stage."

" Must have one built," Marie insisted. " We royalty, you know, can't mix with the *herd !* "

" Royalty ? "

" Didn't you know ? Well, I've kept it quiet up till now—I'm not just Marie Lloyd any more—no, I'm done with that. The Duchess of Hoxton, from now on ! "

By the Wednesday night that " Princess Barbarola " was only too glad to retire to a dressing-room and never emerge from it except to come down to the stage to do her turn and then go back—and shut the door !

Marie was driving down to Bristol from Bath one day, where she was to appear at the Empire. On the way—and, believe me, this is probably the one and only exception when she broke faith with her " boys and girls "—she stopped with Mrs. Burge to visit some friends who lived on the road. Clocks were wrong, time was forgotten, Marie was delighted to meet her friends, and suddenly realized that by the time Marie reached Bristol the first house would be almost over. When they arrived the first house *was* over and the manager was at the stage door in a flaming temper—and rightly.

Marie got out of the car beaming—trying to get ready the " soft answer which turneth away wrath "—and said : " Hello, I'm sorry, I'm a bit late, I'm afraid."

" A *bit* late ! " he stormed. " A bit late ! Do you know that we've played ' God Save the King ' ! "

" Then," said Marie, " play ' God Save the Queen '—and she'll get on some make-up and appear ! "

CHAPTER THREE

Marie's memory—Her dance—The child at the Met—Marie's tempers, and generosity—The cornet player—Her money—The giants.

ONLY lately I heard that Marie Lloyd, as well as the Music-hall Ladies' Guild, had a hand in bringing Doctor Crippen to justice. Although Marie might think very little of Belle Elmore as an artiste she had a certain affection for her and resented—as she always did—the sight of another woman alienating a man's affection from his wife. After Belle Elmore disappeared, at the time Crippen told Mrs. Charles Coborn and Miss Lottie Albert, first that she had gone to America, then, contradicting himself, that she had gone to stay with her sister at Torquay, and thirdly that Belle had died, there was a very big ball given at the Horn's Hotel, Kennington. The famous music-hall society known as " The Water Rats " gave one every year, and the whole of the music-hall world attended. They were great functions, those Water Rats' dances and dinners and outings !

Mrs. Egerton, one of Marie's greatest friends—in fact, a friend of the whole profession—was one of the guests ; and, among others, Dr. Crippen attended with a lady.

Now Marie had an admirable memory for certain things and, having a very pretty fancy for jewellery herself, had often noticed and admired Belle Elmore's. She watched Crippen's companion for a few moments, then went over to Mrs. Egerton.

" You've heard that Crippen told Mrs. Coborn and Lottie Albert that Belle had gone back to America ? Well, the woman with him is wearing all Belle's jewels to-night ! What does that mean ? "

As Edwin Adeler, who tells me this story, says : " Tongues

began to wag, questions began to be asked, and the machinery
was set in motion which led to Crippen's arrest."

I think that it was at a Music-hall Artistes Railway Federation Ball that Marie arrived somewhat early. She, as always,
hated having to stand about killing time. She noticed that
several very smartly dressed men had already arrived and,
gathering them together, suggested that they should have a
" caterpillar " race. Questions were asked as to the precise
nature of this sport and Marie explained that it consisted of
wriggling along the floor propelling oneself by the palms of
one's hands and one's toes. Let me add that all these men were
" leading lights " in the profession and not in any way short of
money. Marie proposed to place a five-pound note at one end of
the room and start them off from the other. Agreed ! Away they
went, wriggling along the floor. I forgot who won the fiver ; but
when they rose their beautiful dress suits were daubed all down
the front with the sticky chalk used to polish dancing floors. It
won't rub off either ! Did Marie know ? That's why she did it !

I can remember her so well at those " pro " dances : always
the smartest woman in the room, always ready to offer anyone
champagne, and more than once accompanied by elderly and
rather shabby ladies to whom she wanted to give a good time.
And, despite the fact that everyone wanted to talk to her, everyone wanted to listen to her, she made it her first business to
see that these rather dowdily dressed friends of hers enjoyed
every minute of their evening.

On one of these occasions it was getting late and there was
the faint sense of flatness creeping over everything and everybody, which comes when people are growing a little bit tired
and yet are not sufficiently tired to go home. Marie was on the
top of her form, talking to everyone, saying most amusing
things, recognizing all her friends and generally the very
centre of attraction. Someone mentioned " pedestal " dancing
and Marie immediately said : " Well, I'll dance on a table
any time." Then there were shouts of : " That's right,
Marie ! You show us ! "

A table was brought and Marie helped on to it. Her eyes
were dancing, her whole face alight with amusement and happiness. She did the prettiest, daintiest dance I have ever seen.
Her little feet twinkled, everyone was delighted—showed
their pleasure—and Marie continued to dance. I think that
she'd have gone on until she dropped if she felt that her friends
were enjoying what she did to amuse them.

Then suddenly the door of the ballroom was flung open and a little crowd of men entered. They had been dancing earlier, but had become bored because they were all of that type to whom ordinary fun and amusement means nothing ! The laughter died from Marie's face, her feet ceased to twinkle, and she held out her hand for someone to help her down. She looked as if a light had been extinguished, as if the curtain had been rung down.

The foremost of the men walked over to where she stood and, standing in front of her, demanded :

" What the hell d'you think you're doing ? "

She didn't even speak, just looked at him. It was the first time in my life I had ever seen Marie frightened. The next thing was the sound of an open hand on her cheek and several of Marie's friends had the fellow by the collar and were hustling him out. I can still see her standing there, her hand laid on her cheek where the blow had struck her, and in her eyes the expression of a child who has been punished for—nothing. I doubt if there was a single person there who didn't feel the horrible indignity of it ; who didn't see that pathetic, startled look in her eyes and realize just what the incident had meant to Marie Lloyd.

But that was many years later, long after the time when she noticed with those exceedingly sharp eyes that another woman was wearing Belle Elmore's jewellery.

So, to switch from that dreadful little scene to something with a touch of comedy. The late Rachel Lowe had a song called " Lucky Duck " and used to carry a pet duck on to the stage with her, under her arm. At certain signals the duck used to " quack " and the bird's interpolations were very much to the point. (This is not the place to tell you what I feel, personally, about any kind of animal act, even if it is only a duck which quacks ; a thing which is, after all, natural enough.) This duck was left in the change-room at the side of the stage. The hall was the old Metropolitan Music Hall in Edgware Road, known affectionately as " The Met."

Marie rushed in, late as usual, and said to the dresser : " Get me a brandy and soda quickly and put it in the change-room." The dresser did as she was ordered. Marie finished her turn, came back into the change-room to get her drink. She found an empty glass and the duck lying beside it. It had flown on to the table and drunk the whole of her brandy and soda—it was helplessly " blotto." I am assured that never again did

that duck quack ! Rachel Lowe's song was never the same
again.

Marie was a great favourite at the Met and here is a story of
her which goes back to the days before she was a great star,
to when she was making headway and was " on her way to
the top."

In those days it was customary for parents who did not belong
to " the business " to apprentice clever children to " managers "
who trained them for the Variety Stage. The child was fed,
housed and clothed at the expense of the manager, who took a
percentage of the child's salary and sent the rest to its parents.
Let me say here that there were many cases where children were
given the greatest care and received the most careful attention,
notably in the case of the children in the " Tiller Troupes,"
who were always in charge of a matron, were fed admirably
and were trained in that style of dancing which has become
famous all over the world.

However, on this particular evening, when Marie Lloyd sat
in her dressing-room making up for the stage, a little child was
crying bitterly. She had made some mistake the previous
evening, or at rehearsal, and had been scolded and smacked
for it by the woman who was in charge of her. This woman
stood over the child, hectoring and bullying.

" Stop that ! Do you hear ? Stop it ! If you don't you'll get
such a thrashing as you've never had in your life."

The little fair-haired woman, who was busy making up,
looked round and asked : " What shall I be doing ? "

" What will you be doing—when ? " demanded the irate
lady.

" While you're giving that kid the thrashing of her life ? "

" Minding your own business, I should hope."

The other nodded. " That's right ! That's just what I shall
be doing ! You touch her and see what happens, that's all."

Then to the child : " Stop crying, my ducks, or you'll spoil
your make-up. No one's going to touch you while I'm here.
I'll look after you this week."

Later the little girl sidled up to Marie as she stood on the
stage and asked what her name was.

" My name ? Marie Lloyd."

Now that little girl was Hetty King, one of the finest " male
impersonators " ever seen on the halls. She told me that story
and said : " I shall always remember how happy I was that
week. Just to go down and know that she'd be there—even

if she didn't say very much to me." And curiously enough, they never met each other again. Passed in and out of music-halls, were at the same balls and entertainments—but never spoke to each other. Yet Hetty King told me that when Marie died she was conscious of a real and personal loss.

In case some of these stories seem almost "too good to be true"—let me say that every single one has been given to me by people who have wished to co-operate with me in trying to make this tribute to Marie. These are not "Someone told my friend who told me"; they are, every one, told by people who knew Marie—and loved her.

I have said that she had faults—her temper was violent and sudden; she was apt to be unreasonable; she had little real discrimination when it came to choosing some of her friends; she was always open to flattery, and she hated ever to admit that she had been wrong. The greatest mistake of Marie's life was made because she refused to admit that it *had* been a mistake. The spirit of bravado was very strong in her, and often she refused to reject people, worthless people, simply because "every man's hand was against them." That may be called loyalty, but it is loyalty carried to a foolish extreme; it is loyalty which has degenerated into sheer obstinacy and a refusal to admit that you can have made a grave mistake.

Her generosity was unbalanced—let's admit that, but remember that it did not come from a desire to "buy" popularity; it came from a genuine wish to make everyone happy. She liked to give people those unexpected little luxuries, which do, after all, make life so much more pleasant. And here I refer to a letter which comes from my very dear friend, Mrs. Martin Adeson. She and her husband used to do a remarkably funny sketch called "Doctor Maud's First Patient." He played the old "gas man," come to cut off the gas because the rate hadn't been paid. I remember the "gag" was: "I've come to cut it off," and the subsequent misunderstandings were very funny. Martin Adeson played with Harry Gratton in that famous sketch "The Plumbers"—that's an "evergreen," and I wonder someone doesn't revive it. For the character of the Brethren of the Lead Pipe still remains unchanged. I can hear the "tag' of that sketch now, with the water pouring all over the stage and the two plumbers agreeing, hands on hips, pictures of undisturbed inefficiency: "Well, it looks like a *burst* ter me, Bill."

Clarie Adeson (Clara Bernard she used to be) tells me of an

occasion when they were on the bill with Marie at the Pavilion, Glasgow, which used to be one of the finest investments you could make. Shares in the Glasgow Pavilion were something more than merely "gilt edged"—they were smothered in gold ! Marie arranged a motor trip for all the women on the bill—the men were excluded. Before they started, she drove round to the best milliner's in the town and insisted on buying every one of her guests a new hat. There was only one stipulation : "Have whatever you like—only don't ask the price ; that's my business ! "

They lunched at one of the big lake-side hotels, and Clarie says the soup really was terrible. Marie tasted it, grimaced, and called the waiter. "Tell the manager that I want to speak to him ! "

The waiter returned with the message that the manager was engaged, and couldn't come. Marie replied : "You tell him that Marie Lloyd wants him and if he doesn't come to me quickly—I'll come to him." He came. Marie showed him the soup.

"Look here, unless you're keeping it a dead secret—what is this ? "

"Soup, madam."

Marie said : "There you are—you said it was, didn't you, Clarie ! Now, tell me, what kind of soup is it ? "

"Pea soup, madam."

(That gave Marie an opening which she couldn't resist and led to the manager repeating the name of the soup slightly more loudly and distinctly, and Marie saying : "Oh, I beg your pardon ; my mistake ! ") Then she repeated : "Pea soup—now I'm something of a cook, and I'm going to give you a hint. When you want to make pea soup, be reckless ; use *three* peas and damn the expense."

Mrs. Adeson tells me another story, too. It was at a famous West End hall, and when Marie went in to dress she found a pretty little " serio," who was the first turn, sitting on the stairs, crying. Of course, Marie had to ask why, and try to find out if nothing could be done to stop the girl's tears.

The story was as follows. The musical director who had rehearsed the girl's music in the morning had left the orchestra at the end of the overture, letting his deputy conduct for the unimportant first and second turns and saving himself for the " stars "—among whom was Marie Lloyd, who came on later. The deputy conductor had done his best, but he had taken the girl's music at a different tempo ; she had been all at sea, and the act was ruined. She had come off with hardly a hand, and what was even more tragic—and, believe me, these things are tragedies to a vaudeville artiste—there had been an important agent in front to watch her turn who had promised her future dates if she went well.

Marie fired off a few questions. " Left the orchestra did he ? The low down so-and-so ! I see ! You think the deputy can conduct, eh ? He's not a wash-out ? He's all right, eh ? Only wants to get the tempo right ? Can you fix it so he does ? You can. All right, cock, come and see me when I'm off."

She, Marie, sent for the manager.

" I don't like your conductor. I won't have him in the orchestra for the rest of the week. His deputy can conduct—he's all right."

" But, Miss Lloyd—you let him conduct for you before. You've never objected to him before. What's wrong ? "

Marie shrugged her shoulders. " I—don't—like—him ! See ? If he goes into the orchestra for the rest of the week, I don't go on at all. I'll take a holiday. Got that ? "

" But why, Miss Lloyd ? "

" You tell him what I've said," Marie replied. " I lay you a fiver he'll know why."

The conductor did know why, and no management dared refuse to comply with Marie's demands ; there is something in being the Queen of Comedy, you can have your orders obeyed ! Later the little serio came round.

Marie said, patting her shoulder : " There you are ; don't you worry any more. Give me the name of your old agent and I'll see that he comes down again this week to see you, and I'll explain to him exactly what went wrong this evening." And she did !

There was the cornet player who came in at the wrong moment in one of her songs. She was furious, rushed back to her dressing-room, stormed and raved ; she'd not have that sort of thing ; she wasn't there to have her work ruined by— well, you can imagine what she said. Finally : " Send the cornet player to me. I want him."

He came, a shivering little man, and the storm broke over him. " Keep out of the orchestra for the rest of the week ! Got that ? Don't let me see your face down there when I go on or, by God, I'll come down and drag you out by your wretched neck ! D'you think that they pay me my salary to have my work mucked about——" *ad lib*, and with several choruses into the bargain.

The sequel was this. The conductor said : "Oh, she'll have forgotten all about it by to-morrow, and you can slip back. We know her tempers, but they're soon over, and she forgets."

However, for once Marie didn't forget, and the next night she sent word down to the orchestra room to know if the cornet player was there, and if he was, they were to keep him out of the orchestra or she wouldn't appear. Things were serious ; the conductor began to get rattled and to "hedge" a little. It was so inconvenient, and he told the cornet player that if he couldn't help making these messes and muddles—well, the sooner they got someone who could, the better. The wretched little man got white and shivered a little. He was very poor, he was married, his wife wasn't too strong ; and the answer he got from his chief was : "I can't help your troubles, ole man."

He gathered up the remnants of his courage and went to Marie's dressing-room. Might he speak to Miss Lloyd ? He was shown in. He explained. He was nervous, he admitted it, he wasn't a bad player, in fact he'd even managed a bit of orchestration now and then for a few of the smaller pros. He was afraid that he was going to get the sack——

Marie, scowling, said : "And a bloody good job, too ! "

He was an engraver by trade, and there wasn't much doing. The theatre work made all the difference, because there was the missus and four children——

Marie, her scowl getting less evident, said : "Four ! Blimy, you're not only careless when you're in the orchestra, eh, cocky ? " And if he got the sack, well, he didn't know quite what would happen.

"Sack ! Who says you're going to get the sack ! You get back into the orchestra, and—wait a minute—here's something for the missus and the kids. How many did you say, forty ? Oh, only four ! Send the conductor to me and get back to your work." Then, that impulsive frankness which was how Marie " wiped out " everything and made you swear that there never had been, and never could be anyone like her : " I'm sorry, old man. I was—you know—bit nervy, bad temper—call it what you like. Forget it, and don't worry ; it's all right."

Sure enough, it was all right. The conductor was offered champagne, he was told that she blamed herself, that the cornet player was very little short of being a great artiste—and that was that !

For years afterwards, whenever she visited that particular hall, at the rehearsal on Monday morning, she would peer down into the orchestra and call : " Hello, how's the Captain of the Forty ? " The little cornettist always spoke of her as one might have spoken of a stern but eminently just god, dealing out punishment when it was needed, but always ready to grant forgiveness.

There she was, at the time of which I am writing now ; she was still under forty ; she had already earned well over a hundred thousand pounds—and spent most of it. There again, the old question came up—how ? No doubt she helped her father and mother ; she had certainly given her family a hand whenever necessary ; she was educating her daughter, Marie Courtney ; she kept a house-boat and a house in town, but none of these things will account for the spending of that colossal sum of money. Her jewellery was good, but never excessive. She would never have " put her money into diamonds," as poor Millie Payn did ; she never kept up the almost regal state of a Harriet Vernon, and though she liked to live well, to have the best—didn't she say : " I always hold with having it, if you fancy it " ?—yet her real tastes were Bohemian in the extreme. I have it on the best authority, that of her sisters, that during these years Marie might have obtained for herself a social position and financial security had she wished. Social position which might not have been " in the first flight," but which would certainly have been well up in the second.

Rich young men-about-town, wealthy stockbrokers, and at least one peer of the realm, to say nothing of a couple of millionaires, laid siege to Marie's heart—and failed. She was a bred in the bone Bohemian, as much of a die-hard in her own likes and dislikes as anyone, and these men with money and position who were perhaps just a little inclined to look down their aristocratic noses, and lift their well-formed eyebrows at Marie's " old dears," and " uncles " and rather shabby, out-of-work pros—had only to show disapproval once. Marie's quick blue eyes missed very little, and her admirers either accepted her, complete with her entourage of old friends and " adopted " relations, or the curtain fell on them and didn't rise again.

The money she had earned, by sheer hard work, by her art, her energy and vitality, had most of it vanished. What did it matter ? There was plenty more where that came from ! She employed an agent, but after the first few years, during which time George Ware made her bookings, she didn't need one. Later, Walter Bently, who died only a short time ago, worked for her, and for a very brief period the late Ernest Edelsten, who had booked her when she played her last tour in America, and, in fact, went over on the same boat. She later used to have her bookings done by her brother, Johnnie.

She first let Johnnie make her bookings when she was "chained" down to £100 a week. Johnnie was then Bar Manager at the Empress, Brixton, and Dick Burge—who was an astute fellow, and a very good friend to Marie—suggested that she should let "Johnnie have a pop at booking her." Marie immediately said to her brother : "Now then, show your quality ! I've got January the eleventh out. Let's see what you can do about it ! "

Johnnie offered her to Charles Reade, who had just that morning booked Vesta Victoria, but who sent him on to Jack de Frece, who had recently opened an agency. Johnnie demanded a salary of two hundred and fifty for the week, and got it. Marie opened at Longton, in Staffordshire, vulgarly known as "Poland." Marie was delighted ; Johnnie left the Empress and, from then on, managed the major part of her work.

The big turns like Marie, Tich, Cinquevalli, George Robey and Vesta Tilley were "gifts" to agents. There was no need to press managers to engage them, as had to be done with some little unknown act. If the hall was sufficiently large, if the weekly takings would stand it, those stars were always wanted. They earned big money, were no trouble and paid their percentage every week. They were money for jam !

At this time the character of the halls was changing considerably. Under the auspices of such men as Edward Moss and Oswald Stoll many of them had been, if not actually rebuilt, at least reorganized. There were cleaner dressing-rooms, the stages were improved, the lighting was overhauled, and new seats were installed. The old chairman had gone long ago, and drinks were no longer served by perspiring waiters during the performance. Music-halls were no longer places to which no respectable woman cared to go—even when accompanied by her husband or someone else's. Music-halls had become less blantantly vulgar, and even in the lower class halls the old " raw " dirt was not regarded with approbation.

The American Invasion had begun, and artistes (though

many of them had little or no right to that title) were flocking to England. Agents dashed over the Atlantic and came back with new acts, new turns, many of them billed as " super attractions " for a week and then disappearing—and rightly— into the limbo of forgotten things. I remember the great Valesqa Surat coming over to England ; I remember her first night at the Palace when she carried a bouquet of Parma violets costing something over a fiver. The Palace audience " stopped and looked and—didn't—listen " ; at least, not with any great attention. I forget whether she finished the week or not—any- way, she never came back again to England. " The boat sailed Wednesday ! "

American turns were the rage, and several good Lancashire and Yorkshire turns studied the accent, changed their names and appeared as " Broadway's Bouncing Boomers " or " New York's Nuttiest Novelty "—and found their salaries leaping up from ten pounds a week to fifty. It was one of those inexplicable ramps—and, like most ramps, it had its day and fizzled out. There were exceptions, of course. The great R. G. Knowles, a brilliant man and a fellow of great culture, came over long before this Invasion. I speak of the majority who were " stunts " and doing nothing more than putting up a bluff. Once that bluff was called they disappeared.

In the midst of this turmoil, when many artistes asked them- selves if they ought not to " get new material with an American flavour," Marie Lloyd went on as she had always done, singing songs which suited her and letting the American craze run its course.

She had long ago given up her semi-childish numbers : " Whacky whack " and " There they were " ; she had cul- tivated a more sophisticated style : the " smart " songs which gave her so much scope. She wore magnificent clothes and delivered those songs with just the right degree of " sauce." This was the period of her career when she was singing : " Every little movement," " The Piccadilly Trot," and " The Coster Girl in Paris."

I have always given it as my opinion that at this time there were certain " fixed " stars who, in their own particular lines, could not and never have been equalled by anyone. They were, and have remained after many years, unique. Poor Dan Leno had gone or, naturally, he would have been included. They were—at the time of which I am writing, about 1908—Marie Lloyd, Cinquevalli, Little Tich, and Vesta Tilley. Those

four people, though they might have their " off days " when
they were not at their best, held their supremacy to the very
end. Cinquevalli—who died of a broken heart—never altered,
he was always the World's Perfect Juggler. Tich was never
anything but a " Bill Topper." Vesta Tilley left the stage in a
blaze of glory ; and Our Marie died in harness, as popular,
and as deserving of her popularity, as she had ever been.
Truly, " there were giants " on the music-hall stage in those
days.

CHAPTER FOUR

" SOME GREAT MISFORTUNE TO PORTEND,
NO ENEMY CAN MATCH A FRIEND

SWIFT

The rift widens—New impressions—Marie makes a break—
" Methinks, my lady . . ."—Command performance—The
Queen of Comedy—America and liberty—The woman with
the whip—The death of Alec Hurley.

THE rift was widening. Alec Hurley had been quite
genuinely in love with his wife ; it was obvious to
everyone, during the early years of their marriage, that
he had been devoted to her. The consensus of opinion is that
in his heart he never ceased to love her and that later he
regretted his mistakes bitterly. At the time of which I am
writing now he had reached that stage which occurs in so many
marriages, when a man begins to " take his wife for granted."
The first glamour has died, the first fine rapture is past and,
though it may be possible that a deep and very real affection
remains, those little attentions which once meant so much have
begun to be disregarded.

Alec was away working in the provinces a good deal, for he
was never a " planet " in the music-hall sky as Marie was, and
many of his dates took him out of town. While he was away
and she was working in London, or when both of them were in
different provincial towns, matters continued on a fairly satis-
factory basis. Marie was never at any time that unreasonable
type of woman who is jealous of the work which takes her
husband away from her side, neither was she the kind of wife
who expects her husband to be for ever catching late trains
from Manchester or Liverpool so that he may spend a few
hours with her. She would have regarded that kind of thing
as utterly stupid and detrimental to his work.

When Alec was at home, working in or around London,
matters were less easy. Marie liked to have him with her on

these occasions, she liked to entertain largely and lavishly, and she liked to have her husband with her when she gathered her friends together. Alec was a popular fellow and he, too, enjoyed going about with his friends and having a good time. Probably his love of amusement became something of a habit and Marie awoke to the fact that she was being more and more left to her own devices. She was lonely, she resented the fact that Alec did not seem to care very much what she did or where she went and, most of all, she resented the fact that he did not appear to realize that she longed for his companionship, for the old comradeship and evidences of affection.

It may have been that he was nothing more than careless and rather selfish ; it is quite probable that it never occurred to him that he was neglecting her. One thing is certain, that later he realized his mistakes and regretted them sincerely.

Now, though it is a fairly true statement to say that Marie had no enemies, yet no one can attain the position to which she had climbed without leaving behind some mean-spirited souls who watch the successful achievements of others more fortunate than themselves with bitter jealousy. There exists, too, a certain type of person who lives by making mischief, to whom scandal is the breath of life, to whom slander is more than meat and drink. There were plenty of such people on the halls at this time and many of them were only too delighted to run to Alec and assure him of their regret and deep sympathy that Marie and he were not " getting on."

As a matter of fact, until these people began to drop their distilled poison in his ears Alec had been very happy indeed with her. Any unhappiness had been on her side, not on his. I have stated that he was a popular fellow and deservedly so ; he was also a very pleasant person, possessed of reasonably good looks, friendly and kind-hearted ; but—and I knew him fairly well, remember—he was weak. Weakness is not an uncommon fault, but it is one which may have far-reaching results ; and when people came with their tittle-tattle of Marie to Alec, instead of ordering them out of his dressing-room, this weakness of his asserted itself. He allowed them to talk, while he listened. Among other things these charming people insinuated that while Alec was working hard in the provinces Marie was enjoying herself, going here, there and everywhere in London.

I remember once when Alec was working one of the South Coast towns Marguerite Broadfoote and I went round to his dressing-room to see him. We found two people there, a man and a woman, both Variety artistes. They were engaged in their favourite amusement—stirring up trouble for other people. With a damnable air of frankness and good-fellowship they were recounting to Alec that : " Someone told me . . ." and " I did hear last week that . . ." and apparently everything they had heard and been told related to Marie Lloyd. They laughed a good deal, they referred frequently to Marie as being " a real sport," " a proper lad," and as " not caring what anyone says or thinks." Under their laughter, under their amusement and their air of harmless merriment was the inference that they couldn't help sympathizing with " poor old Alec." That was where his weakness showed itself. Instead of ordering them to speak frankly ; instead of telling them to put their cards on the table and then " calling their bluff," he listened, and gradually it became evident that, in his heart, doubt began to take root and he really felt that he was a badly used fellow.

The stories ended, as all such stories do, with the assurance : " Mind, Alec, old boy, neither of us wants to say a word against Marie. We'd never do that, only somehow it does seem a shame when you're out in the provinces, working so hard, that——" *ad lib.* Alec, by that time, was in that almost hypnotic state which comes to people who are not really particularly intelligent and who don't use what brains they have sufficiently. He was, in fact, rather like poor little David Copperfield in the capable hands of Mrs. Heep and her son Uriah !

" No, I know you'd never say anything against Marie. I know that," he said. Marguerite, the most gentle creature in the world, who admired Marie as an artiste and loved her for the generous, great-hearted soul that she was, spoke up.

" But that's just what they are doing ! " she cried. " They are talking against Marie, and they know it. That's what they've come here to do. They're too cowardly to speak plainly, so they're telling half-truths, which are the most damnable of all lies, and you know it. Alec Hurley, I'm ashamed for you ! " And with that, like the celebrated duchess, she " swept out."

Only, unfortunately, everyone did not take that line with Alec, or he might have come to his senses and everything might have ended quite differently. He was weak, Marie was reckless, and the breach between them grew wider and wider until it was impossible to bridge it. He neglected her ; she was lonely and she hated loneliness. She was, in addition, a very proud woman, and the thought that Alec preferred, or seemed to prefer, other people's company to hers wounded her dreadfully.

She tried to talk to him, but—as we have seen—Marie never found it very easy to keep her temper ! Alec responded with some of the exaggerated and fantastic stories which had been retailed to him, trying to justify himself, hiding behind those lying tales which by this time he had almost persuaded himself to believe. Marie, intolerably hurt, flung back her old challenge to him :

"Well, if I've got the name—I might as well have the game ! "

There were fresh starts, matters were patched up, armistices were arranged, but the old confidence in each other was shattered. It was evident to both of them that what had made their marriage such a success originally existed no longer. Marie Lloyd watched her second marriage prove itself a failure.

Marie knew everyone, and among her friends were a great number of racing people. Two of her sisters married men who were in that particular world—married most successfully and happily. At her huge Sunday parties you might meet any amount of jockeys, and among them a young Irishman who was making a very fine name for himself in the racing world. He was sought after by owners, he was stated to have " judgment and pluck," and he had already a considerable number of successes to his credit.

Marie found him rather shy and retiring. She scarcely spoke to him, for her Sunday afternoons and evenings were always crowded, and she was always surrounded by people. The Irish jockey came again with his racing friends, and still made very little impression on her.

Then one Sunday he arrived with an accordion under his arm. Marie shouted with laughter. She felt, somehow, that it was in keeping with his shyness and quietness to play an accordion. In itself she regarded it as a slightly comic instrument and one which gave forth music which was melancholy in the extreme. However, his friends praised his playing, and it transpired that he could sing as well as play. He was persuaded to play and sing, which he did with considerable talent. Marie was delighted.

She might, herself, sing songs in which all sentiment was lacking, but she loved music, and her heart was easily touched. Her pleasure at those Irish melodies is an additional proof of her innate simplicity. She might tell stories which were distinctly *risqué*, she sang songs which had a distinctly Rabelaisian flavour, but simple people, simple sentiment, and simple old songs never failed to bring out the softer and more gentle side of her nature.

I can imagine her listening, with her blue eyes a little moist, to "Believe me if all those endearing young charms," "The meeting of the waters," or "The last rose of summer," and almost blaming herself for not having been sufficiently kind or attentive to this young Irishman who played so delightfully.

Marie might appear to be a complete woman of the world ; she was the world's greatest comedienne, but she had remained in many ways still the "Little Tilly Wood" of the Fairy Bell Minstrels ; she had not changed materially since the days when, wide-eyed, she told the great "Drurylanus" that she had always imagined his magnificent theatre was a barracks.

So Alec Hurley drifted out of Marie's life, and what she had honestly believed to be the great romance of her life ended. Gradually the memory of Alec Hurley became obliterated, and Marie slowly realized that she had found again all that she had once discovered when she met Alec years ago. Life had renewed itself once more, and she was wildly happy. She said quite frankly : "I'm forty and no woman knows what falling in love can mean until she's forty." It was springtime over again, and she was—she announced it with a queer little touch of defiance—"going to be happy."

She was at the top of her profession ; she was working magnificently, sought after, popular, and beloved. She had fallen in love, quite desperately, whole-heartedly, and there was something almost splendid in her complete assurance that she had found that Philosopher's Stone which was to change everything into gold.

Mr. Dillon was still riding in those days, and at one race meeting Marie went down to see him ride. She looked wonderful, by far the best-dressed woman on the course. She was on the top of her form, delighting everyone with her daring witticisms. The horses were going up to the start ; Marie stood at the rails, and as Mr. Dillon rode past, she stopped him, held up her face and kissed him before everyone. The crowd —Marie's public, Marie's "boys and girls"—roared with delight. They admired her pluck, loved her for her disregard of everything and everybody except the man she loved. They yelled :

" Bravo, Marie ! Good old Marie ! "

When Mr. Dillon won the Derby, riding " Lemberg,"
" Fairie " Cox's horse, Marie stood in the grand-stand and
cheered herself hoarse. " I feel as if I owned the horse myself ! "
she told everyone, adding that smile of hers which could be
utterly charming and completely confiding : " What a horse—
and what a jockey ! "

Marie was a good sportsman ; there was no " hedging "
with her. When she made a break she made it clean and
complete. She never tried to run with the hare and hunt with
the hounds, never grumbled because she could not eat her cake
and have it. There was that essential decency about her which
made her look facts squarely in the face. Alec had failed her ;
she had tried reconciliation, she had attempted to make new
starts—nothing had come of these. Very well. She cut Alec
out of her life, and she cut clean. He was not asked to help
her to obtain a " fake " divorce ; he was not asked to shoulder
some fictitious blame, to send her hotel bills and supply " necessary evidence." That was not Marie's way. Alec Hurley
was free to take what steps he wished ; she made it clear
that she expected no " special treatment."

And while we are touching on the matter of divorce, here is a
little sidelight on Marie's character, sent to me by Mr. Pearce
Gervis, giving his impression of her. It is so often assumed that
any woman who has been married, divorced, and re-marries,
takes these things lightly. There is so often a kind of sneer on
the faces of those good people who say with twisted lips and
acid tones : " I see that So-and-So is married *again !* I don't
think her divorce was made absolute more than a month ago !
How curious some people are." I have heard this type of
person say : " Marie Lloyd ! She made a habit of getting
married, didn't she ? " My reply has generally been unquot-
able, but very much to the point. However—to get back to Mr.
Pearce Gervis's recollection.

" During the latter part of the war, one of my best pals had to
divorce his wife. Naturally, he was given the care of the child—
about four years old—who was to be handed over to him at his
solicitor's office in Bedford Row. He asked me to go with him.
I remember that we took the child to lunch at Scott's, of all
places, and then on to The Oxford to the matinée, where Marie
was appearing, because my friend knew her and wanted to show
her his kiddie. I stood outside the dressing-room, but Marie
sent for me to go inside. I can picture her now, sitting in a sort

of wrap, with her 'make-up' a little smeared. She turned towards me as I went in and I saw that her eyes were wet. She had the child on her knee.

" ' Poor little beggar ! ' she said. (At least, that's how we'll ' report ' her words !) ' This is the rotten part of divorce ! '

" In the taxi, on the way to the station, the child said : ' Was that my grandmama ? I like her ! ' "

One other remark of Marie's he recalls.

" I don't care a damn what they say about me," she said, " *so long as they say it !* "

And lastly, his final comment, because here is the verdict of a man who is not a sentimentalist, who is a very successful business man, and a writer of considerable ability and humour : " That was the woman all over ! She was wonderful ! "

Marie had no set religion. She lived her beliefs. She never denied help to any religious order if they asked for it. Salvationists, Protestants, Nonconformists, and Catholics were all the same to Marie, provided they wanted help and asked for it without getting " mealy-mouthed." I knew a Catholic priest once—he is dead now, and there is no reason to give his name. He was one of those " obscure saints " who work and live for their religion. He loved the halls, and he loved to go behind the scenes and talk to everyone. Talking one evening to him, he told me that he had ventured to " call on Miss Marie Lloyd."

" How did she receive you, father ? " I asked.

He said : " As any lady would receive someone who called on her in friendship. How else would she have received me ? "

He said that he sat in her dressing-room for half an hour and that as she began to talk easily to him, a slightly unconventional word would slip out now and then. Every time she said : " Sorry, I didn't mean to say that. I don't mean anything by it, y'know. I mean, I don't say it because I'm trying to offend you."

She had a good opinion of Catholics, and gave a magnificent altar-cloth to the Catholic Church at Golders Green because she admired Father Bendon, the priest in charge, who gave his life to the building of that church.

I once spoke to her of a certain scandal there had been on the halls. I won't give the details here ; sufficient to say that it set a good many people talking, talking what Marie called : " All that damn *pure* stuff ! "

She said : " Look here—how can I tell ? It's not my game, see ? If it was, then I might be able to give an opinion—the

same as everyone else is so ready to do now ! What I do say is
this—poor devil ! And I mean it, too. Maybe I do—you do—
we all do—things that are just as bad in our own way."

I said, tritely enough, something about " He who is without
sin—— " Marie said : " Believe me, if only people would live
up to that there'd be a damn sight fewer bricks flying about.
The trouble with all this mud-slinging is that nine times out
of ten it never hits the person who deserves it."

That was typical of her. Live and let live. She lived her own
life, and she was perfectly willing to let other people live theirs—
as they wished to. She lived up to the only creed she knew :
" Do as you would be done by " and " Forgive us our tres-
passes as . . ." and she used to like to stress that last word,
" as we forgive them that trespass against us."

So the third act of Marie's life opens at her own beautiful
house in Golders Green. It was one of the most faultlessly kept
houses I have ever seen—and I am something of a " housewife " myself ; whatever could shine shone, whatever would
polish was polished. Marie might be, indeed was, a Bohemian,
but hers was the Bohemianism which has nothing in common
with untidy houses, badly served meals, unwashed hair and
dirty necks ! She was meticulously neat in her person ; she
would spend endless time and care upon those little details
which go to make a well-dressed woman. Her cupboards were
miracles of neatness, her wardrobes and drawers were models
of tidiness. Her taste—like that of her sisters—never deviated
towards the merely flashy, and her house was in keeping with
her clothes. It might be " Liberty Hall," but it was kept and
run by one of the most " house-proud " women who ever lived
—Our Marie.

Her sisters tell me that often she would walk into the kitchen
and say to her servants : " Let me have a look at those shelves.
I like to know that they're properly scrubbed. Never mind
putting clean paper over the dirt, let's see if it's clean underneath." Often, too, until her health began to fail, she would
take a scrubbing-brush and soapy water and show her staff
how she " liked cleaning done. Get into the corners, the
middle'll clean itself."

For those first months after her separation from Alec, Marie
went everywhere. She was working better than ever, and
assured everyone she met that she had never been so happy,
never been so utterly content. And everyone accepted what she
said ; everyone was delighted that she should have found the

happiness which she deserved. Then someone whispered : " Methinks my lady doth protest too much," and you realized that perhaps, after all, Marie was rather stressing the fact that she was so *completely* happy, so *entirely* content. No one suggested it to her ; everyone who knew Marie Lloyd too well to risk the explosion which would have been the result. Marie resented interference in any way, and she never listened to criticism of the people she liked, much less those she loved.

In 1911 the music-hall came into its own. Sir Oswald Stoll coined an apt phrase when he said : " The Cinderella of the Arts has gone to the ball at last." The King and Queen were to attend a Command performance at the Palace Theatre. The programme was to represent all that was best and most typical of the Variety stage.

The list of artistes appeared and Marie's name was not included. Everyone asked why ? Even now, when " pros " get together and " fight their battles o'er again," they are still asking—why ? Marie, who had been recognized as England's foremost comedienne, who was the highest salaried woman artiste on the halls ; she had " topped " bills for years, and she was the Idol of the Public. If there existed a fear that her songs might be too " risky "—well, Marie was sufficiently clever to have toned them down and still kept them brilliantly witty. Her songs, as they stood, were no more suggestive and outspoken than those of half a dozen other performers. She was terribly hurt that she should have been rejected—and no wonder.

If the omission was due to the fact that some long-faced busybody had spread some whisper of scandal concerning her private life—well, very few people on the halls or on the Legitimate stage attain a great measure of success without some breath of scandal touching them. Actors and actresses, comediennes and music-hall artistes live in a fierce light. Their every action is noted and almost automatically exaggerated. In addition, the fact that " A " has appeared in the Divorce Court does not make him one whit the worse as an artiste ; or because Miss B. married and discovered that she had made a mistake, which she proceeded to rectify, her voice need not suffer in the least. The private life of artistes is their own business. Affection may make their public take an interest in that life, but it ought not to bias them one way or the other with regard to the work which that artiste offers to them.

However, whatever the reason was, Marie Lloyd's name was

not included ; and on the great night everyone who appeared
seemed—to me at least—to be slightly oppressed by the
presence of Royalty. The number of warnings given at dress
rehearsal in the afternoon had been overdone, and everyone
was nervous and inclined to be temperamental.

The brilliant artiste, Mr. George Robey, seemed to lack his
usual spontaneous wit and sparkle. Harry Tich, always rather
touchy, let his nerves get the better of him and refused to stand
in the big scene at the end of the show, when Harry Claff—
looking like " Lohengrin "—sang " The King." Ida Crispi
and Fred Farren " packed up " and didn't appear at all because
someone expressed a doubt whether it was " quaite naice " to
roll Ida up in a long strip of carpet at the end of their " Yankee
Tangle." Vesta Tilley had disinterred an old song, " Mary and
John," which didn't suit her inimitable style nearly so well as
some of her later numbers ; and altogether, except for Joe
Boganny's Lunatic Bakers, who were completely at their ease
and very funny, I found the performance, as I have said, very
dull.

And at the Pavilion, a few hundred yards away, Marie Lloyd
was appearing, billed as " The Queen of Comediennes," with a
slip pasted on the bills announcing that " every performance
given by Marie Lloyd is a Command Performance by order of
the British Public." Always after that Marie was billed as
either " The Queen of Comediennes " or " The Queen of
Comedy "—and no one had a better right to those titles, and
no one ever treated their subjects better than " Our Marie "
treated her " boys and girls."

Then came an offer for America and Marie accepted it.
The engagement was made by the late Ernest Edelsten, who
was her agent at the time. Marie, accompanied by her maid,
sailed on the *Olympic*. Mr. Dillon was also one of the passengers.

Before she sailed Johnnie Wood, Marie's brother, always far-
sighted and possessing sufficient courage to speak to her frankly,
advised her against certain matters which he felt might
ultimately be prejudicial to her in the American engagement.
Marie refused to listen. As always, she said that her own business was her own business and that—provided she worked well,
" delivered the goods " at whatever music-hall she was engaged
to appear—her private affairs mattered to no one.

The crossing was not particularly encouraging for a woman
who was going out to face some of the most critical audiences in
the world. Marie's nerves, never her strong point, must have

been fairly tried by that trip across the Atlantic. She knew that great things were expected of her ; she knew that her world-wide reputation would take some living up to, for much is forgiven the small artiste, while the star must always be at the top of his or her form.

The journey ended and Marie—who had been depressed and miserable during the trip—looked forward to landing and meeting her sister, Alice McNaughton, with considerable excitement.

On the landing-stage a man came up and spoke to Marie. He said that he had met her some years previously at the Tivoli. I have never known his name ; I doubt very much if Marie knew it.   He was one of those sharks who call themselves " journalists " and go about " seeking whom they may devour," searching for little bits of news which they will turn to their own account if possible.   To such creatures a scrap of news which may be twisted into a scandal is the very breath of life !

Marie, friendliest of souls, was delighted to see him.   The fact that she didn't remember him in the least, that she had in all probability never seen him before, mattered nothing to her. He was someone who knew her beloved London !   That was enough.   She talked and chatted, told him where she was to appear and how anxious she was to please the American public.

" But I didn't see your name on the passenger list, Miss Lloyd," said this delightful ex-Londoner.

Marie, with that engaging frankness of hers, told him why. She had nothing to hide, there was nothing furtive or secretive in anything she did.   It would never have occurred to her to lie or make excuses for anything which she felt was her own personal affair, a matter which affected no one except herself.

The gentleman, seeing some fame—or infamy—for himself in this bit of news, hurried away.   I don't think that Marie ever saw or heard of him again, but within fifteen minutes Marie was arrested and taken to Ellis Island. Her sister Alice came forward immediately and stood security for her, for the authorities demanded £600.   Marie was subjected to questionings of the most humiliating description before she was set at liberty.

How Marie, decent, reckless, kindly, never counting costs or looking ahead, ready to live each day as it came and thinking no ill of anyone, must have hated it all !

Where her other friends were at this moment, why everything was left to Alice McNaughton and Marie to see through alone, is difficult to understand.   How it was possible for such a thing to have happened at all is astonishing.

She told me that when it was all over reporters crowded round asking for her impressions of America, her opinions and ideas.

"One of them said to me: 'What is your opinion of America, Miss Lloyd?' I said: 'Come over here,' and took him to the window. By craning your neck you could just catch sight of the Statue of Liberty. I pointed to it and said: 'See that? Well, I think that your idea of humour is—grand!'"

She added: "And believe me, if that rule of theirs had been in force in England, half their Vaudeville artistes would never have dared to start, never mind trying to land!"

The night she opened she was terribly nervous. She felt that the atmosphere was antagonistic, that they were not going to like her and that belief sapped her vitality. There was a certain Englishman who was in New York at that time. He was in charge of the swimming-bath on the *Olympic*, and years before had been in Variety and had known Marie very well. Like the rest of her public he loved and admired her. He gathered together every steward, sailor, engineer, bar-tender, and Turkish bath attendant he could find on the boat, and every man-jack of them were in the theatre when Marie walked on to the stage. She was greeted with shouts of: "Good old Marie!" "You're all right, Marie," "London's with you!"

She went magnificently. Possibly some of her essentially British humour did not "get over" to the New Yorkers, but her reception was excellent. True, one of the critics managed to excel himself in courteous criticism when he wrote: "Marie Lloyd looks like a grandmother and talks like a scrub woman." Well, if American grandmothers can manage to look as Marie did at that time their beauty parlours and face-lifting *salons* must be the finest, and busiest, in the world. She toured America and Canada, toured regally as Marie liked to travel, with sleeping-cars and parlour-cars, and wherever they halted any English performer living or working in the district was welcome. Even on a train Marie contrived to keep open house.

Still, there were long-faced Puritans at work, and in Alberta a newspaper editor chose to make disparaging remarks concerning Marie in his paper and also in public in the "bars" of the town. The tales, which were scandalous and abominable, reached Marie's ears and she was furious. She was a little woman, but she didn't know what fear meant. She bought a dog-whip and announced her intention of giving the man the thrashing which he deserved ; then called on him and administered the thrashing !

And during this time Alec Hurley was lying ill at Jack Straw's Castle at Hampstead. He had pneumonia, and from the first it was evident that he had very little chance of recovering. He talked constantly of Marie, always with the greatest affection.

There is one of the queer things of life. That clear realization which comes when it is too late. Alec might have tied Marie to him for life. He might have had her with him at the end, which is one of the things the poor fellow wished so often, if only he had known how to appreciate her goodness, her essential generosity while she had been his wife. When it was too late he realized and would have given all he had if she could have come to him. Only life doesn't stand still while we make up our minds and learn to see only too clearly the mistakes we have made ; and by the time Alec Hurley understood what he had lost—and understood, too, that he need never have lost that happiness—Marie was in the United States and he was dying.

" Tell Marie—because you'll see her again and I shan't," he said to a friend a few days before he died, " that I love her as much now as I did the first day I saw her. She knows how much that is."

Alec Hurley died and Marie married—while she was still in America, I think I am right in saying—Mr. Diilon, and so began what was really the last chapter of her history.

CHAPTER FIVE

Racing—Cards—Bransby and " Rubio "—" Bachelor's Button "
and the rent books—" A tenner to hear the King's voice"—
Ascot clothes—" Poor Joe "—Marie's motor-cars—Hats—She
gives advice : more than once.

THERE are still people—those clever people who
always know everything—who will tell you that the
reason why Marie Lloyd left so little money was
because she had squandered all her substance on betting and
gambling. This is as untrue as many of the other things which
are said about her. Marie never was a gambler. She liked
to bet because it added a little excitement to life ; she like a
smart race-meeting because she loved pretty clothes, liked
to wear them and to know that she created a sensation. She
loved the colour, the movement, the excitement of a race-course,
and no matter what people may say, there is no one who doesn't
get something of a thrill from the knowledge that seventy per
cent of the crowd know who they are and nudge each other as
they pass.

On a race-course everyone knew her. It was : " Marie
Lloyd ! There—in the black hat," or a little lower down the
social scale : " Look, that's Marie Lloyd, y'know, who sings
those saucy songs ! " and lower still : " Blimey, theer's Our
Marie. Looks a treat, don't she ? "

I remember once going to a very smart meeting, and as we
walked along seeing a little crowd of well-dressed men gathered
round someone who was hidden from us. My companion said :
" I bet that's one of the big musical comedy stars ! " I said :
" I bet it's Marie Lloyd ! " And it was ! Marie, dressed
beautifully. I remember that she carried a lace parasol with
a very long handle, and if anyone knew how to make the best

of a parasol she did. She was laughing, showing those very white, rather prominent teeth which were such a marked characteristic of her vivacious face. One of Marie's " good days "—and towards the end, God knows, there were only too few of them.

Her sisters say that when they were young Marie liked a game of cards and invariably lost her money to them because—and here is a point which is so typical of her in everything, not only in playing cards—Marie would never " throw in her hand." If it held nothing high except one ace, Marie would announce : " Well, I'll go Misere," and throw the ace under the table !

It was inevitable that the two sisters who married jockeys should be interested in racing : Gracie, who married George Hyams, and Maudie, the youngest, who married " Whip " Wheatly ; and, naturally, there was a certain amount of racing atmosphere about the family home. But Marie's betting was limited. One of her sisters says : " A fiver was the limit " ; but I fancy that there were times when she went a little higher.

Bransby Williams told me this story of her at Aintree, one Grand National. He says : " Marie was there with her crowd of hangers-on as usual ; Marie paying for everything ! She met me with some well-known racing men, stopped me, looked me up and down and said : ' Hello ! *You've* taken to racing have you, young cocky ! What do you fancy, eh ? ' In those days I knew so little about racing that I did not know how to approach a bookie, I had bets on with my friends, ' people who were in the know '—or thought they were. I told Marie that I had seen a horse I fancied. ' Well, keep on fancying ! ' she told me. ' And keep your " spondulicks " in your pocket. What's the horse, anyway ? ' I told her that it was ' Rubio,' a rank outsider, which made her roar with laughing. However ' Rubio ' won and—I *had* kept my ' spondulicks ' in my pocket. The price was sixty-six to one. Next time I met her she asked me how I'd got on, as she was certain that I hadn't taken her advice. I told her. ' Well, I dropped a packet,' she said, ' so we're even losers—I put too much on the wrong horse and you put nothing on the right one ! ' "

At Ascot Mr. Solly Joel once gave her a tip that " Bachelor's Button" was going to beat the unbeatable "Pretty Polly." Marie had her usual fiver on it. " Bachelor's Button " won all right, but at a very short price, and Marie really cleared very little. However, the *Star* got hold of the story, and there was a long paragraph to the effect that Miss Marie Lloyd, thanks to the advice of Mr. Solly Joel, had won an enormous amount, etc. etc.

Then, as her brother Johnnie says : " The rent books began to come in." You know the sort of thing : " I am in great trouble, deeply in debt, and I enclose my rent book to prove to you," and so on.

Johnnie Wood says that when he was Marie's manager one of his daily jobs was to open these letters and return the rent books, always with a ten-shilling note enclosed. He says that no one will ever know the number of "rent book pensioners" Marie had on her list. Their rent books came along with beautiful regularity, and were returned promptly, always with the same enclosure. He says that very often he never showed these letters to Marie because they distressed her so, only carried out his orders and dealt with them.

Once, at Kempton Park, Marie said that she'd give a tenner to hear the King's voice ! King Edward was there and this sudden desire got firmly fixed in Marie's mind. She would hear his voice—it was worth a tenner ! She sidled nearer and nearer to where he was standing, talking to a lady. At last Marie was near enough to hear what he said. " Such-and-such a horse couldn't possibly lose." That was all she heard and that was enough. She put a tenner on the " King's choice "—and it lost ! You should have heard what Marie had to say then about " giving a tenner to hear the King's voice " !

She gave it as her opinion that probably that was why they beheaded Charles the First. " I expect he gave them too many ' certs ' that were never in the first three." Always afterwards when King Edward's name was mentioned Marie used to say : " I don't doubt that he was a good king—all I know is that he was a rank bad tipster ! "

All the bookies knew her, and at one meeting there were six runners in a certain race. Three of them quoted at even money and two others at six to four, leaving one outsider. Marie sauntered up to a bookie and asked what price he'd lay on the outsider.

He smiled, recognized her, then said with great heartiness : " Well, Miss Lloyd, as it's *you*," there was a long pause, during which he sucked his teeth and thought hard, " as it's you, Miss Lloyd, I'll take you six to four to a little bit."

Her father, still alive and " going strong " at eighty-eight, likes to have his little daily flutter. He told me this summer with immense satisfaction : " I brought off a treble—think of that ! Yes, and won two pounds ! "

Alice tells me that the other day he complained that he had some difficulty in masticating his food. Alice said : " Well, father, you ought to let us get you some new teeth ; then you'd be all right."

" New teeth ! " he exclaimed. " At my time of life ! Nice thing—new teeth at eighty-eight. For someone else to wear when I'm gone, eh ? Not likely ! "

A grand old man, John Wood, who told us with minute detail of his visit to Italy years ago, when he went to spend a holiday with his " one-time " boss, Luigi Corti. Even remembering several Italian words and sending Alice out to the car to shout " *Buona Sera* " to us as we left ! Ask him about his family. He can tell you story after story : tell you which was the prettiest, the best-tempered, the hardest worker, and end with : " Marie, well, she was a bloody marvel at everything."

Here is a typical " Marie Lloyd " incident. I had this from Charles Russell, the well-known turf accountant of Edinburgh. He knew Marie very well, and admired her tremendously . One Ascot Charles Russell arranged to meet Marie at Waterloo and escort her. Believe me, any man of taste and discrimination would jump at the chance, for she was always magnificently gowned, in addition to being the best company in the world. He arrived at the station—himself very much " got up " for Ascot—and found Marie looking a picture, but not alone. With her were three elderly and—let's admit it—exceedingly dowdy ladies. She was full of delight because she was giving them " a day out." Charles Russell says that not to put too fine a point on it they looked terribly un-Ascot. They were very Early Victorian, with " tippets " and " bugles," and he thinks that one of them wore a bustle !

Marie had a telegram from Steve Donoghue telling her to back his mount, " Square Measure." They got to Ascot ; Marie only cared that her three elderly friends should have a good time.

She put twenty pounds on " Square Measure " and smaller amounts for her friends. It won, and Russell was paying over after the race when he noticed that they were standing exactly in front of the Royal Box. He saw, too, that the King was drawing the Queen's attention to the little group. Whether he recognized Marie, or whether he was amused by the appearance of her three elderly friends, Charles Russell could not tell.

He said to Marie : " Now *don't* look round, but the King's seen you ! " Marie promptly did look round, and insisted that her friends should look round as well. The King continued to smile, and Marie said afterwards to Charles Russell, with immense satisfaction : " You know, it made their day for them, having the King smile right at them like that ! ".

He says that Marie often told him that if she could appear in a " straight " play her ambition was to play the part of " Poor Joe " in *Bleak House*, the part made so famous by the " Vital Spark "—Jenny Hill. No one could have played it better than Marie could have done, because, with that generous nature, she would have given full value to those words : " 'E was very good to me ! " No one ever did anything for Marie without gaining gratitude quite out of proportion to the small service they might have been able to render her.

And here, at this juncture, I am going to take a leaf out of that excellent book of " Billie " Boardman's, *Vaudeville Days*, and mention a subject which would have been very near—indeed, *was* very near—to Marie's splendid heart.

The music-hall profession have their own Institution where those " old pros," for whom life, through ill-health or other misfortune, has gone hardly, may find a home which is a home.

This is no cold, efficiently run, dehumanized concern. It is a fine house, with beautiful grounds, every comfort, and where each resident has a private room, which they can furnish more or less as they wish. There are very few rules, very few restrictions—it is a Home in every sense of the word. But homes need keeping up, and so if there are any of you who, after reading this attempt to put Marie Lloyd before you, feel that you would like to, or could, help this very splendid institution, send whatever you like, send whatever you can, to Harry Marlow, Brinsworth House, Staines Road, Twickenham.

The residents have sent me so many letters, so many stories about Marie, they have written such magnificent tributes to her kindness and generosity, that I felt impelled to write back and ask if they would give me the privilege and honour of asking them to " send out for one " and have it " with Marie Lloyd." By return of post came a letter from Flo Hastings, full of good wishes, and positively breathing content and happiness. That " by return of post " is illuminating.

When I began this book I wrote nearly a hundred letters asking those people who had known Marie to send me their recollections of her. The replies have been touching and rather wonderful, but the absence of replies from various " stars " has been remarkable. As I wrote various letters, I could hear Marie's voice saying, with a sort of chuckle : " No good writing to her, Micky, she's never liked me," or " Good Lord, have you gone crazy ? You don't suppose that ' Her Royal Highness ' will bother to send you back a reply to any questions about *me*, do you ? " And, sure enough, they haven't replied. Those people for whom Marie would always have found praise, to whom she would always have given the most frank admiration, have never even bothered to answer my letters.

But the " rank and file "—and not only the rank and file, but the real " pro," the good trouper—have taken trouble not only to write themselves, but to get their friends to send me letters. Well, I may feel a little " sore," but I believe that Marie would only shrug her shoulders, and say :

" Feel sore, you silly fool ; what have you got to feel sore about ? They've always been like that. Anyway, look here— here's a letter from Arthur Prince, and Harry Claff, and Bransby, and dear old George Graves, and a whole lot more. Let the rest of 'em go to the devil ! "

However, that's only ventilating a private grievance, and let's get back to Marie, who would have told me to " shut up and get on with the doings."

Of course, the moment that motor-cars were a practical proposition Marie Lloyd had one. A little red Panhard coupé. That was the smart thing to have ; Harry Tich had one, Marguerite Broadfoote had one. They were two-cylinder, and it used to take us half the day to get down to Selsey from London. To go there and back in a day was considered an adventurous feat. Marie had her red Panhard, and she had her young brother, Sidney, to drive it. She dressed him in black leather, and very smart it was too ; only with Marie's affection for " spit and polish," the poor lad had to clean the whole suit with " Nugget " boot polish !

Sid was driving her up Brixton Hill one day, on her way to a luncheon party—perhaps driving up to George Barclay's magnificent house, where his wife, Kate Carney, had a piano which was the replica of one made for Queen Victoria. Over it hung a portrait of Kate Carney singing her celebrated song : " Three pots a shilling."

The car was behaving badly, and a very old, rattling four-wheeler passed them easily. Marie leant out of the car and shouted to Sid : " What the hell is the matter with the damned thing *now* ! " Sid replied in the language of the perfect chauffeur, which is unintelligible to anyone who is not versed in " mechanical " lore : " Oh, it's the piston—the dynamo— the carburettor—and the clutch—— " The car stopped. Marie, by this time, was in a perfect frenzy of annoyance. " Oh, good God," she shouted, " talk *English*, can't you ? " Leaping out, she looked at the car as if she hated it. Then, with a gold mesh-bag set with rubies, banged on the bonnet, shouting : " Damn you—go home, d'you hear ?—blast you, go home ! "

They were wonderful cars in those days. This Panhard held four gallons of petrol. Sid says that he once drove Marie, with Gertie Miller and Lionel Monckton, to Richmond from town. They had to stop and " fill up " three times before they got there. The petrol-tank was so placed that the moment you began to run uphill, unless the tank was really full, no petrol came through, it tilted away. I have known cases when the only way to get up a fairly steep hill was to reverse and go up backwards !

They once left Manchester for Brighton at five in the morning. The car behaved in its usual way, and they arrived at Brighton at half-past nine on Monday evening, Marie in a perfect fever because she had " missed her turn."

Though she could lose her temper wildly, entirely and unreasonably, there were times when she remained perfectly good-tempered under circumstances which would have made the average woman swear. She was going off one morning to lunch with some friends at Romano's. The car was at the door. Marie emerged, dressed wonderfully, wearing a huge picture hat. She advanced towards the car, put her foot on the step and turned to smile and wave at whoever was seeing her off.

" Good-bye—I shan't be late for dinner," and dived into the car. The door was narrow and the hat was simply " shot off " her head. She picked it up, looked at it, more in sorrow than in anger, and said : " Well, of all the—— However ! " and, picking it up, bowled it into the car and got in after it. She drove away, still smiling, with the hat—a veritable *pièce de résistance*—lying on the floor.

I remember once, though which hall it was I can't recall, anyway, it was in the provinces : Marie was putting on a new song, very nervous, as usual, and wearing a huge hat. Now, it was one of those hats that won't " stick on," and it was obvious that it was irritating her and adding to her nervousness.

The stage manager, a young fellow, was terribly anxious to " make things right " and keep her happy and content. Marie came down, and as she stood talking, the hat, which had a lot of feathers on it, tipped over one eye. Marie pushed it back, and said : " Gawd ! This hat'll finish me ! "

The little S.M., trying to be helpful, said : " I wonder that you wear it at all, Miss Lloyd ; I should think it's going to worry you."

Marie spun round and fairly spat at him. " Who asked you to think ? What d'you suppose I bought the damn' thing for ? To keep under a glass case in the dressing-room—or what ? You—wonder ! You—*would* wonder something b—— silly ! "

The poor little fellow crept back to his prompt corner and didn't say another word. Music played, Marie—again settling the hat at the right angle, with a last injunction that someone should " hold the words " and " watch " her—went on. The hat rocked and twisted, Marie twitched it straight, and again it lopped over one eye. At last, she pulled out the pins which held it, and flung it down, pointing to the prompt corner and saying to the audience : " It's his fault—that stage manager of yours. He made me nervous of the thing before I came on ! " The audience roared, Marie finished her song and all was well. When she was going back to the dressing-room, the little S.M. came forward to give the hat to her maid.

Marie said : " Blimey, I don't want to see that damn thing again ? You married ? You are ! Well, take it home and give it to your missus from me." Then more good-temperedly : " You were quite right, cock—the —— hat was no good at all. To-morrow I'm going to wear a cloth cap—peak to the back ! "

Just before one Ascot week I was talking to her and asked what she was going to wear. What was she going to wear ! She'd got a wonderful hat, Paris model, black, covered with sequins and ospreys. It was a hat over which Marie became positively lyrical.

Later, Ascot over, I asked her what sort of a time she'd had. Not a bad time, it appeared. " But," and her face clouded, " did you see what some damn fool paper said about me ? You didn't ? Miss Marie Lloyd looked very handsome in a *black jet bonnet*. I ask you ! He might just as well have said that I'd been found drowned in a pair of elastic-sided boots ! "

Talking of someone once, she said : " But her clothes ! I've never seen anything like them. She always looks to me as if she was dressed out of Clarkson's back shop." If any of you can remember what Clarkson's back shop looked like, can remember the air of dust and general dinginess which overshadowed everything, you will realize what a splendid simile that was.

There was once a very well-known comedienne who, though she still held her own on the halls, was past her first youth. Marie was talking to her one evening, and this woman confessed that she was very unhappy. Marie asked why, and was told that she didn't feel that her husband loved her any longer. He'd grown tired, took her for granted, came home late, and scarcely spoke a word.

Marie nodded. "I see. Has it ever struck you what you look like when he does come home? Face covered in grease, eh? I thought so! Hair in those iron fenders, eh? I knew it! Still reeking of grease paint—oh, yes, you do! What sort of night-gowns do you wear? No, don't tell me, I know. Cotton —what they call Horrocks' Longcloth, with long sleeves and a bit o' embroidery round the neck, and a great iron button! Yes, covered with linen once upon a time—about the same time that Hyde Park was in a flower-pot. Now—listen! What's the matter with a little bit of parsley round the dish? You've got money; well, off you go to-morrow and get yourself a real night-gown. Something with lace, insertion, fluffy, you know. Throw your iron fenders out of the window, and take the grease off your face. Little scent, little powder, bath salts—there you are."

A few nights later the lady arrived at the music-hall looking more wretched than ever. Marie full of enquiries. This was the story. She had been out the next morning, she had bought a *crêpe de-Chine* night-gown—"Good, too, Marie. I paid twenty-five bob for it." (Marie piously murmured: "Good God!") "Got some powder, and scent."

Marie asked: "What scent—Jockey Club or White Rose?"

"Neither, some foreign name—sort of Indian! Very strong."

"I see. Go on."

"I didn't put my hair in curlers; I bought a boodwor cap. I got home early and put on this lovely night-gown. Well it happened that Billie came home early that night. He walked up into my room, and he didn't half stare. I said: 'Oh, Billie, you *are* home early.' He said, in a funny sort of voice: 'You didn't expect me so early, did you?' I said: 'No, I didn't.' 'No,' he said, ' that's *just what I thought*, gettin' yourself up like a prize rabbit.' Oh, Marie, it was hours before I could make him believe that I hadn't been waiting for someone else. I shan't ever wear that horrible night-gown again."

Marie nodded. " No, you're right," she said. " I was wrong. You stick to your high necks and iron buttons. You and Billie have both got—Horrocks' Longcloth *minds*."

She once said : " You could cover a sow's ear with silk purses, and the damn bristles would still work through."

She was very fastidious about clothes, and Sid said that on one occasion he went with Mark Leslie to see her in her dressing-room, and she looked him up and down with disapproval. " Don't like that suit on you at all, Sid. Give it to Mark, and I'll get you a new one." Sid says that she was always doing that, and that she bought him quite literally dozens of new suits —just because she was dissatisfied with the one he was wearing at the time.

Here is a story which goes back to the time when she and Alec first went to America. It is sent to me by George Hurley.

He says : " I saw them off from Liverpool and three weeks later was over in New York myself and looked forward to seeing them. Before leaving England, as it was November and I knew how cold it was going to be in U.S.A., I bought myself a really fine overcoat. Melton cloth, double-breasted, with smoked pearly buttons ; this was all the fashion in London at the time. Arriving in New York I went straight to the hotel where I knew Marie and Alec were staying and marched in wearing my new Melton cloth overcoat. I felt very pleased with it, conscious that I was wearing something very smart indeed. The moment Marie saw me—and there were quite a lot of people there— she shouted out : ' My God, you can't wear that thing here. You look like some old London cabby. Come with me and I'll get you a coat that you can wear and look decent in.' She took me off, down Broadway, and went into one of the smartest and most expensive shops. There she bought me a splendid coat lined with fur, the same as everyone was wearing —who could afford them—in New York at the moment. I forget what she paid for it, but it was a very large sum indeed. My own coat was carefully packed in a cardboard box and we walked out on to Broadway once more. When we got outside Marie caught sight of someone who looked on the ' needy ' side, shabby and shivering. She took the box from me and said to this old fellow : ' Want a coat, old chap ? Well, here you

are.' The man stared at her ; he must have thought she was
mad or playing a joke on him. ' No, it's on the level,' she
said. ' Get inside it, you look blue ! '

"I said : ' Marie, dear, that's a bit thick. That's my good
new Melton cloth coat you've given away ! "

"She promptly replied : ' What's the matter with you,
greedy ? I've just bought you a new one—damn it, you can't
wear two, can you ? ' "

Fred Barnes tells a funny little incident of once when Marie
was staying at Bristol. She was then at the Royal, but later she
always stayed at Mrs. James', where she used to take the whole
house. However, on this occasion she was at the Royal, in a
splendid suite of rooms. Fred Barnes—only just beginning, in
those days, to make his way—had a tiny room right at the top of
the hotel. Marie asked him down for a cup of tea. They had
just begun when Aunt Betsy, Marie's aunt, arrived. Complete
with bonnet, mittens, dolman and bow under her chin. She
looked round and said : " Nice little place ! Make the most
of it, my gal, for it won't last for ever, mind you." Then all in
same breath, without a pause anywhere : " I just seen the
best pair o' boots I ever *have* seen—three-and-sixpence, real
beauties. Mind if I ask my friend in, Marie ? " A moment
later in came her friend, a little old lady of eighty-seven, very
like Aunt Betsy in general appearance. This new-comer
didn't open her mouth for about half an hour, and then said
quite suddenly : " My word, Marie, ain't you getting fat !
I never see such a be'ind on anyone in all my life."

Marie shouted with laughter, but Aunt Betsy was furiously
indignant and rose, saying to her " girl friend " : " Now look
here—I asked you in here, an' now I'm agoin' to ask you *out !*
Bussom—yes, but be'ind—no, never ! "

This was the Aunt Betsy of whom Marie cabled when she was
in Australia. She sent a cable to wish the whole family a Merry
Christmas and added : " Whatever you do don't forget to pay
Aunt Betsy's insurance." Daisy Wood says that the insurance
was only about sixpence a week and the words in the cable
must have cost nearly as many pounds as the insurance cost
pence.

Marie—and Fred Barnes tells this story against himself—once
stood near him at the side of the stage at the London Pavilion and
looked him up and down, her expression quizzical. He was
wearing his immaculate tightly waisted coat, beautifully creased
trousers, snowy white shoes and hat, and his make-up—well,

Fred has always affected a slightly " pink and white " make-up, with eyelashes built out like the " park palings."

Marie leant towards him and whispered : " Boy, you've forgotten your brassière—don't go on without it whatever you do ! "

CHAPTER SIX

Among the stars—Thec hildren at Hoxton—The orphanage—
" Barnardo's Home—now shut up ! "

OUT of the mass of material which has been sent to me
by people who wish to join in paying their tribute to
Marie Lloyd comes a delightful impression by Charles
Valvo, one-time ventriloquist. He has written this impression
in scenes—as surely a good " pro " should ; and I have
inserted it here, only adding a line here and there in order to
make some of the music-hall technicalities clear to the non-
professional reader. To me, it is not only a good picture of
Marie, but of music-hall life in general.

" Ladies and Gentlemen ! Mr. Charles Valvo !
' At Rehearsal.'

I had played the Empress, Brixton, several times before,
though as a general rule my work lay in the provinces. It is
difficult for anyone who is not ' in the business ' to understand
what an important matter it is when your provincial artiste
gets his chance to appear on the same bill with stars. Not those
stars who are only shining because they are topping the bill at
Wigan or Hanley ' for this week only,' but the stars which go on
twinkling every week in every year. I was full of expectancy,
hope, trying to have confidence in myself. It was helpful that
I knew the various important men at the Empress and that they
knew (and perhaps liked) me. There was the manager, Mr.
Grimes ; Charlie Johnson, the conductor ; and Ted, the stage
manager.

I arrived on Monday morning for rehearsal, after a long and
tedious journey from Bradford. I got out my band parts,
carried the books down to the stage and set them down.

(Let me interpolate here that it is the custom to carry down
your band parts, stand them on the stage, close to the footlights
and then they are handed down to the members of the orchestra
in the order in which they have been put down. It's a case of
" first come, first served.")

' I'll be the first to rehearse,' I said to Ted as I placed my
books in the proper place.

' You won't,' he replied. ' Marie called early, put her books
down and went straight out again.'

I suggested that we might slip across the road, and asked if he
cared to come with me. ' I'd like to, only I daren't be long ;
we've got a huge bill this week—three big " tops." There's
Marie, then Harry Lauder—who is now Sir Harry (if you're
not angry !) and Joe Elvin doing his Hampstead Heath stuff ;
and you know that takes a bit of setting up.'

And while he was talking I was eyeing that little pile of books,
each one marked ' Marie Lloyd ' ; eyeing them with a kind of
admiring awe, and into my heart was creeping a sort of fear of
this ' big bill.' I had known it happen before. The big people
demanded—and rightly—the best places on the programme and
the public wanted to listen to them. Those were the people
they really paid to come to see and hear. The smaller turns had
often to go to the wall ; their acts were often cut, they were
shoved on immediately after the overture or immediately before
the bioscope—just ' make-weights.' My act—ventriloquial—
never could be heard in either of those positions, because in one
the public were all coming in and in the other they were all
walking out.

However, Ted and I walked over to the bar opposite and had
a drink together. He set down his glass, glanced at his watch
and said :

' I'll have to get along back, Charles. Lots to do.'

' Oh, no you won't ! ' We both turned at the sound of the
voice. ' You'll just wait long enough to have another with me.
And you, too, cocky. What are you staring at ? Never seen
a female woman before ? Anything wrong with me, eh ? Have
another look ; it's all my own—teeth, hair—all complete.'

I flushed like a schoolboy, but somehow a warm kind of
friendliness seemed to radiate from her. You felt that she liked
you and wanted you to like her.

I said : ' I once worked at the Middlesex with—with a lady
who was rather like you. Only she was much taller. It's some
time ago——'

Ted interrupted : ' I shall have to go,' and as he passed me he whispered behind his hand : ' It's Marie—Marie Lloyd.'

I honestly hadn't realized it. True, I had once worked on the same bill with her, but I had only seen her on the stage, when she looked almost tall, with magnificent clothes, a tall diamond-headed stick—just the Queen of Comedy.

I began to stammer out an apology. ' I'm sorry. I didn't know—what I mean is, Miss—er—Miss Lloyd.'

' Marie,' she said. ' I'm Marie to everyone. Just that—without any trimmings. So we played together at the Old Mo, did we ? What's your act, cocky ? '

I told her I did a ' vent ' act and then I found that I was telling her all about the good times, and the bad ones, and how much I hoped from this week at the Empress and hoped that some agents might come in and see my work ; but—it just came out with a rush—I admitted that I was afraid that I should be squeezed out.

' You see, on a bill like this, I'm always on early turn and everyone's waiting for the stars and I don't think that I shall get much of a chance.'

She looked at me reflectively. ' No. If only you could get in somewhere between me and Lauder, or Lauder and Joe—it's difficult. Still, hold on to that ; you've got your chance and you're going to take it ! See ? There's more downs than ups in this business, I'll give you my word. You've come from Bradford, eh ? I've heard people call it the " comedian's grave," which only goes to show they never worked Sunderland ! And you thought that I was taller, did you ? Shows you what Louis heels and a stick of Leichner can do. (Leichner is the celebrated grease paint.—N. J.) Makes a difference—ever seen Lashwood off the stage ? You'd be surprised ! Well, there's Charlie Johnson getting his band together and I must rehearse. I don't usually rehearse here, only I'm putting on a new number to-night and I want to hear what the band parts are like. So long, cocky, and don't forget—you're going to get your chance !

She went off, leaving me conscious that my fears had gone. She had reminded me that I was going to have my chance and that I must take it. Somehow, all day I carried with me the memory of those very blue eyes and that atmosphere of friendliness which surrounded her.

I was putting out my stuff in the dressing-room, with my

' vent ' doll sitting watching me with his staring eyes, when a deep voice behind me made me turn.

' Who uses this dressing-room ? '

' This ? It's my room,' I said. ' I share it with another fellow, a comic singer ; but he's not down yet.'

' There's the three of you, then ? ' he said, pointing to my doll. ' Now Ah'm goin' tae ask you a favour, it won't cost you anything, wull you oblige me ? '

Again I stammered, flushed, again my old fear of the great stars swept over me. ' I'll be d-delighted. If—er—there is anything I can do—I mean—it will be a pleasure.'

His manner changed ; it became bright and very brisk. ' Weeel, this is the way o't. My brother has tae mind the car, because if he leaves it the bairns all come round hootin' the horn an' mak'in' a great set tae. Noo, ma room is at the far end o' the corridor, an' I want tae pit ma changes here in this wee room o' yours. You can just look after them, an' gie me a haund wi' them. Then yer can bring ma stick an' bonnet tae the wings an' haund them for me whiles I need them. Noo, can I rely on ye tae dae this every evening ? Then at the end o' the week, ye shall hae a fine signed photo o' me in Heilan' costume, eh ? '

I was recovering from this strange proposition when Ted stuck his head round the door and said : ' Valvo, you're wanted in the office.' My heart sank. I knew what it was going to be. I'd faced it before. The manager would say—quite nicely : ' Oh, Valvo—sorry, old boy ; but we shan't be able to fit you in. The programme's too crowded and something or someone's got to stay out. Of course, you'll draw your salary just the same. Bad luck, old man ; but you do understand, don't you ? That's right then—a week's holiday for nothing.'

I was shown into the office. There was Mr. Grimes and, at the table, working at a programme with times attached, one of the queerest-looking individuals I had ever seen. One eye was half-closed, the other seemed to work quite independently of its fellow ; a turned-up nose, a wide humorous mouth and quick speech and vivid gestures. It could only be—the great Joe Elvin.

Grimes said : ' Sit down Valvo.'

Joe Elvin began, talking very quickly, firing off short sentences like a machine-gun. ' Valvo ? 'Morning. Want you to help us if you will. Big bill and Lauder *wants* a full stage ; Marie has a *right* to one, and I *have* to have one. It's the last change that's the difficulty. Lauder will have finished, my stuff has to be set. We've been trying to find a way out. Can you work in front of the tabs?'

(This means, could he work in front of the big velvet curtain, so that they could be busy on the stage, setting, while his act was in progress.)

I said : 'Yes, sir. I can work anywhere. I only need a chair to put my foot on.'

'Good! Now in discussing it with Marie—she tells us that you're a friend of hers, by the way—she suggests that you come on after Lauder and before me, working in front of the tabs. See? How long do you do? Ten minutes? Could you, to oblige us, make it eight? You sing? Finish on a song, good again! When I come behind you and clap my hands, you break into your song, will you? Now, how does it go? The "dumb" show, then Marie, then Lauder, then you, Valvo, and then me. That's all right and thank you very much.'

I came away, my head whirling. I was placed in among the stars, I had got a position on the bill which was better than my wildest expectations. Joe Elvin had thanked me, implying that I had been useful—and Marie had told them that I was a friend of hers! That night I worked as I had never worked before, and I worked—for Marie.

The show over I walked into the bar. The bar at the Empress had—at least in those days—no licence, but there was always a bottle circulating somewhere. I felt timid, more than a little nervous entering the bar among all the leading lights.

The moment she saw me Marie shouted : 'Come in, don't stand there. No one's going to eat you. You're as shy as Jack Pleasants. Now then, who's got that bottle? I want a drink for a little pal of mine, he's done Joe Elvin a good turn to-day and he deserves a drink.' Then, drawing me on one side, she whispered : 'Over there, the man with the beard, that's Tom Pacey ; the other's Ernest Edelsten. They've both seen your show and I've talked to them both about you. Go and carry on the good work. Remember those are the fellows who can make you or break you.'

I went over, offered my card to the two important agents. Pacey said : 'Useful act. Come and see me in the morning, at eleven.' Edelsten said : 'You've played the Broadhead, eh? Come and see me to-morrow.' I thought that night as I walked home to my digs : 'Last night I was among the factory chimneys and to-night I'm among the stars. But there's one star that outshines all the rest—Marie.' I had met an idol, without a single enemy, an actress without a mask ; and for the rest of my life, even if there have been ' more downs than ups,' I have carried that memory, that she called me her ' little pal.'

If only I could write a book I would make her my heroine. I would call it ' The Bohemian Lady,' because she is one of the few people who succeeded in being a good Bohemian and a lady—and, believe me, it's a pretty difficult feat. I can just imagine Saint Peter, at the Pearly Gates, saying : ' Oh, no, my dear ; you don't have to send in your card for a seat— there is one waiting for you. There always has been a place for you, everywhere. Now—Enter, Marie ! ' "

I have given you that rather long letter because it shows a good many things, makes clear many others. That is probably the only time in his life that Valvo ever sat down and tried to put his ideas on paper. He did that ; took immense trouble and great pains to write that for me from Brinsworth, where he now lives. In his letter to Harry Marlow he says : " I've written this because I felt it to be my duty—to Marie." In addition, that letter gives you a picture of Marie at her very sweetest and best—fighting for the under-dog, using that very quick and active brain to find a way by which this little provincial performer could be given his chance. That's not enough for her, as ever she had to give with both hands ; and so she greets him as " her little pal " ; she tells everyone that he has done the great Joe Elvin a good turn and she makes it possible for him to meet two important agents in circumstances where he was—virtually—under her wing.

In short, this letter is as good a picture of Marie as you can want, and it's true.

That story is on a par with one which was told me in the Trocadero by an old waiter, long since gathered to his fathers. Twenty years ago he was growing pretty old, his feet bothered him a bit, but he was a good waiter and I used to enjoy a chat with him.

He said to me one day : " Last night we had Our Marie in ! Treat, it was. And did she look beautiful. Like a queen." (I may tell you that this waiter was known as " Ould Pat.") " Glory to God, the clothes av her, the joo'ls, the lovely smile, thim eyes like bits of summer sky. T'ey was all crowding round her, and her wid a word for all av thim. I watched, I listened wheniver I got the chance, an' I t'ought : ' Ah, but you've niver seen her as I have, down in Hoxton.' "

He told me that Christmas after Christmas she went down there, with dozens of pairs of boots of all sizes, for the poor children. Oh, well, let " Ould Pat " tell the story !

" Down she'd come—in her car, wid a chauffeur. They'd stop, an' she'd get out. Thin she'd start. It was to wan : ' For the love av God get me a chair ! ' ; to another : ' Don't stand staring like a fool, get me another chair ! ' It was : ' Bring me this—— ' an' ' Dam ye, find me something else.' Dressed like a queen and swearing like a coster. Thin—the children 'ud come round an' there was no more swearing, no more shouting. She stopped being a queen, or a coster ; she was just a grand lady who loved the kids loike as if they'd been her own.

It was : ' D'this pair fit you ? Now they don't at all, for your toes are nearly poking through already. It's a size larger you're wanting ' ; or ' Here, what wrong with you ? Chilblains. Take this half-crown an' go to the chemist for something to make thim well. Thin your boots 'ul fit.' That was the way av her. Joking wid the kids, making thim laugh, an' herself wiping away her tears wid the back av her hand while she talked wid thim. They admire her whin she's dressed like a queen in a restaurant, wid her tongue as smart as bedad, but down Hoxton way—they love her."

What happened once at Southend when she was working there ? She saw a long line of children, in charge of a matron. Forty or fifty of them orphans sent down to have a week at the sea. In a moment Marie had decided. A holiday—holidays ought to mean a " good time " ; children loved cakes and sweets and sugary buns. They should have them. She spoke to the matron, asking if they might all be taken to a café near by and regaled on all those sweet things which are joy to a child's small soul.

The next day the same thing happened and on the Saturday, for the last time, the bairns were entertained by Marie Lloyd. She talked to the matron, asked questions about the home, the food, the financial side ; she wanted to know everything. Then, almost defiantly, as Marie always spoke when she was going to do something stupendous, she said :

" There's something in this envelope. To help a bit. Poor little kids. You know, for little extras, eh ? That's right. Good-bye—God bless you."

She left them, went back to her work, which for that week she had done for nothing ! That envelope contained Marie

Lloyd's weekly salary. A cheque for two hundred and fifty pounds.

Her motto—only she didn't know it, and would have stared if you had suggested it—ought to have been : "What I saved —I lost. What I had—I spent. What I gave—I have."

Rich people, important people, only mattered to her if they were amusing, but poor people, old people, shabby people and children—they always had the key to Marie's heart, and anyway—what did anyone want with a key ?—that door was always left open.

Near her house in Golders Green there was a Catholic college, and these young boys used to interest her a great deal. Marie had no set religion ; dogma meant nothing to her ; formalities would have been inexplicable to her, creeds would have " made her head ache." I fancy that she would have obtained a certain satisfaction from splendid vestments ; she would have been carried away by the pure notes of a boy's voice, and the thunder of an organ would have stirred her deeply—but the religion that is brought out once a week and carefully locked up in the four walls of a church for the other six days would have annoyed and irritated her.

I was in the garden with her one morning, and she pointed out this seminary to me and asked several very pertinent questions with regard to priests and the priesthood. I answered them to the best of my ability. Marie looked doubtful and shook her head.

"Too clever for me, Micky. I only know that facts arc facts."

Just at that moment two of these lads came round the corner. Marie saw them and said : " Damn it, I shall tell them ! Oh, yes, I shall. I don't believe that the poor little blighters know what they're letting themselves in for. I don't care what you say—it's not right."

" I should leave them alone," I said. " They know what they're doing."

However, she persisted, and as they drew near, she hailed them.

" Are you two boys priests—or going to be priests ? "

Rather shyly they admitted that they were.

She went a little nearer to the two lads. " Now look here," she said, and I could never convey the kindness in her voice, " I know quite a lot that pr'aps you don't know. I've been going into this business of—priests. You're both only a couple

of kids. You don't know who I am—my name's Marie Lloyd,
and I'm old enough to be your mother. Listen, here's a bit
of advice. Think it all over before you decide, see ? Don't let
anyone bounce you into it. Think—it—well—over. Good
luck, cockies."

The two slightly bewildered young men raised their hats
and walked on. Marie turned to me, filled with pride at having
done the right thing.

" Poor kids," she said. " Someone ought to tell them, after
all." Then, " I wonder if they get enough to eat in that place ?
Damn it, I might just as well have asked them to come in and
have a bite ! "

When some old judge asked in court (because a slightly
facetious barrister had said : " As Marie Lloyd would say "),
" Er—who *is* Marie Lloyd ? " Marie's comment was : " That's
a judge, mind you ! Silly, damned ignorant old fool."

Years ago there was a question of Marie being injuncted
over some dates. She had been booked to appear at—let's
say, for the sake of argument—Crouch End Hippodrome and
The Empress, Brixton. After the Monday night she found
that it was impossible for her to work both places, and she only
worked one. The management at the other were naturally
furious, and there was a case about it.

Marie contended that she could prove her case. The Strand
was up at the time, and this made the journey additionally
difficult. She was questioned by a very smart young barrister.

" You are a Londoner, I believe, Miss Lloyd ? "

Marie nodded. " Hoxton."

" You know London—I take it—fairly well ? "

" Like the palm of my hand."

" Then, knowing London as you do, how far would you say
that this journey is from one hall to the other—as the crow flies?"

Marie cocked her eye at him. " Not being a bird, it's difficult
to say, but I know with the Strand in the state it is at present,
I'd hate to have to try to hop it."

There was a story going round London at one time concerning Sir Herbert Tree, who was reputed to have asked the
late Fred Terry if he thought that his daughter, Phyllis Neilson
Terry, would like to appear to play lead in a certain production
" in my beautiful theatre " ?

Fred Terry replied that he fancied that she would and they
began to discuss terms. Two hundred a week was the figure
suggested.

" Two hundred ! " Tree cried.   " Why, I can get Marie Lloyd for a hundred and fifty ! "

I told that story to Marie, who replied with tremendous seriousness : " Who said that ? Sir Herbert Tree ? He *can*, can he ! Let him just try, that's all ! "

There is the story about the tripe. The scene is a very hot Saturday afternoon in the big room at The Oxford. No one likes working a matinée very much at any time, and when the air is hot and stuffy, when, as fast as you put your make-up on it gets greasy and horrible—everyone loathes the matinée and curses the late Sir Augustus Harris, who is supposed to have " invented " them.

In the big change room were gathered on this particular Saturday Gladys ffolliott—lounging in a chair, with her monocle screwed into her eye, her beautiful boots stretched out in front of her, gently swearing about the weather, Marguerite Broadfoote, lovely, gentle and one of Marie's most sincere admirers, and myself, hating the heat as much as any of them. Into the room Marie arrives and joins in the Hymn of Hate against " afternoon shows." May, the dresser, fat and comely, panted as she moved about.

Then Miss Victoria Monks arrived. Now Marie admired Vicky Monks as an artiste, but upon this particular afternoon tempers were apt to get frayed and nerves were rather raw. Victoria Monks carried a small, rather damp-looking parcel. Marie said, in her most offensive voice : " What have you got in that bundle ? " (a quotation from one of Charlie Austin's sketches).

Victoria Monks said : " Tripe. What's the matter with it ? "
Marie replied : " Nothing except its age."
" It's fresh ! "
" *Was*, once upon a time, perhaps. It's horrible now."

Marguerite tried to turn the conversation by launching forth into a long and rather dull explanation of how tripe was cooked in Scotland. Marie interpolated that she wished to God this tripe was in Scotland, and she wouldn't give a damn how anyone cooked it. Vicky Monks scowled and began to breathe forth threatenings and slaughter. Gladys ffolliott, Irish to her backbone, sat upright, her eyes suddenly bright at the prospect of a row.

The row began. Vicky Monks stated with admirable clarity just what she was going to do to Marie if she said another word about the tripe. Marie asked what particular word she wanted

and expressed her willingness to say it at once—then the storm
burst. Gladys ffolliott smiled and offered to take bets as to
who would win ; Marguerite Broadfoote cried and begged
them to kiss and be friends. Finally, in desperation, she picked
up the packet of tripe and hurled it between Marie and Vicky
Monks. The window was wide open, the tripe didn't touch
either of them, but flew through the window and was lost to
sight. In five minutes it was all over. Marie sent for drinks
and in no time everyone was talking and laughing as if no
such thing as tripe had ever existed.

There was a knock at the door. May opened it and there
stood the barman from the Blue Posts opposite.

" I come ter know," he said, " which lidy 'ere slung that
tripe ? It come in through the open winder, 'it a lidy
customer o' mine on the mouth and she ain't 'arf annoyed
about it. Says it's ruined 'er bonnet."

Gladys ffolliott, sardonic and calm, asked : " What sum
does she give as the amount of the damage ? "

" 'Arf a quid—not ondly the bonnet, it's the shock to 'er
system."

" I see. Come on, Meg, pay up, my dear."

Meg, thankful to get everything over so peacefully, paid her
half-sovereign contentedly enough. Marie laughed : " There
you are, ducks, that's what comes of being so—lady-like ! "

There was an ability to put things behind her, with Marie.
She never bore malice, she never blamed people, the only thing
that used to really rouse her scorn was when anyone pretended
to be something rather more " beyond reproach " than Cæsar's
wife. That used to produce real indignation on Marie's part.

" That—pure—stuff ! " she used to say scornfully.

I remember once a certain little lady, whose life had been
anything but—shall we say—conventional, who was enlarging
on her dislike, her abhorrence and abomination of anything
which deviated from the straight and narrow path.

Marie listened, heard how one woman had behaved dis-
gracefully, how terrible was the life led by a second, and how
abominable were the actions of a third. The whole tirade was
on the lines of : " I thank Thee that I am not as this Publican."

Marie nodded. " Yes—what a shame, isn't it ? "

" What's a shame, Marie ? " asked the little lady, expecting
sympathy and approbation.

" Well, when you feel like that, when you've always lived so
nicely, been so—pure—and such a little lady, too ! Then to

think what people have been calling you for years. It's damn'
awful ! "

" Call *me ?* What do people call me ? "

" Doctor Barnardo's Home—I've never called you anything
else ever since I can remember. *Now—shut—up !* "

CHAPTER SEVEN

" THE FAME WHICH SONG BRINGS——"

OVID

Her songs—Who wrote them—Nerves—Her clothes—Her one
patriotic song—The three sisters—Tragedy and comedy.

MARIE'S songs may be divided into three classes. The
first, when she began her career and sang songs
which enabled her to wear clothes which were almost
childish, and songs which were—even with their spice of
" naughtiness "—suitable to her extreme youth. The second,
when she sang " smart songs," wearing magnificent dresses,
hats which made you hold your breath, and everything as
elegant as possible. Then, thirdly, when she began to specialize
in her " character " songs, wearing shabby clothes, but always
—mark this—clothes which were eminently suitable to the
character which she was portraying.

There was none of your careless artiste about Marie. If
she was playing an old char, then her clothes, her handbag,
even her shoes were in the " the part." I remember once
going to see a performance of *The Merry Wives of Windsor*,
when Mistress Page and Mistress Ford were played by two
very well-known West End actresses. When they pranced and
danced, which they did to the almost complete exclusion of
everything else, their full skirts swung and swayed, displaying
most beautiful and expensive *crêpe de Chine* underwear!
Marie Lloyd would never have made that mistake.

Her songs were written for her by various song writers, and
with all due respect to them all, those songs were never really
very outstanding affairs. They were good vehicles for Marie's
genius, that was all. They might have been given to a dozen
artistes and they would, in all probability, never have been
heard of again. But, in Marie's hands, they became electrical,
vivid, and astonishing.

George Le Brun wrote for her, so did George Ware, who was

known by Marie as "The Old Reliable," and was also her agent for many years. There was one, Lytton, a schoolmaster from Greenwich, who wrote her some good numbers, and there was Hollitt, who wrote : "Eh—what—rather ! "

Marie had no difficulty over her songs. Writers knew what she wanted and she knew even better than they did. Songs were easy for her. Her brother Johnnie maintains that of all the people who wrote for her, Le Brun was the best. He could take a little bit from this song, another little bit from that and make them into a sort of medley which suited Marie admirably. Le Brun had written so much of her material that this "judicious mixture" of his various songs merely stressed Marie's characteristics. In short, he gave Marie a menu which was never entirely different, and yet was so well arranged that neither she nor the public ever tired of it.

In her early days she learnt easily. Her mind was quick and retentive, though she always suffered from "first-night nerves," and once told me that she was nervous every single time she went on.

"The day that I'm not nervous," she said, "I shall leave the business, because I shall know that I'm not any damn good."

I have always contended that she was right, and that your artiste who is nervous, provided they know their work, provided that their technique is good and that they can control their nerves, will give a far better, far more brilliant and sensitive performance than any other. Your player, singer, music-hall artiste who boasts proudly : "I've never been nervous in my life. After all—what is there to be nervous *of ?*" rarely "gets there." They are too self-satisfied, they have too much assurance, and their performance will be "blunt" and insensitive.

I once heard a woman tell Marie that she "didn't know what nerves were. After all," she said with a certain complaisance, "what's the need ? The curtain is bound to come down sometime ! "

To which bit of brilliance Marie replied tersely : "That's what I fancy the poor —— audience feel when you're on."

Her earliest success, as we have seen, was "Throw down the bottle," but after all, this may be regarded in the light of a "free song," which was probably a bit threadbare when Marie first sang it. Then later, she, knowing nothing of songs, song writers, free songs, and those which were specially written and paid for by certain artistes, just sang whatever songs took her fancy. I have told how she narrowly escaped prosecution over this lack of knowledge.

Then came her first songs, songs which were hers, written to suit her. She sang them, dressed rather like a big doll, with a lace-trimmed bonnet, and with her hair very curled, looking—just what she was—a child.

That veteran of Variety, Mr. Charles Coborn, writes to me saying : " I think it was in the year 1881 that I first saw her. She came to the London Pavilion, where I was engaged. I remember her singing and dancing in a short yellow satin dress, and being much taken with her perfect assurance and style, I at once prophesied a future for her, as I had a naturally keen eye for the real stage goods. I know what her life was—full of vicissitudes, and ended too soon. I saw her on the stage many times and always admired her work. She always bore the name of a good daughter and sister, and· her many works of kindness and generosity were of widespread repute." Mr. Charles Coborn has made some error in the date here, for Marie was only nine years old in 1881. He admits that he is writing from memory, and probably the date was several years later. I suppose Marie's first performance at the Pavilion must have been about 1888. Only, such is my respect for The Grand Old Man of Variety that I cannot bring myself to alter what he had written.

To this first period of Marie's songs belong her " semi-childish " numbers, though the children impersonated in these songs were slightly more sophisticated than the average child. There was : " I hate the horrid schoolboard, so does brother Jack," which gave her an opportunity of indulging in one of those refrains which in themselves meant nothing, but which handled by Marie—meant, just whatever she wished them to mean.

" Nothing but a whacky, whacky, whack, whack, whack."

Sheer rubbish, as were the lines which followed, but which Marie transformed into something pungent with meaning.

Another was : " There they were, the two of them on their own," concluding with : " They gave me half a crown to run away and play, Hi-ti-iddildy, hi-ti-iddildy, hi-ti-iddildy aye."

That semi-idiotic refrain, sung in Marie's voice, with Marie's inflections, could convey unutterable things, could make people giggle, grin, and force the puritanical to wonder " if we ought to have come to hear Marie Lloyd after all."

Then there was her first really great success : " The boy I

love sits up in the gallery," which probably laid the foundation
of that queer, personal affection which for more than thirty
years existed between her and the "boys and girls in the
gallery."

Then came the second period, when Marie wore dresses, hats,
shoes, and carried sticks and parasols which were designed to
startle everyone by their magnificence and smartness. She was
a brilliant designer of clothes, she knew just where a skirt
should be looped, exactly where a diamond buckle would have
its full value, the precise angle at which a hat should be worn—
in fact, how to get the greatest possible effect.

Her stage clothes were almost part of her songs. She never
wore a costume which did not, in some way, "belong" to the
song she sang. Her flair for *décor* was perfect and, what is more,
no one ever saw Marie in a dress from which the first glory had
departed. Whatever she wore must be not only the acme of
smartness, but it must have that crisp freshness, that real
elegance which can only come from exquisite cleanliness.

I have seen many performers go on the stage with velvet
dresses well spotted- down the front with the remains of odd
sandwiches, carelessly manipulated glasses of stout, and they
have assured me that "it 'ul never be noticed from the front."
I have seen voile and *crêpe de Chine* which was soiled at the edges,
torn here and there, satin shoes which looked dingy, and artificial flowers which were well past their first stage of pristine
freshness—the wearers have always gone on with the sublime
conviction that "it doesn't show," or "after all, the song's the
thing that matters, not the dress." All those silly little worn-
out clichés which are so pleasant to the people who use them,
and which mean no more than most well-worn, threadbare
remarks of a like nature.

Marie never indulged in that kind of self-deception. Apart
from the fact that it was never in her nature—any more than it
is in the nature of her sisters—to wear clothes which have
become "old performers," which have come to carry the
marks of battle. Her clothes, like everything which she
possessed, like her home, had to be always in that state of crisp
freshness which, believe me, never fails to show "from the
front."

There are still what are known as "dress acts"—acts in
which the songs are nothing, the personality of the singer
matters even less, but where the clothes are the attraction.
Everything is subservient to them. Provided a woman can

spend sufficient money on her dresses, that she can wear them
" with an air," such acts may attain a certain amount of
popularity for a time. Marie's work never degenerated into
a " dress act," her clothes were—as I have said—part of the
décor, part of the production, but her essential art remained
the thing which attracted, held, and delighted.

To this second period belong then, the dresses, the diamond-
headed sticks, the Louis heels, and the long strings of pearls
which Marie Lloyd knew how to use as no other artiste has ever
known. Marie could convey anything by her use of that long
string of pearls. I can't tell you how, I could scarcely tell you
what she did, I only know that, as you watched, you were
conscious that you were watching an artiste, an actress who
might claim to rank—and justify her claim—with Bernhardt,
Duse, Patrick Campbell, and Ellen Terry.

There was " My Directoire Gown "—with Marie looking
superb, her dress slit up the side to show a particularly shapely
leg, gartered with diamonds. If I am not mistaken this was
the first song in which she used her celebrated diamond-headed
stick.

> " Do you think my dress is a little bit—m-mum ?
> Not too much of it ?
> If it shows my shapes just a little bit,
> Well, that's the little bit the boys admire."

Where did the art lie in that ? It's more or less rubbish, not a
single brilliant turn of phrase—nothing. I don't know if I can
tell you. I have a record made specially for me by Alice, Daisy,
and Rosie Lloyd. Rosie sings this song which I have just
quoted, and she possesses that gift of inflection which is one of
the Lloyds' " master cards." There are moments when she
sings that song that she *is* Marie. Just as there are when Alice
or Daisy sing other songs of Marie's. The art of that song lies
in nothing but the inflection. That " eh ? " is not " Ay " at
all, it is merely an *enunciated upward inflection*. It might be
written as : " Ump-ah," it might be written in half a dozen
ways, and it means : " Do you think my dress is a little bit—
well, you know what I mean, rather " naughty," likely to make
the conventional mind shake, and likely to make the unconventional mind sit back and take notice ? "

There used to be a joke, made originally at the expense of
some producer, in which he was supposed to have said : " You
see, I want you to come down here and pick up this book—

conveying, as you do so, that you have been left a fortune by your uncle, your mother's brother, who has recently died in New Zealand, where he has been sheep farming for twenty years with great success."

Believe me, the Lloyds could have done it. Marie actually used to convey almost as much in one single line, in one utterly "unwritable" exclamation, in a single little movement.

It is impossible to recall all her famous "hits," but others which belong to this period were : "The Piccadilly Trot" (which was one of the first times she ever portrayed—though not in dress, but merely in her voice, a couple of her adorable old "drabs"), "Every little movement has a meaning of its own," "Twiggy vous," "Wink the other eye," "You can't stop a girl from thinking."

In "The Piccadilly Trot," after she had for two verses dealt with her "Berties and Gerties" you had a flash of real Cockney humour. "I remember the 'Aymarket when theer *was* 'ay, not chaff!" In "Every Little Movement," how well she acted. Miss Maudie Brown, who went to bathe, and was noticed by "Reggie."

> "She didn't smile or frown,
> Just threw her *peignoir* down"

(and you saw it being slowly dropped from Maudie's female form divine—saw it as it slowly billowed, a mass of lace and frills round her feet—when Marie sang the song) :

> "'Oh, I'm here-ah,' cried Reggie, 'if you fail.'
> And in less than half a wink,
> Maudie, dear, commenced to sink.
> Every little movement tells a tale."

Her "Coster Girl in Paris" was a fantasy which Marie made reality. Red, white and blue satin, red, white and blue feathers, she was the embodiment of every coster girl's ambition. She was "London, east of Algate pump," she was the life of the Whitechapel High Road, she was the spirit of the Old Forester's Music-hall, she was the personification of that vitality which makes your coster the past-master of repartee. She had been to Paris for a honeymoon, and though at school she had been taught to speak French :

> "Parley-vous, and silver plate, an' mercy an' we-we,
> When I came to look around,
> Then in Paris soon I found,
> Why even little kids spoke French much better'n me."

Again :

"We went to a music 'all, an' a lady she was singin',
An' all the blokes was laffin'. Bill says : ' Come art ! '
I says : ' Shan't, first I can't make out what they got ter laff
    abart ! '
An' some bloke turns to me an' says, ' Well, it's a good job that
    you carnt.'
Still, I'd like to go again, to Paris on the Seine,
For Paris is a proper pantomime,
An' if they'd only shift the 'Ackney Road, and plant it over theer,
I'd like to live in Paris all the time ! "

There was her famous " Oh, Mr. Porter," in which she
appeared as the embodiment of injured innocence, a song which
—because some of us heard Marie sing it before the tabs at the
Alhambra, will never cease to be charged with tragedy. There
was her little bit of real " impertinence," when she sang a song
concerning the young lady who spent her quiet hours contemplating the vegetables in her garden. That song which gave
the late Sir Henry Tozer blood to the head, and storming into
Marie's dressing-room he demanded that she changed the
offending line immediately. Marie, wide-eyed, trotted out her
old remark that there was nothing in her songs which need
offend, and that she was not responsible for people's " dirty
minds "—however, she *would* alter the line.

She did, and the insertion of the name of another vegetable
didn't really make the song any better from Sir Henry's point
of view ! Whenever there were rows, whenever irate managers
asked Marie to remove this, or delete that—they had to get up
very early in the morning to get the better of her. Only a few
days ago, Miss Maidie Scott—herself a delightful artiste— reminded Alice Lloyd of one occasion when Marie and she were
on the bill at the Palladium. Maidie Scott was singing her
celebrated " Green Apple Pain "—" those two little boys they
were singing—ohh-oo ! " Marie was singing a song called :
" The End of a Perfect Day." Mr. Marner, the manager,
objected to a line in Marie's song, and came round to tell her
that she must cut it out.

Marie said : " My song ! My words ! My gestures ! Always
picking on me, aren't you ? Yet what about Maidie Scott's
song. Green apples, pains, ' ooo-er ' and all the rest of it.
What's that but a rude song ? It's a—*lavatory* song, that's what
it is ! "

Then came the war and Marie sang her one and only patriotic

song, and what a good song it was, too ! Marie had never been
one of those artistes who bawl topical stuff, who scream about
John Bull and " God bless——," whoever is the Prime Minister
at the time ! I doubt if in the South African War she sentimen-
talized over the Yeomanry, or the C.I.V.'s, and she certainly
restricted herself to this one patriotic song in the war—but it
was real. A coster woman, this time lacking silk and satin, just
a fine, buxom East End wench, who has been frightened that
her " bloke " might not join up, and who is delighted when he
does.

> " Once " (she sang) " I thought yer meant to grow a Derby curl,
> But they cut it orf and shoved it in your chest."

Then :

> " I do feel so proud of you, I do honour bright,
> I'm going to give you an extra cuddle to-night.
> I didn't think much of you, till you joined the army, John,
> But I do like you, cocky, now you've got yer khaki on."

And, to finish, one of Marie's inimitable little dances, with a
tall fellow in uniform—who I fancy was her brother Johnnie,
though I can't be certain. Nothing particularly intricate, just
the sort of thing a coster woman might very well dance to the
music of a barrel organ, on the pavement with her bloke. A bit
of East End life—a real character study.

Then, a little later—for Marie didn't " hang on to her songs,"
and when their day of popularity was over they went, were put
on the retired list—she gave us : " I shall never forget the days
when I was young." The first time I heard her sing this was
at a matinée at the Palladium, and she looked adorable. She
wore an old-fashioned dress, almost a crinoline, with a little
parasol which she carried open over one shoulder.

> " I shall never forget the days when I was young.
> Oh, it don't seem so very long ago,
> Since I used to twist my feet, to the organ in the street,
> I shall never forget the days when I was young."

As you listened to her, you felt certain that " it certainly could
not have been so very long ago "—she looked so young, and
so very pretty.

There was her famous " talkie " song, " Woman's Opinion of
Man," one of the most brilliant songs ever written for her, and
delivered as only Marie could have delivered it. That fine actor,

the late Leslie Faber, who heard her sing it at the Alhambra (and for reasons which I shall make apparent later, I should like to make a special note of that—at the Alhambra, three weeks before this beloved artist made her last appearance), said to me that this song was " a compressed three-act play," and that he had never witnessed a finer and more beautiful performance.

She took The Three Ages of Woman. The first, " seventeen, only a flapper," who regards man as a hero, " for his trousers are creased and he wears a tall hat," she thinks that he is waiting to provide her with " chocolate creams in a palace of dreams."

" Fancy," Marie used to say. " Chocolate creams and a Palace of Dreams—I don't think."

Then, woman's opinion of man when she's " twenty-five, now a young lady," despite whatever she may say (" and she vows she won't marry, though if a man says : ' Wilt,' she'll wilt, you bet "), " man is a creature she looks on with awe, she really can't think what he's wedding her for——"

> " But her ma says : ' The dunce, I can tell her in once——
> I've had some.' "

And " the last stage of this strange, eventful history "—as sung by Marie Lloyd, " when her age is a matter of guessing, she powders and dyes and makes up her eyes, ah, and she has to be careful when dressing."

> " Great, oh, she's great—is the woman of umpty-eight,
> A lot she's endured from the thing they call—man,
> Still, if to live life o'er again she began,
> Would she live it again, would she play the same game ?
> Well—(and listen there for Marie's marvellous, half-amused,
> half-cynical laugh) . . . *Rather !* "

Then came her character studies. James Agate says :
" When she came to the portrayal of elderly baggages, she refrained from showing them as Pendants to her courtesans. . . . She gave happy life to battered harridans ludicrous in the sight of man, if not of God. She depicted the delight of humble life, the infinite joy of mean streets."

A great deal has been made of the fact that Marie adopted this form of character work towards the close of her career, a great deal of most astounding rubbish has been talked, and idiotic inferences drawn. Men who knew nothing of her, who would have never been able to understand her had they met her every day for a month of Sundays, have, with strong mental spectacles, tried to pry and peer into a mind which was so far above them that they were as capable of understanding Marie —as I should be of understanding the whole Theory of Relativity.

I have read with a sort of sick disgust some of these gems of cheap journalism. Marie—"realizing that she was growing old, determined, with that honesty which has ever been one of her dearest traits, to show herself to her public as she really was. No smart woman of fashion, but an old, grey-faced, tired woman."

As Marie would have said : " Old—grey-faced—*nothing !* "

Old—at fifty-one, fifty-two ! Did Ellen Terry still play " Juliet " toward the close of her career, does Mrs. Patrick Campbell still play " Magda " and " Paula Tanqueray," does Miss Lilian Braithwaite still play " juvenile heroines "—and Miss Marie Tempest still sing " A Goldfish swam in a big glass bowl " ? —of course they didn't, of course they don't—because they are artistes, and the fewer the limitations of a great artiste, the more conscious is the real artiste of those limitations. So Marie·played her " drabs."

To pretend that Marie wished to " show herself to us, as she really was," is the most utter nonsense. Marie disliked anyone knowing " what she really was." Long after her real joy of life had gone, long after she had suffered, had known disappointment and disillusionment, Marie showed a brave face to her public. Marie never *did* become " old, and weary, and grey-headed," Marie at fifty-two was an amazingly smart and pretty woman. Those of us who knew her, have seen her ill, heart-broken, have seen her—with her head on her arms—crying bitterly in her dressing-room. Some of us have seen actual proofs of what she had gone through, sufficient to break the spirit of a less courageous woman. That was her own business —and it remained her own business to the end !

Don't let us try to attribute reasons for her songs which never existed. She liked " character work," and only when she had reached maturity did she feel able to draw upon her know-ledge, her observation and her art to portray her old Cockney women.

Looks are one of the assets of an actress—be she Variety or Legitimate Stage—and she uses them as part of her stock-in-trade. Would anyone expect Miss Gladys Cooper with her beauty to prefer playing some old hag, to the heroine of a play by Somerset Maugham ; or Miss Marie Tempest with her chic, her ability to depict " smart " women, to cast herself for char-women parts, however well she might be able to play them ?

Marie Lloyd, then, used her looks, her ability to wear clothes, to deliver daring lines to make herself " The Queen of Comedy." Only when her position was assured could she embark on those masterly character studies in which her artistic soul delighted. Then, she called to her aid all the knowledge which she had gathered, all the observations she had made, all the little touches which she had studied and gave us pictures which were true and entirely life-like. It was not a matter of age it was a matter of artistic knowledge, and suitability.

In addition, let me remind these " sob stuff merchants " that Marie never indulged exclusively in " low comedy " songs. At the Alhambra she sang : " Woman's Opinion of Man," another number which for the moment I have forgotten, and lastly, " One of the ruins," ending with " Oh, Mr. Porter."

Years ago she produced one of these " elderly women " numbers : " You're a thing of the past old dear," I forget the date, but it is many years ago. Didn't Marie once sing : " Good Old Iron," which was, and is, because her sister Alice still sings it, a character song ?

> " Good old iron, never been known to rust,
>   A little bit fruity on the crust,
>   Well, I'm no chicken, but underneath the moon,
>   The fellows say I'm no good because,
>   I'm not so young as I uster was,
>   But don't forget, the older the fiddle, the sweeter the tune."

Her two most famous character songs were : " The Cock Linnet " and " One of the ruins that Cromwell knocked about a bit."

The former, the elderly lady, who has been watching the home packed into the van because it's " moving day." What a character ! By the time Marie had finished her patter, " nothing was hidden from you." The whole life of the woman was laid open for you exactly as Marie contrived to do in that other remarkable song : " A little of what you fancy does you good." In fact those three elderly drabs—the one in " A little of what you fancy," the old dame in " The Cock Linnet," and the slightly more antique one in " One of the ruins," were sisters, and if one could have met them all at once—if one could have listened to their conversation, to their confi-

dences, what an entertainment, what an education it would
have been.

The first, admitting that she likes a " little 'oliday, ah, an' we
always 'as one, my old man an' me," then last year he " sprung
up a noo idea when he saw the ladies bathing in the sea." He
said : " What a man requires is change of—everything, an' 'e
oughter take 'is 'olidays alone. Away from every day-affairs."
(" Mark that, there was a bit of sauce for yer, if you like.")
" So," says the first of the Three Sisters : " I said—Well, if
you'd like a little fortnight on yer own——"

> " I always 'old with 'avin' it, if you fancy it,
> If you fancy it, that's understood,
> But if that's your bloomin' gime, I intend to do the sime,
> 'Cause a little of what you fancy does yer good."

The second tells of moving day, the terrible way the removers
handled the furniture. " Rite away they broke the—well, the
nicest bit of china wot we'd got."
At last :

> " Away went the van with the 'ome packed in it,
> An' I follered after with the old cock linnet,
> But I dillied and dallied, dallied and dillied,
> Lost me way and don't know wheer to roam,
> And——" (confidentially to her two sisters) " a' course I had to
>   stop, an' have a little drop of tiddley——
> Now I can't find my way 'ome."

Lastly, in desperation, she announces that if she could get " in
it "—pointing to the cage she still carried, " I'd sleep with
the old cock linnet."

Then the third sister, a real roystering old crone, devil-may-
care, take the rough with the smooth, face life with your head up,
sort of old dear, recounts what happened " Outside the Cromwell Arms, last Saturday night," she was one of the ruins that
Cromwell knocked about a bit ! There is a great deal more to
it. She came over all " queer like "—tired, and sat down in
the grass—and not alone. Commercial traveller, the gent was.
Only when he left her did she look for her purse and discover :
" I've been buzzed ! That's what comes of sitting in the grass
with a commercial traveller."

It wasn't what Marie—as any of her characters—said, it was
the things she left unsaid, and filled in the silences with the
most minute wink, the least twitch of her eyebrows, the smallest

and most telling gesture. That was the difficulty of watching Marie's act—it was too much, there were too many wonders, too many bits of side play, you were fearful that you might miss some gem while admiring another, afraid that while you tasted the fine flavour of one dish which she offered, some other dish might pass untasted.

If you listened to her diction—admirable, as is that of all her sisters, where every vowel is given its full value, and the " end " of every word is cut off smartly and exactly—you might miss her expressive hands, you might allow the twitch of an eyebrow, the lowering of an eyelid to escape your notice, you might not observe the twinkle of her feet as she did a few steps quite perfectly.

She was not one artiste, she was half a dozen. She did not sing a song, she acted a play for you, comedy or tragedy, for her character songs so nearly became pathetic, the line between her comedy and tragedy was so fine. As she herself said of Dan Leno :

" If we didn't laugh at him—we'd cry our eyes out."

CHAPTER EIGHT

" . . . IN NOTHING ELSE SO HAPPY—REMEMBERING MY GOOD
FRIENDS "

SHAKESPEARE

Her appearances—The change begins—" Winkles for tea "—At
the munition works—A soldier said . . . —A poem on Marie
Lloyd—Gossips—The case of Dick Burge—The auction sale.

FOR many artistes the war was an opportunity, and they
took it. They organized concerts, they got others to
work for them, and they saw to it that a great deal of
fuss was made over them. As ever, the people who did the real
work got little or no advertisement. A great actor—I say that
advisedly—wrote to me some stories of Marie not long ago.
He referred to concerts which he used to have each Sunday
at a certain theatre of which he, at that time, was owner.
Until then I had never heard of those concerts, and yet there
they had been " every Sunday afternoon for months, for the
Tommies." He was one of the people who " got on with the
doings," and did nothing for the sake of what he might get
out of it.

That, too, was Marie's attitude.

I doubt if during the whole of the war she ever neglected to
send flowers to the hospitals. I know that after a birthday of
hers every flower which had been given to her was sent
immediately to the T.B. hospital at Colindale ; I know that
whenever she was on tour in the provinces, whatever bouquets
were handed to her, went automatically to the local military
hospital. I know that she, despite the fact that she was far
from well, gave her services Sunday after Sunday when she
appeared at charity matinées.

I happen to know that she hated many of these. While she
loved giving her services, while she would cheerfully sing to
wounded men, to munition workers, she loathed the kind of
functions which were organized with the object of getting as

many " names " as possible on to one bill, when the leading
light—often a society woman—knew nothing of Marie Lloyd,
and barely knew and understood the favour this great artiste
conferred on her by appearing.

I have seen Marie—having travelled up from Liverpool and
having to leave again on Monday morning to open at Bristol for
the following week—arrive at some big music-hall for a Sunday
concert. The back of the stage crowded with elegant males and
females, who, as Marie passed, barely turned their heads to look
after her. I have known her shown into a dressing-room devoid
of any comfort, without an arm-chair, and—she has been left
there. While some young woman, probably playing lead for
the first and only time in a West End theatre, has thrown tem-
peraments, and demanded this, that, and the next thing before
she went on to recite (" and how ! ") some hoary-headed old
chestnut like " If," or a long pathetic ballad which begins :
" At some place or other down on the Rio Grande," and
which dealt with a young woman who was trampled to death
by mad cows. When she finished, a crowd of well-dressed
women would crowd round chattering and exclaiming :

" *Dar*-ling, you were *won*-derful ! I shall never be able to
thank you enough. Lov-ely, angel. I don't know how you can
remember it as you do. Who comes next ? My dear—Marie
Lloyd ! I believe she's terribly vulgar ! I don't know where
she is—the stage manager will find her, I suppose."

Marie didn't care. She liked those concerts where people
were " matey," where she met her friends, where people, who
were fine actors themselves, recognized her as a great artiste.
That is why, I am certain, she was always glad to work for Sir
Seymour Hicks. I cannot imagine that in his theatre Our
Marie was treated like a " first turn " at Saint Helens or
Longton.

I think that it was at a Sunday show in London that I first
realized that Marie was ill. Not that her work suffered, she was
better than ever, she danced beautifully, her voice was splendid,
she had the same grasp of technique—but there was a change.
A change not in her work, but in Marie herself. Something
very subtle, something that might not have been apparent to
anyone who did not love her very dearly. She was more
serious, and on this particular afternoon I remember saying to
poor Lauri de Frece, that her smile—that lovely wide, generous
smile, which used to light up her whole vivid face—had
changed.

He said : " I've noticed it. It never seems to touch her eyes now."

It was that afternoon, too, that she stopped pretending for a minute. Marie, the most honest soul in the world, was—in one thing—the greatest bluffer in creation. She bluffed everyone, she never scrupled to lie, and lie and lie—because she had too much pride to not wish to hide—or try to hide—what was becoming pretty patent to everyone.

People suspected, people chattered, we heard this and listened to that, some of us even heard things which we would have preferred not to know—and Marie, gallant, decent, far-too-loyal Marie went on with her lies, smiling that smile which never succeeded in reaching her eyes. There were even people who heard that " she has no one except herself to blame," and were fools enough to believe it. There were people who shrugged their shoulders, and hinted that Marie was " horribly extravagant," that nothing really affected her very much. " Don't tell me ! " these folks said, " I listened to her the other evening at the side of the stage at the Oxford " (or the Pav. or the Holborn or the Met., as the case might be) " laughing and joking. That woman hasn't got a care in the world ! " Poor Marie, you were too good an actress.

So on this particular afternoon I sat in her dressing-room until it was time for her to go down to the stage. We spoke of two women—her friends and mine, one of whom was recently dead. Both fine artistes, both sweet, kindly women, both desperately unhappy. Neither of them possessing the ability to stand up against personal unhappiness and the ill health which followed.

Marie—her face very grave and tender—said : " Poor dears —and what grand women, both of them ! Killed, really, y'know. Their work—killed, hope, happiness—all taken from them. Oh, yes, I know E—— is still alive—or trying to pretend she is. I don't know what they said that M—— died of, I don't know what they'll tell us killed E—— but I know ! Broken hearts. Just that." There was a little pause, then she went on : " You'll lose another of your pals the same way, Micky. See if you don't."

I stared, then said : " Marie—you don't mean——? "

There was that old flare of temper, the old resentment that she had allowed someone to see what lay beneath the mask. As always, she vented that temper on the person nearest to her at the time.

" Mean ? " she said. " Don't stare like that, you fool. Mean —I mean nothing at all ! Hundreds of people die of broken hearts. This is a nice way to be talking when I've got to go on and make them laugh in a minute ! Damn it, can't we manage to be a bit cheerful, not chatting about death and broken hearts and all the rest of it. Haven't you heard any new stories this week—well, come on, tell me ? "

Three minutes afterwards we were " swopping " stories, and Marie was laughing—at least her lips smiled.

Soon after, she was standing at the side, joking with Lauri de Frece, laughing at Jimmy Lindsey, who was stage-managing for the afternoon, looking like the Marie we knew, as if she hadn't a care in the world. I remember her asking Jimmy and me if we'd care to drive back with her. " I've got pints and pints of winkles for tea ! " she told us as an added inducement.

That was the afternoon when she said to me—in a queer kind of off-hand way that was, if you hadn't known Marie, almost insulting :

" Why don't you come and travel round with me ? You might just as well. I don't see that you're doing much good in London making those damn munitions. I'll give you as much as they give you at that damn place. Go on, you'd better."

" I don't know. There'd be nothing for me to do, would there ? "

" Plenty to do. You might write a few letters for me—I never write any. Look after me, book rooms—oh, there'd be plenty to do."

But I was ambitious and selfish, and I wanted to " have a career " and all that sort of silliness that one believes in when one isn't very old. I don't suppose for a moment that I could have really done anything to help her, that I could have made life easier, only—well, I ought to have tried. And I didn't.

I was supervisor of a munition factory in those days, out at Willesden. I liked to get a little show for the " boys and girls " every Friday dinner-time and I used to get all sorts of kind folk to come down and do a short entertainment. Dick Tubb came, Thornley Dodge, Datas, Murray Pilcer and his band, Jimmy Lindsey and many others. I asked Marie if she'd come, adding : " Mind, I don't suppose you'd care to. It's a longish way, after all—just for half an hour." Marie said : " What's the matter with you—always supposing something, aren't you ? That's the trouble with you, you always know such a hell of a lot about

everything ! Why shouldn't I come ? I'll come next Friday·
'Course I will. Have I got to be very ' starchy,' or can I just
—let myself go ? "

She came as the works " buzzer " blew twelve. For some
munition workers she didn't know, had never seen, she had
dressed gorgeously. Furs, and ospreys in her hat, pearls—she
looked a picture. What concerned her most was—would her
chauffeur be able to get some lunch ? I'd arranged for that.
I asked her to come and have some food. Rather nice
food, too, I remamber, for my cook—who stood six feet
four, and had five brothers in the Guards, all taller than
herself—had worshipped Marie from the audience for years.

Marie praised the food, but she scarcely touched it.

At half-past twelve she was ready to go on. The works went
mad ! They beat on the tables with knives and forks, they
yelled " Good Old Marie ! " and generally gave her a great
reception. And what did she give them ! One of the boys in
the works played for her, and she sang song after song ; she
pattered ; she was at her very best. When they went back to
work at one, she sat in the canteen with me for some time,
talking, and I thought she seemed terribly tired.

Then : " Well, I must get along."

I led her through the works, where the belts were whirling,
the drills humming, and where an air of bustle reigned. Now
I knew what the boys and girls would do. Whenever they
wished to show appreciation, whenever they wanted to give a
little additional applause, every man-jack of them, every man,
every girl, every little lad on the capstans beat on the nearest
piece of iron with a hammer or spanner or whatever was
handy. The noise was deafening ! Marie started, clutched
my arm, and I explained that it was a compliment.

" Whew ! " she said, " it's damned awful. Let me get out
of it."

But she walked the length of the works, smiling, turning this
side and that, laughing at the men, bowing to the girls, because
if you have learnt your job as a Queen, you know how to greet
your subjects. Only when she reached the door did she swing
round, and laughing, her whole face alight, she shook her fist
at them, shouting as she did so : " For Heaven's sake—stop
it—you devils ! Good-bye."

I believe that if anyone in that factory had dared to speak of
Marie Lloyd without due respect, he would have been laid out
with a spanner, or thrown into one of the ovens. I know that

he would have been dealt with very promptly by Big Liz
Mitchell, Bob Harward, Harry Boyes, Harry Burleigh, Joe
Mintin, Bill Eastwood, Tom Woollet, or "Simmy." To say
nothing of the Sergeant, who was an old Grenadier Guardsman,
who saluted her that day when she left as if she had been some
member of the Royal Family paying a state visit.

To the soldiers she was goodness itself. Her dressing-room
was always open to the rank and file. She would always
listen to them, ask them questions, offer them advice, and find
cigarettes and a drink for them. Here is a letter which came
to me some weeks ago. I don't know the writer, he doesn't
know me. His knowledge of me is confined to a certain book
I once wrote, called *Me*—and I have a very shrewd suspicion
that he liked that because Marie was mentioned so often.

" I am sending you the enclosed photographs," he said, " of
dear Marie Lloyd. I hope that you will be able to make use of
them. To me she was the sweetest woman I have ever known.
During the war I was in the London Scottish, and Marie was
appearing at Chiswick Empire. We were billeted at Richmond.
I called to see her very late one evening, just before eleven, and
it was much later than that when I left her dressing-room. But
it was not too late for her to drive me down to Richmond, and
she was very tired and worried that night. The wife of Eli
Hudson, of the Hudson Trio, was very ill, and she was terribly
upset about it. She had all her flowers those which were given
her that night, sent off at once. Nothing ever ' thought out,'
just the feeling of thinking of others which was natural to her.
That is why everyone loved her. I shall long to read a book
about her.—Yours faithfully, Alfred Gibbs."

In 1917, when everyone had to produce ration cards, Marie
went to Edinburgh. Of course, being Marie, she arrived there
without her cards, and was half-demented to know what she
could do. She sent for Charles Russell—who has appeared
before in these pages—and explained the position. He was one
of those fortunate people who could invariably get additional
supplies, and he came to Marie's assistance. Her comment was :
" Seems to me that I do a damn' sight better without ration
cards than with them."

It was during the war that Marie was honoured by having a
poem written about her by no less a person than Mr. Rudyard
Kipling. This poem was afterwards included in his book
entitled : *The Years Between*. While the poem itself is not essentially amusing, while—in fact—it might not make any great

appeal to those friends of Marie's who loved her and admired
her work, it produced an amusing sequel.

The poem is called "A Recantation," and has for its sub-
title : "To Lyde of the Music-halls." I can only suppose that
"Lyde" is an attempt to reproduce Marie's surname in the
dialect of a cockney. The second verse runs thus :

> "Ere certain Fate had touched a heart
> By fifty years made cold,
> I judged thee, Lyde, and thy art
> O'erblown and overbold."

The poem continues :

> "But he—but he, of whom bereft
> I suffer vacant days——
> He on his shield not meanly left,
> He cherished all thy lays.
>
> Witnessed the magic coffer stocked
> With convoluted runes,
> Wherein thy very voice was locked,
> And linked to circling tunes."

I should have liked to ask Marie what "convoluted runes"
meant. She'd probably have said : "Here, here ! We don't
want any of that ! Keep the party clean ! " It's taken me over
ten years to realize that the expression means—(" I'll give you
two guesses," as poor Arthur Roberts used to say)—gramophone records ! Well, I think that I am right in saying that
Marie only made three double-sided records in her life—for
I have them all—so the "magic coffer" wasn't exactly
overflowing !

Now listen to another couple of verses, for in them is the
point of the story.

> "Never more rampant rose the Hall,
> At thy audacious line,
> Than when the news came in from Gaul
> Thy son—had followed mine.
>
> But thou didst hide it in thy breast,
> And capering took the brunt,
> Of blaze and blare, and launched the jest
> That swept next week the front."

Thy son—whose son ? Marie never had a son. Capering—

when did she ever "caper"? However—there's the poem, and here is the sequel.

I forget the exact year—probably about 1926—anyway, by that time Marie Lloyd had stopped singing, and the world was the poorer for her loss. I read in a paper that a Kipling Society was in progress of formation, and the notice continued : "It is not generally known that Mr. Kipling wrote a poem to the late Miss Marie Lloyd." I wrote to the secretary of the society to ask where I might obtain this poem, stating that it would be of considerable interest to me, as Miss Lloyd had been a friend of mine.

I got a very stiff letter in reply, telling me that if I wanted information I must join the society, and adding that the valuable piece of special knowledge could only be given to members.

If Marie was here now I could tell *her*—though I can't tell you in cold print—what in effect I said in my reply.

Some months later I had a letter from this secretary, saying that as I had stated that I was a friend of Miss Lloyd's, would I kindly supply the name of her son—and his present address, as the society wished to communicate with him.

(I had by this time unearthed the poem, and read it with no great pleasure, though the reference to this mythical "son" amused me. Also as the verses stated that "thy son had followed mine," I felt that the implication was that he had "gone west.")

I answered that Miss Marie Lloyd had one daughter, but no son, and this being the case, I still didn't understand how (*a*) he could have died in France, and (*b*) why they should want his address. They replied, like the man in *Alice in Wonderland*, "very stiff and proud," explaining that they felt it most extraordinary that I should state that Miss Lloyd had no son, *when Mr. Kipling had written a poem about him.*

That was how a certain type of person always behaved about Marie.

I have heard the most startling stories told concerning her, told by people who had never seen her, and certainly were never likely to meet her. The sort of story which always begins :

"My dear, I know for a fact—" and goes on something like this : "My dear aunt, Mrs. Higginbottom of Surbiton had a maid whose brother was in the police force, and *he* told *her*, and *she* told *me* that Marie Lloyd is never allowed to go on anywhere, without at least two policeman standing in—what is it called ?—the flies—no, the arcs, no, no—what ?—oh, yes, the wings—to listen to what she says. I believe at the first improper word they simply go on the stage and arrest her ! "

Or : " Marie Lloyd is an old woman. I happen to know. My Aunt Sarah Ellen saw her in Mudcum-on-the-Slush in 1854, and she was—my aunt assured me—at least thirty then ! "

As I once heard Mr. George Lansbury say, when some long stor' was retailed to him : " They say—well, let 'em say."

That—in effect—is what Marie used to say.

According to some of these old gossips, Marie had been married twice as often as Henry the Eighth, her escapades would have filled any adventurer with envy, she had lived a life of such wild extravagance that it sounded like the *Arabian Nights*. She was spoken of as a cross between the Queen of Sheba and Ninon, with a dash of Jezebel and Cleopatra ! As she herself sang in " Woman's Opinion of Man "—" Dear, dear—what rot ! "

At the end of the war some person of importance gave a dinner to the Theatrical and music-hall professions, to make a public acknowledgment to them of their services during the war. This huge function, with a reception, dinner, and everything else imaginable, was given on the night when " Dick " Burge passed away.

I must digress here to say a word about this remarkable man. His life and that of his wife have been more or less bound up with the whole Wood family. You will remember that Bella Burge actually worked with Alice Lloyd—as the Sisters Lloyd —in their early days, and it was when she married Dick Burge that the act ended.

Richard Burge—though he was always known as " Dick "— was a boxer and exceedingly popular. In 1902 the celebrated Goudie Bank Scandal came to light, and Dick Burge was arrested, along with Marks, Mances, and Goudie. Dick Burge stood his ground and refused to turn King's Evidence.

Dick Burge was cross-questioned by Mr. Gill, K.C., and " emerged from the skilful examination very badly." Now, remember that it is quite astonishingly difficult for a man of Dick Burge's calibre to emerge " very well " out of these examinations. He was not a man of great education, he was probably highly nervous, and very distressed at the position in which he found himself. How far he was guilty or not is no concern of mine, sufficient to say that he stated that he was in no pressing need of money, that in eight years, from his boxing,

he had made £30,000, and he added that he had not been
" *hard up for ten years.*" Various witnesses came forward,
including Mr. John Nathan of Covent Garden, who testified
that he had known Burge for many years and had always
found him to be highly respectable. " That was," said Mr.
Nathan, " Burge's general reputation."

He pleaded " not guilty " ; he got ten years' penal servi-
tude. The report reads : " Burge took his sentence very badly,
breaking down completely in the court."

That sentence is one of those reporter's clichés which always
seem so astonishing to me. If a prisoner breaks down, then he
" took his sentence very badly," if he does nothing, then he
" retained a stubborn and callous attitude." It's a case of
" Heads I win, tails you lose."

He served seven years, having three years remitted through
his exemplary conduct, and owing to the fact that he saved a
warder's life when he was attacked by another convict. He
took The Ring in the Blackfriars Road—where his wife, Mrs.
Bella Burge, is still happily in management—served during the
war, did a tremendous amount of recruiting, and when he
died, at the end of the war, one of the first telegrams of condolence received by his widow was from King George V. He
left the reputation of having been a splendid friend, and a man
of great integrity.

In *The Life of Lord Birkenhead*, by his son, you may find the
following sentences : " The other defendant, Burge, received
the same sentence." " The big boxer broke down in tears.
He was, incidentally, a brother-in-law of the famous comedienne, Marie Lloyd, whose sister he had married shortly before
his arrest." Which goes to show that even the sons of famous
lawyers may make mistakes. Of course, Dick Burge was no
relation to the Lloyds, neither was his wife one of that family.

However, to get back to Marie on the evening of poor Dick
Burge's death. She was terribly upset, for the whole family
loved him, and always speak of him with the greatest possible
affection. Marie felt that it was her duty to be present at this
dinner of official recognition. She arrived late—Marie was
always late for everything except her work—and found a
well-known theatrical artiste on his feet. This is the type of
speech which he was delivering to the assembled company :

" I can assure you, my Lord, Ladies, and Gentlemen, that
whatever I—that is, whatever—*we* have been able to do during
the war, it has given me—er given *us*—the greatest possible

pleasure, to feel that I—I mean that *we*—have been able to do my—er—*our*—little bit to mitigate the lot of the soldiers and sailors. And I can only assure you that whatever I—er—er, whatever *we* have done——" and so on, *ad infinitum* and *ad nauseum*. Marie listened, Marie's eyes grew stormy, she frowned and waited. The gentleman sat down. Marie was on her feet. Remember that when Marie wanted to make a speech, there was no one who could make a better and more pointed one.

"My Lord, Ladies, and Gentlemen, you may not know me. My name is Marie Lloyd. I don't advertise, I haven't had my photograph taken for years. I only want to say that, apparently, in this war neither poor old Ellen Terry nor poor old Marie Lloyd have done anything, in fact no one has done anything —*except* the gentleman who has just spoken to you. This is not strictly correct. That's all. Thank you."

She didn't wait, she simply walked out. Not that Marie ever wanted thanks and public recognition, she disliked being " smarmed over " as much as she liked being flattered. She was an honest person, and her resentment on that particular evening sprang originally, I am certain, from the recollection that her friend, Dick Burge, who lay dead, had done so much, and that she compared the essential modesty of the dead man with the somewhat grandiloquent remarks of the speaker. Had the speaker mentioned Dick Burge, had he referred to his public services given so loyally ever since the outbreak of war, Marie would have been the first to have applauded, and to have assured everyone that : " Say what you like, old —— (whatever was the gentleman's name) is a fine fellow ! May not be much of a speaker, but his heart's all right."

She said to me once, after the death of that fine actor and playwright, H. V. Esmond : " I saw that Miss Moore'd lost her husband. I thought of writing to her, but you know I hate writing letters, and anyway, I expect that she had dozens. When you see her, you might just—well, just say : ' Marie Lloyd's very sorry,' will you ? "

She never wrote letters if she could avoid doing so. She'd spend any amount of money on a telegram or a cable, but how she hated writing letters ! I have one of hers, it only covers one side of a sheet—otherwise the only specimen of her writing I possess is the signature on a photograph. Very characteristic writing it was, too ! Bold, generous, nothing " niggly " about it, full of vitality, and very clear.

She was entirely lacking in conceit. That was one of the

reasons she loved flattery. It stabilized her, gave her that confidence which she lacked fundamentally. Oh, she could "swank" with the best, she could "throw her weight about" as much as anyone, she could be arrogant and overbearing, but underneath it all there was a simple, genuine nature. She was loyalty itself. Her friends were her friends, and Marie didn't care whether they lived in a slum or a palace. Probably she would have preferred them to live in a slum, so that she could have paid to remove them immediately to a palace! She never cared what people wore, what anyone said concerning them. In fact, Marie might have been the female model of the "Thousandth Man":

> "Nine hundred and ninety-nine depend
> On what the world sees in you,
> But the Thousandth Man will stand your friend
> With the whole round world agin you."

And again:

> "Nine hundred and ninety-nine can't bide
> The shame or mocking or laughter,
> But the Thousandth Man will stand by your side
> To the gallow's foot—and after!"

And Mr. Rudyard Kipling hit off the character of Marie Lloyd more correctly in that poem than he ever managed to do in "Lyde of the Music Halls."

I remember—and this is one of those little incidents which keep crowding into my mind when I write of her—after a Sunday show, when she was tired to death, longing to get home and rest, an auction sale was in progress. During the war it was customary at many of the "Charity Performances" to have these auctions. Pounds of butter, a couple of chickens, a half-pound of tea, a pound of sugar, anything which at the time was difficult to obtain, would be put up for auction. On this occasion Lauri de Frece was the auctioneer. His voice was very bad, he had caught cold, and was straining his throat terribly, holding this comic auction.

"A pound of fresh butter—only came up from the country this morning—five shillings—half a sovereign, fifteen shillings—a pound—any advance——?"

Marie, watching him from the side, called: "Two pounds!" and got it. Later, a pair of chickens; again, with his voice growing more and more hoarse, he encouraged the audience to buy.

" Two pounds—and ten shillings—fifteen—two fifteen—three——"

" Four pounds ! " Marie Lloyd again.

She called to him : " Got much more stuff ? "

" Two more lots, Marie."

" Right—put the top price on them and I'll have them whatever they are. I can't bear to hear you rasping your voice like that." Then, to some elegant lady near her, Marie explained : " Damn it, his voice is his living ! I wonder that anyone allowed him to do this . . . silly auction ! It's horrible ! "

She didn't particularly want the butter, chickens, and the two unknown lots—but she knew the value of an artiste's voice, and she was going to spare if it she could. That little kindness probably cost her a tenner—it would have been just the same if it had cost ten times that amount !

When the war ended, Marie Lloyd received no decorations, her name was not mentioned in any official lists, she never became entitled to add several letters after her name—and she didn't care ! She did all that was in her power, and the thanks of the soldiers and her friends were her reward.

CHAPTER NINE

Langley Levy and "The British Army in Flanders"—Mabel
Thorn—Marie buys more hats !—Late again—Two nippers
—Who is like Marie ?—Sees me act—What Julia Neilson says.

THERE have been times when I, writing this book,
have felt that it would be impossible to come to the
end of it, because every day letters arrive with new
stories, fresh recollections of Marie. There seems to be no end
to the people who wish to help, who wish to identify themselves
with this attempt to pay tribute to her.

Yesterday came a long letter from Langley Levy, Editor of
the Johannesburg *Sunday Times :* " So you're writing a book on
Marie Lloyd, well, may I be here to read and review it."

He then goes on to tell me, in a long letter, many recollections of Marie herself. Many of them cannot be used here
because they belong to that period of her life when acute
unhappiness had laid its hand on her, and when her outlook
on life had become so coloured by that unhappiness, that—well,
sometimes it seemed as if the Marie we had known, laughed at
and laughed with, had ceased to exist.

However, here is a typical little verbal sketch of Marie. Here
is a " snapshot " which illustrates her sudden bursts of fury,
and shows how quickly she emerged and became herself again.

She was playing " Boy Blue " at the Shakespeare Theatre,
Liverpool. The first time she ever played principal boy.
Langley Levy (who in those days wrote lyrics and " locals " for
many pantomimes, and wrote them sufficiently well for Robert
Courtneidge to empoly him—which, believe me, is saying something, for " The Guv'nor " only wants the best whatever his
purpose) was in Marie's dressing-room, seated on a big dress
basket. She had gone down to the stage and told him not to go
until she came back, leaving " him after a quick one, and a

short, racy chat." He waited, and as the door opened to admit Marie, the stage door-keeper came running down the corridor and handed her a telegram.

Marie came into the room, opening the telegram and forgetting that Langley Levy was still there, seated on the dress basket. Marie opened the telegram and read that her house in London had been burgled, and that quite a quantity of plate had been stolen.

" Then she swore, whole-heartedly and without reck of my presence. She swore like Billingsgate, like Newport Market, like the Mile End Road, and like the British Army in Flanders. Suddenly she became aware of my presence, and looked up, smiling, her expression very whimsical. ' Don't mind me, cocky, but my house in London has just been burgled.' "

He told me, too, of another incident which—though a certain tragedy underlay it—is valuable because it shows that almost childish attitude of mind which was typical of Marie sometimes. This was when she and Alec were very much at cross purposes. Langley Levy entered Romano's Bar in company with a well-known comedian, who said : " Now wait a minute and you'll see Marie and Alec both come in." Sure enough, in came Alec and took up his position at the end of the bar furthest from the Strand ; a moment or two later, Marie entered and stood with her little group of friends at the other end—nearest to the Strand. Both eyed each other, as Langley Levy says : " Obviously quite unable to decide whether they should hurl insults at each other or make advances towards a reconciliation. Each talked loudly *at* the other, throwing covert glances with the object of judging the effect of their various verbal shots." He adds : " It was really rather pitiful, because their thoughts were so apparent, and neither of them attempted to conceal what they were trying to do."

In case you should get the entirely erroneous idea that Marie's generosity, Marie's goodness of heart lay in spending money wildly and rather uselessly, let me tell you one or two of what you might call her more simple kindnesses.

Here are two stories sent to me by Majorie Lotinga, that clever artiste who, even if you have not actually seen her, you have probably heard on the air. Marjorie Lotinga's mother was Mabel Thorn, one of the famous theatrical family. Now, Marie had a positive mania for buying people hats. Probably she knew that this particular form of feminine adornment

made a tremendous appeal to women in general, and knew
that nothing gives a woman such a sense of " confidence " as a
new and, if possible, expensive hat. This happened at Glasgow,
where Mabel Thorn was dressing in a big room with six other
girls. Suddenly the door burst open and Marie dashed in
waving a cheque. Someone had paid her a debt for seven
pounds ; she waved the cheque in proof. No wonder she was
delighted, no wonder she felt that it was an " occasion "—
people rarely paid Marie Lloyd what they owed her. Anyway,
Marie was seven pounds to the good and she decided to celebrate, and to make this celebration not with the stars, but with
these young girls of no particular importance—at that time.
The next day, she told them, they were all to go with her and
buy new hats. In the morning Marie was waiting, Marie who
was always *almost* late for everything which concerned herself !
—at the theatre with two cabs. She drove with the girls to
the best milliners in Sauchiehall Street, and everyone was told
to choose a hat. As a matter of fact Marie helped considerably,
and not one of those hats cost under five guineas. The bill
was thirty guineas. She then took them all out to luncheon,
luncheon with champagne.

The same thing happened once in Bristol. The daughter of
that Mrs. James at whose house Marie used to stay so often
opened a dress and hat shop. The first week this shop opened
Marie was in the town, and visited the place. She bought
twenty hats, right off the stands ! Looked at all the dresses,
said half a dozen times : " That's a nice dress ! I'd like one
exactly like that ! Can you make one ? " the owner of the
shop told my friend who visited her to obtain " stories " of
Marie for me. " They were most of them quite ordinary
dresses. I was only beginning, I didn't make such good things
as I do now, and Marie could, of course, have bought nothing
but the finest models had she wished. But she made you feel
that she *really* wanted them, and not that she was just trying
to do you a good turn."

To return to Marjorie Lotinga, and one of her mother's stories.
Mabel Thorn was working the Middlesex, now the Winter
Garden Theatre, once upon a time : " The Old Mo." She
was working two halls, and rushed in rather breathlessly.

In addition, she was not strong at the time, as she was
expecting the birth of her first child in a short time. The
stage manager was nervous, inclined to shout his orders and
admonitions.

"Now, Miss Thorn, hurry up there. You're on next, and Miss Marie Lloyd follows you. Don't waste time, please, you're almost late as it is."

Marie saw, heard, and stepped forward. This must have been one of the rare occasions when Marie herself arrived at a hall with more than two minutes to spare !

"No, she doesn't go on before me. I'll go on first, and she can have my place. That's all right—that's how I want it."

Thus she gave Miss Thorn the best place on the bill, and devoted the three minutes before she herself had to go on in helping this delicate woman to dress. Giving her time to recover from her nervousness, to get a little rest and so do herself justice when she went on.

And remember that a position in a music-hall bill is a thing calculated to a nicety, a thing which your star has had to fight for, step by step, climbing each rung of the ladder slowly and painfully. The "star turn" is not a "movable feast"—it has a "fixed and never changing quality"—but Marie gave her position away when it suited her.

When her own baby was little, Marie was working, of course —she was in great demand, and went back to her work the moment it was possible. But because she was working, her baby wasn't neglected. It was carried down to the hall, and Marie, when she finished her first appearance, sat with the little thing in her dressing-room—for those moments, not the successful comedienne, but just an ordinary woman whose child's physical welfare means so much to her. She could have afforded to pay expensive and efficient nurses, but—that wouldn't have been good enough for Marie ! She never grudged spending her vitality on her audiences, and she certainly didn't grudge spending it on her child.

She always put off leaving home for the theatre until the very last minute. Her brother Johnnie tells me that. And he knows, for at one time he used to drive her brougham, in the days before everyone had a motor-car. He says that when she was appearing at Drury Lane, Marie lived at Lewisham, and was always late starting for the matinée—then known as the "morning performance." "I was going along fairly fast," he says, "when the rug covering my knees blew off and was whirled into the street. Marie saw it, flung down the window, and shouted to me : 'Don't stop ! Don't stop ! We'll buy another later !'" He says that she used to often "make up" as they drove along, and she realized that they were late.

At the big London halls, whenever she was on the bill,
I remember that there was always a certain amount of tension
until it was known that she was actually in the theatre.

Those of you who have only known the halls in their
"Decline and Fall" cannot imagine what they were like in
the height of their glory. "The glory that was the Pavilion, the
grandeur that was the Oxford"—wonderful days. Such bills,
such artistes, such a hurry and bustle. At the Oxford, the stage
manager, always a little worried and anxious, people coming
down to place their changes ready in the change room, people
coming to ask questions, dressers hurrying backwards and forwards, broughams driving up, driving away, the electric bell
signalling to the orchestra, the heavy swish of the tabs as they
fell—it was a little world of its own inside the stage door.

Standing at the door which cut off the passage and stage door
from the stage, you might hear the shrill young voice of the call
boy upstairs as he announced to the various artistes that their
time was near.

"Mr. Malcolm Scott—the Zigeuner Quartette are on their
finish." A moment later : "They're coming off, Mr. Scott,"
and Malcolm Scott, tall, heavy, with that queer, ugly, humour-
ous face, and in the costume of "Catherine Parr" would
come down the stairs, twitching his wig straight as he came.

"Call Mr. Tich." (Stage managers, everyone, knew better
than to call him "Little Tich !")

"Mr. Tich is down, sir."

There, sure enough, was Harry Tich, small, unobtrusive—
or *apparently* unobtrusive, for never was there a man and an
artiste who demanded so much deference, so much attention,
or who could be, on occasion, so difficult. Mr. Tich would be
deep in conversation with someone, and presently the call boy
would draw near and whisper : "Mr. Scott's on his finish,
sir."

"Very well."

"Call Miss Lloyd."

Away would go the boy and return, "Miss Lloyd's not in
yet."

Silence. The S.M. looks at his watch, looks at Tich who is
just going on, and he tries hard to pretend that he is not worried
over the non-arrival of Miss Lloyd.

"Miss Lloyd in yet ? "

"No, sir—I just been to see."

Tich has finished his first song, he has gone on for his second

—still no sign of Miss Lloyd. Tich changes for his last number, changes into a ballet skirt, he is going to sing " I am the queen of the fairies."

" Miss Lloyd's just driven up, sir."

The tension relaxed—she was there ! No need to panic, no need to send the boy flying upstairs to tell some other artiste to " stand by, Miss Lloyd's late." The door on to the stage swings open, the Queen of Comedy enters, with a dresser, probably her mother and a sister, maybe two of her sister's little girls, and a few friends. Signs advising you that : " No one except the actual artistes and their dressers are admitted to the stage " meant nothing to Marie.

" How long have I got ? "

" Mr. Tich is just coming off, Miss Lloyd."

" Love us ! We ran it fine that time ! All right ! "

Tich is off—he listens for a second to assure himself that the applause is all that he could wish, then with a nod and possibly a brief word of greeting, the great little man walks briskly off the stage. Marie pulls a bow straight here, smooths her gloves, jerks her head towards the disappearing figure of Mr. Tich and says : " Always talks such a lot, that fellow, eh ? "

The S.M. says : " Ready, Miss Lloyd ? " his finger on the bell.

Marie, those nerves of hers beginning to assert themselves, snaps out : " Ready ! I've been here *hours !* Get on with it ! "

The music begins, Marie's *ad lib* is playing, she moves nearer the entrance and disappears. The thunder of applause tells you that she is—on. Marie Lloyd hasn't kept her public waiting.

In the old days of the broughams, the carriages and pairs, she was leaving the Tivoli one night with George Graves. The usual little boy was there, with the brush and tray, making the street tidy, according to the L.C.C. regulations. Marie was in the middle of some story when she caught sight of this little lad. She stopped, watched him for a minute, then called to him :

" Garn ! You horrible little sparrow starver ! Ought to be ashamed of yourself ! "

Another evening she came out of the same hall and waited for her brougham to draw up. Two little London street arabs were standing near the door, and she heard the following conversation :

" Thet's er ! Yus, it is—thet's Marie ! "

"Thet's Marie ! Blimy, you said as 'ow she was loverly !
Said as 'ow she was puffickly 'eavengly ter look at ! "

"So she is ! I sed so an' I still sai so."

"Gor' luv us, I call 'er a 'AG ! "

"You do, do yer. Then I calls you a b—— liar."

Marie moved forward quickly, a hand on each of their
collars. The brougham was told to wait further down the road,
and she propelled them both, half-laughing, half-frightened,
to the nearest coffee-stall. They were ordered to eat—to drink
hot cocoa with far too much sugar, the kind of cocoa that
children love ; they were given buns and sandwiches, their
pockets were stuffed, and only when they could neither eat
nor carry any more did she allow them to leave the stall.

"So you think I'm perfectly heavenly to look at, do you ? "

"Yus, I do, an' I sed as I did ! "

"And you, cock, you think I'm a hag, eh ? "

The child shuffled his feet. "Well—I don't care whatcher
look like, I sai this—you're a proper toff, a reel lidy."

Marie grinned—on occasion she could grin like a naughty
schoolboy. "I'll tell you something. No woman cares about
being a toff, or a real lady—every one of them wants to be told
they *look* heavenly. Now—remember that, both of you."

Somewhere in the world—unless they were blown out of it
between 1914 and 1918, there are two cockneys who probably
still tell their own little children of the night when " Ar Marie
give me an' my little pal a proper blow art ! Not 'arf a blow art,
neither, it was too. We 'ad cocoa, an' caike, we 'ad——" and
so the story will go on, and other little " nippers " will wish that
they might hang round the old Tivoli Stage Door, and meet
" Ar Marie." Only now there is no stage door, with the steep
incline that made it so difficult to drive down ; there are no
artistes, no orchestra, only a few cinema operators. I wonder
if at times, if one could see sufficiently clearly, there are not
ghosts who enter the door that doesn't exist in reality any longer.
If you might not see Tich, smart with a curly brimmed topper
and the red ribbon of the Legion of Honour in his buttonhole, and poor George Formby with George Bass, agreeing
that the damp night air was trying to both of them, 'Gene
Stratton stepping lightly down the paved passage, little Dan
Leno with his great melancholy eyes and wide, flexible mouth,
R. G. Knowles, Tommy Dunville, Dutch Daley, lovely
Queenie Leighton, and the magnificent Harriet Vernon,
Marie Duggan flinging back a joke to someone over her shoul-

der, dear Marie Kendal, and lastly—if one could sense the sudden stir, the whirl and rush, as Our Marie arrived, as always, only just in time !

You don't know what you miss, you present generation who only know the " no-longer-silent drama " which inhabits the old palaces of Variety. They are wonderful, the production is magnificent, you have good—if only they wouldn't use the Vox Humana stop quite so often on those super-organs— music, comfortable seats, ash-trays and everything for which you can wish except the personal contact, except the friendship which existed between the old Variety artiste and his or her audience.

We used to quote the sayings, sing the songs of R. G. Knowles, of Florrie Forde, of Marie Lloyd. You never remember anything your " film favourites " say, you might remember a theme song until the next one comes and drives the last tune but one out of your head ! No one ever says : " As Greta Garbo says in ——." You only hear people repeat, *ad nauseam*, in what they believe is a " Garbo " voice : " Ay wanner be be a-loaone." True, you quote Miss Mae West—believing that you are speaking American—or Miss West's adaptation of American, but generally those quotations mean nothing in particular, or they are intended by the people who say them to mean only *one thing* in particular. I always feel sorry for Mae West, she has so many bad imitators, and she is such a good —though slightly limited—artiste.

I had been out of England for nearly five years, I went back to hear : " You must see Mae West, you'll love her ! My dear —she *is*—Marie Lloyd. The American Marie Lloyd."

Marie had a sense of comedy, so has Mae West : Marie was audacious, so is Mae West : Marie wore magnificent clothes— magnificently, so does Mae West, and that is the sum-total of the likeness !

I was assured that Miss Lily Morris was " exactly like Marie, in her type of work." Again I went, hopefully, again I failed to see the slightest resemblance, except that Marie sang cockney songs and so does Miss Lily Morris.

There is one person and one person only who is in the least like Marie Lloyd—always excepting Marie's own three brilliant sisters and Clarice Mayne in her imitations—and that person is not a music-hall artiste at all. She is one of the greatest actresses in England, she can act without speaking, as Marie could. She can convey everything in a little movement, but

a turn of her head, by a little smile, by the twinkle of her eyes.
She can use her hands, as Marie could, and she could come on
to the stage and make you believe that she was eighteen—if she
wished—as Marie could have done. That actress is Miss Marie
Tempest, and her art, in another sphere, in a different setting,
is the same art as that which Marie possessed.

But the rest, the poor, pale imitators, the silly little fools who
think that they can imitate Marie by singing indifferent cockney
in a slightly husky and entirely artificial voice, those impertinent
people who announce over the radio : " Aye shell naow
attempt to give you a sleight impression av the late Mess Maree
Lloyd——" they ought to be forcibly prevented from making
such " poppy-shows " of themselves, and for traducing a
great artiste. If you want to know what Marie was like on the
stage, go and listen to her sisters, Alice, Daisy, Rosie. If you
want to know what she was like off stage, persuade them to let
you go into their dressing-room between the " houses," and
you may get a correct impression of Our Marie, and her wit,
wisdom and kindness of heart. For the rest, there is only
one word : " Out ! "

That kindness of heart ! Here is a picture of Marie, a later
picture, when she was growing just a little tired. When—oh,
well, we won't go into that here, because this is a very pleasant
memory. The tragedy will not be content to be shut out much
longer in this chronicle, and let's make the most of what good
times there are left.

It was in Bristol. I was playing there in Ian Hay's *Safety
Match*. The company was Robert Courtneidge's, and was
under the management of that dear old man, the late Robert
Arthur.

I looked at the bill of the music-hall, there were no names I
knew, which disappointed me a little. I felt that Bristol had
grown a little dull. Then one morning my landlady said to me
that Marie was in the town. Not working, she was doing a cure
at Bath, and driving backwards and forwards. She was
staying at Mrs. James's, where she stayed so often.

I went round. I remember that Arthur Prince, the best
ventriloquist either you or I will ever hear, was with her. I
remember too that he was wearing a particularly admirable
suit of plus-fours, which suited him remarkably well.

Marie wasn't well. That was evident. She looked tired and
she sounded tired. She was dispirited, the old sparkle seemed
dimmed, except at moments when it would flash out suddenly

as bright as ever. Just flashed, then the cloud would come
down again, and all the brightness would die.

As I was leaving, I said, very tentatively, because I have been
properly brought up to realize that you don't assume that great
stars want to come and watch your performance : " I suppose
you'd be too tired to come and see the show to-night ? "

The old Marie showed for a second. " You suppose ! I've
never known the time when you weren't *supposing* something—
or *thinking* something or *knowing* something ! Who says I'll be
too tired ? Of course I shall come. Who's your manager ?
What—Robert Arthur ! Oh, he knows me all right (as if all
England didn't know her !). Ask him to let me have a box.
I'll be there."

And, sure enough, she was, and in her seat in the box before
the curtain went up, and stayed there the whole evening, leaning forward, listening intently, applauding everything. Marie
was never the " typical dead-head " who, having been given
a seat by the management, sits watching with a supercilious
expression, and goes away to tell everyone that " it's a frightful
show at the theatre this week."

I went round after the show, for I was off just before the final
curtain, and Robert Arthur gave me permission to go to Marie's
box—" as it's to see Miss Lloyd," for to go in front of the house
is a most unprofessional thing to do.

Marie was watching the end of the play. I sat down next to
her and waited. The moment the curtain fell she turned to me.

" There's a little bottle of champagne there waiting for you."
I drank the wine, and—I could do with it. I'd played a longish
part. Marie said : " It's a splendid play, I've enjoyed every
minute of it." She added some very apt and just criticisms
on the acting and construction, for Marie knew as much as
anyone about stage plays. Then, rather nervously, because
she was always quite honest, I said : " Er—did you think I
was all right ? I mean—do you think I shall make an actress ? "

She turned, smiling, and patted my hand with hers, she had
the prettiest hands in the world, small, well-shaped and wonderfully soft. " You—you don't need to be an actress. You're
a b—— artiste. You're all right."

Generous Marie ! Too big to ever be patronizing, ready to
put you on the same level as herself. Anxious to give praise,
and able to couch that praise in words which would mean the
most to you.

Now to finish this chapter, to round off Marie's praise of an

insignificant actress with the praise of a great actress for Marie.
I am going to quote it fully, because I know just how it would
please her. I can hear Marie's comment on this letter.

" Forgive me for not having answered your letter more
quickly, but I have been a little poorly with acute neuritis,
and so I fear that my letters have been neglected.

I don't know that there is anything for you in my several
meetings on various occasions with that most wonderful Marie
Lloyd. I used to meet her at Westgate, many years ago when
she was appearing at Margate.

We always had enthusiastic little chats over our plays, which
she adored, and she always invited me to come and see her
' turns ' (bless her !) and wonderful they were. She always
played ' to me.'

What a *great-hearted* creature !

I wish your book a huge success—which it is bound to have.

Yours sincerely,

JULIA NEILSON."

Dear Marie ! Does it sound sentimental to say that I know
how much pleasure that letter would give you, how your very
blue eyes would brighten, your lips part in a smile (a smile
which *this time*—reached your eyes !) and how, assuming that
" off-hand " manner, you would say : " Who ? Julia Neilson !
Get out—she never wrote that ? Show me, then ! " I can
picture her reading that letter, flushing a little, and then
handing it back, and saying—still trying to make believe that it
didn't matter : " Nice of her ! Listen, let me tell you. What
an actress ! And what's more—a damned nice woman !
One of the people who can afford not to wear frills—get me ? "

After all, there was something of a bond which existed
between these people. Aristocrats can meet on an equal foot-
ing all over the world ; if Julia Neilson, if Sir Seymour Hicks,
dear George Graves, Bransby Williams, have sent me their
tributes, it is because they know that they are saluting a woman
who was on their own level, who was one of the great company
of people, aristocrats of the stage, who are proud to be servants
of the public.

BOOK THREE

CHAPTER ONE

"VAUNTING ALOUD, BUT RACKED WITH DEEP DESPAIR"
                                                    MILTON

Her loyalty—Her bravado—America and Africa—a contrast—Her
    salaries for three years—Figures and facts—Her expenses—
    Illness—The shadow comes nearer—Why ?—What the specialist
    said.

IT is impossible to have a deep admiration, a very real
affection for anyone, to watch that person change—and
change in such a way that it is obvious that mental distress
is the primary cause—and refrain from forming opinions, to
prevent yourself coming to certain conclusions as to why this
or that has happened.

So it was difficult to watch the change in Marie Lloyd and not
feel certain convictions growing with regard to her. It is also
quite impossible to write down all one's private and personal
opinions in cold print, for many reasons. One of those reasons
being that probably Marie would have resented it very
deeply.

I have already recorded the fact that Marie was one of the
most stubborn of mortals, more, she was always the violent
champion of the person whose hand was against every man,
and against whom every man's hand was directed. It might
be patent to her family, to her friends, to her relations that
some person was not a good friend to her. It might be obvious
that she was being duped, cheated, preyed upon, treated badly,
but it was not the slightest use attempting to tell Marie so.
The moment anyone was attacked, Marie automatically became
their champion. The moment people spoke against them,
Marie was up in arms defending them.

To make Marie Lloyd decide to see less of anyone, to make
her realize that she was wasting money and time and affection
on them, the proper procedure was to praise them unstintingly.
Assure her what splendid folk they were, laud their (non-

existent) virtues to the skies, state that they were brilliant, kindly, clever, and utterly devoted to her, and she might reply : " You seem to know a lot about it, don't you ? Mind your own business, what do you want to come shouting his (or her) stock for ? "

She hated to admit that she had made a mistake. She liked to swagger, and pretend and make-believe that whatever she had done was right. I have not the slightest doubt that she prided herself on being a fine judge of character. Then there was another side to her nature. She forgave easily, and that fatal love of flattery made her terribly vulnerable. It was easy to find the chinks in Marie's armour and to either wound her or apply salve to the wound.

With all her quick wit, all her knowledge of the world, her ability to portray character, she remained in many things a veritable child and as defenceless as a child would be. She was like some young person who has learnt the rudiments of a difficult card game, and light-heartedly agrees to play with a gang of sharks ! She lost, they won, and to cover her losses Marie would aver that it was all good experience, and probably add that she didn't care if she had lost, and that she didn't want to win, anyway ! That was how she ran her life !

I said in the last chapter that I wanted to keep out the shadow of tragedy as long as possible, but it will not be disregarded and the time has come when one must face the deep tragedy of this woman's life. One must face the fact that Marie, whose whole life had been a long succession of generous acts and kindnesses, who has left behind her memories which are invariably dear and affectionate, had to face suffering which was all the more cruel because she *would* not, perhaps *could* not, allow anyone to help her.

There are people—those clever people !—who will tell you that she brought her unhappiness on herself, that whatever befell her, she alone was to blame. It's an easy way of accounting for many things, only it does not happen to be correct. Naturally everyone has his own opinion, I have mine —and mine is the opinion which is shared by the sisters who loved her and by the friends who knew her.

However, " look on this picture and on that "—and then judge for yourself.

Marie in America. That visit when she was there with Alec Hurley, when Bransby Williams tells us of her dinner to celebrate the birthday of the King of England, and " to show them that we're British." She is the life and soul of every party, she laughs, spends money, people hang on her words and repeat her sayings. She is the embodiment of gaiety.

Now consider a visit to South Africa some years later. Admittedly she is older, but age does not touch any of the Lloyds particularly heavily. They are not a family who grow old quickly. Their father, at eighty-eight, can still laugh and enjoy his jokes and his little "flutters," his papers and his meals. Her sisters? I cannot see that they are any older in appearance, in their ability to sing, dance and present their act to the public, than they were five, ten, fifteen, even twenty years ago.

Africa, and with Marie on the bill are two people who ought to have kept her "merry and bright"—there was the beautiful Queenie Leighton, one of the most charming women imaginable, and there was that delightful man, that brilliant personality, that kindly character, "Dick" Knowles—the famous R. G. Knowles. In a photograph of them all taken together, does Marie look as if age was weighing heavily on her? On the contrary she looks just as she had looked for years.

Yet—and though I cannot give the name of my informant, let me quote this letter : " I couldn't believe that it was the same Marie Lloyd that I had known. Pretty as ever, as smart as ever, not a day older, and yet there was a difference. It was as though the sparkle had gone out of the champagne, and I shall never forget the misery in her voice—that husky voice we all loved so much—as she sat and talked to me.

" Are you enjoying South Africa? "

" Me? " she said. " I don't enjoy anything—these days."

I said that perhaps she was tired, blamed late nights and the strong, clear air. " People often feel a little slack until they get used to it," I said.

" Late nights ! I daren't go to bed, I daren't be alone. You know what that poor soul did not long ago—" she referred to a young girl well known in society, who had thrown herself from a third-story window some weeks previously, "—that's what I shall do one day ! I mean it ! What's the good of going on? "

I could scarcely believe that I was talking to Marie Lloyd —Marie who had always loved fun, who had laughed and thought out elaborate practical jokes. It didn't seem possible.

Cissie Lawson told me : " The last time I met her was on the platform at Victoria Station. She stopped and we talked for a

few minutes, she smiled, but it wasn't a ' good ' smile. I mean,
it didn't seem to mean anything, her eyes were terribly sad.'

Bransby Williams says : " Later, I used to watch her smile,
it was the saddest smile I ever saw." Her sisters go further,
they say that during the last years of her life she never smiled.
Alice Lloyd adds : " Not what we call a *smile !* "

There had been a change somewhere, something had gone
out of her life, or something had entered into it.

Had she been a strong-minded, iron-nerved woman, she
might have been able to deal with this weight which lay so
heavily on her. She could have faced her unhappiness squarely,
and with one burst of action dismissed it, dispelled the clouds,
and continued her life as it had once been. She was none
of these things, obstinacy is not strength, stubbornness is not
firmness, the capacity to fly into sudden tempers denotes
weakness, not strength, and Marie was weak in this particular
case. Only once—and here is a characteristic touch—when her
father had been in bodily danger, when he had been hurt, did
she act with sudden and unexpected decision.

This should end, that was over, the other must never happen
again ! And what *did* happen ?

Here's the tragedy of it all. Marie, who " could conquer
others," could never conquer her own soft heart and her own
love of admiration. Marie could never listen to a " hard luck
story " unmoved, Marie never probed and delved and tried
to dissect people's statements, she never asked, like Mr.
Wickfield : " What is the motive."

Instead of ringing down the curtain, keeping it down, Marie
allowed it to rise again and again, on what she always assured
herself was " an entirely new production," and never realized
that it was the same old shoddy drama dished up again and
again.

To say that there are two sides to every story, to talk about
" no one, least of all Marie Lloyd," being perfect, is rubbish.
If you have read so far, and if I have failed to show you Marie's
faults as well as her virtues, then I am to blame. I have never
wished to depict her as faultless, I have rather stressed her
tempers, her extravagance, her recklessness, but I do know
that in the whole of her character there did not exist one atom
of meanness, one trace of petty small-mindedness, and that as
a bookmaker was heard to say after she had died : " Her heart
was as big as Waterloo Station."

The fact remains—and fact it undoubtedly is—that Marie,

during the last years of her life, changed in a way which was terrible and heart-breaking. Not that her work suffered, she was too good an artiste to carry her private worries, her ill health and her changed outlook on life on to the stage. There she was herself, the real Marie, and her public adored her as they had always done.

Of course, she was working too hard. During the year 1919 –1920—and I take that at random—she had three weeks' holiday only. For every other week she was working, " bill-topping," carrying the chief weight of the bill on her shoulders twice nightly. There was a month at the Palladium, then, later, three weeks there, a West End show, demanding new songs, new dresses, and the whole of her show given at the very highest possible standard.

There are some remarkable figures on this sheet—and this is a return made out and accepted by the Income Tax authorities :

Finsbury Park	–	–	£357 for the week.
Southsea	–	–	£347 for the week.
Swansea	–	–	£279 for the week.
Cardiff	–	–	£622 for the week.

That last figure is for a date less than a year before she died, and yet there are still people who wag their heads and tell you that she was " losing her hold on the public." Music-hall managers, combines, agents, are not fools, and to receive over six hundred pounds is to argue that in actual, hard cash you are worth a good deal more.

To go round the country, taking long journeys, Newport to Nottingham, Nottingham to Glasgow, Glasgow to New Cross Empire, is not the easiest way of spending your Sundays, and after all, three weeks' holiday is not a very long time, particularly when it is split into single weeks, in which to recuperate and get jangled nerves soothed and a tired body entirely rested.

Remember, too, that the whole character of the music-hall was changing. They were no longer booming, no longer were agents scouring the Continent and the United States to find new and original turns ; no longer were salaries the inflated affairs which they had once been. The good old times were gone, and with them many of the artistes Marie had known and loved. People had left the " show business," they had retired, and the consequence was that touring was not the jolly " family party " it had once been. There were no longer picnics, outings, parties, the days when touring was really fun were over. Yet Marie kept her place as Queen of Comedy, and her life, like that of most exalted people, must have been curiously lonely.

Let me refer to those Income Tax returns again for a moment.

In the year dating from April 2nd, 1917, to March 25th, 1918, she had two weeks' holiday, and her highest salary was £470 (four hundred and seventy pounds).

Her takings for the year were considerably over seven thousand pounds.

The following year—1918 to 1919—she had only two weeks' holiday, one in July, and the other in the following January. Here her highest salary was at Cardiff, where she had £520, though Newcastle was only a few pounds short of that amount.

The year 1919 to 1920 she had three weeks' rest, in May, and no holiday again until December. This year her earnings were nearly eleven thousand pounds, while the year before they had been a few pounds short of ten thousand. This year her biggest salary was Cardiff with £622.

In 1920 to 1921 the year's total is again a few pounds short of ten thousand pounds, and this year her holidays were three weeks. One week in August, and another two the following February. This year Liverpool paid her £445, and Cardiff twenty-five pounds in excess of that sum.

There are people who will tell you that they know for a fact that (a) Marie never got the tremendous salaries ascribed to her ; (b) that she was losing her hold on the public and that the managers did not want her as they had done some years previously. These figures prove the contrary.

One other small item which is illuminating is that in 1920 she appeared at Edinburgh before one of the most critical audiences in the British Isles, and her salary was £324 for the week.

Of course, there will be people who, in reading those figures, will exclaim immediately : " Then she ought to have saved ! Forty thousand pounds and scarcely anything left ! " The answers to that are the only possible answers to make where Marie is concerned. The first is that she literally " earned money to give it away," and the second is that she had far heavier expenses, far more calls upon her than anyone except her own family will ever know. If they cared to, no doubt they could explain this lack of bank balance, for they saw a great deal that was hidden from the rest of the world, but they were unable to check Marie, as had always been the case since she was a child.

They did what was possible. Two of her sisters bought a house, bought a slightly smaller and less expensive house than the one in which she had lived for several years in Golders Green. They let it to her at a nominal rent, thus trying to safeguard her from additional expense. But Marie was not a child, she was a woman of nearly fifty, headstrong, resentful of criticism and control, and what her sisters and family could do was comparatively little.

When I saw her at Bristol, which must have been in 1920 or early in 1921, it was obvious that she was not only a sick woman, but a very sick woman indeed. Moreover, it was evident that she had no particular interest left, she was tired out, dispirited, and terribly unhappy. She complained of " aches, like rheumatism," said that she couldn't sit still for very long in one position or she " got all stiff." She ate practically nothing. I have heard since, that for the last three years of her life she scarcely ate enough to keep her alive. Her appetite had gone.

One thing remained—her looks. If you hear that she grew haggard, grey-faced, lined, and wrinkled, that is not true. She looked ill, admittedly ; her voice had lost some of its vitality ; her wit only came in flashes, she no longer laughed, and when she smiled it was something which needed a conscious effort, her eyes—those unbelievably bright, blue eyes—were the saddest I have ever seen.

Only her work never altered. Her stage clothes were as perfect as ever, and her new style of song, her " three old sisters," " The Cock Linnet," " A little of wot you fancy," and " One of the Ruins," were three of the most brilliant studies she ever gave to the public.

She began to experience some difficulty in memorizing her new songs. Previously she could learn words with the greatest ease, though she always became nervous when she sang a new number and always swore that she'd " forget every damned line." She never did forget, and now to find that to study new songs meant real concentration and definite effort, distressed her terribly.

It is not making too much of those last four years to say that the fight which Marie Lloyd put up was one of the most gallant things she ever accomplished. She was ill, though no one, except her brother Johnnie, who had heard the specialist's report, and kept that as a secret which he shared with no one, knew that she was quite definitely doomed. Johnnie knew that, Johnnie knew, too, that nothing could save her. Those questions had all been put to the specialist. " Would it save her if she stopped working ? " " Would it make a difference if she laid off for six months ? " " Were there waters she might take, baths, cures, foreign spas which might prolong her life ? " The answer was always the same : " Nothing could make any difference."

She was not old—not yet fifty-two—and her life was finished. She had worked hard since she was fifteen, she had played hard, she had got the last ounce out of life, and she had loved every minute of her success and her popularity. Now, ill and tired, she sat in her dressing-room between the shows, playing patience, twisting this way and that to ease the aching of her limbs, her eyes watching the cards without a great deal of interest, wondering, perhaps, where and when everything had begun to go wrong.

Only when the call boy came down the corridor with his cry of " Overture and beginners," and later : " Half an hour, Miss Lloyd," did she shake off her weariness and turn her thoughts toward the one thing which never failed her—her work and the public which she never failed in all her life.

Years before, when suddenly my own small world had rocked and splintered into bits, I sent for Marie. She came travelling from somewhere in the North—Newcastle, Edinburgh, Glasgow, I forget where, to London ; leaving that same night to go to Liverpool, after spending only a few hours in town.

I can remember seeing the door open, watching Marie come in. Not the smart, elegant artiste, speaking audacious lines, with a gay smile and eyes which twinkled and danced, but a rather short, almost stocky little woman, who held out her arms and cried :

" It's all right, Marie's here ! "

That was what Marie Lloyd said, in effect, so often during those last years, when music-hall business was not what it had been, when houses were less packed than they had been before the war. When managers pulled wry faces over the look of the house, and wondered why so many of the turns lacked the sparkle of the old " pros," that was when Marie virtually cried : " It's all right, Marie's here ! " That was when she forgot that she was ill and tired, and walked on to the stage, catching the attention of the audience and holding it fast. That was when she shouldered the whole weight of her salary—and earned it !

There is in your truly great artiste a queer, additional strength of purpose. There is an ability to fling aside private worries, pains, aches, and general weakness. Once the music is playing, once that illuminated number has flashed at the side of the proscenium arch, your real artiste ceases to be a suffering man or woman, and steps on to the stage in their capacity as " A Servant of the Public."

Old Joe Grimaldi did it, little Dan Leno did it, Dan Rolyat, George Formby, George Bass, poor Ernest Reeves with his broken back that no one ever discovered until it was too late, all of them did their duty as bravely and gallantly as any soldier who won glory, medals and promotion. Marie Lloyd did her duty as gallantly as any of them ! Only for these people there are no medals.

Dan Leno, trying to brush away with sheer concentration those clouds which gathered round his brain, striving to learn his lines and devise new comic business ; George Formby, shaken to pieces in his dressing-room by that cough which tore his lungs to shreds, going on to the stage and joking about his illness with the conductor : " Ma cough's bad tae neit. Ah doot Ah must 'ave consum-ption ! " Gene Stratton flying across the stage, light as thistledown, trying when he sang to hide that increasing hoarseness, and knowing its cause ; and Marie, gallantly going on, earning her salary, sending her weekly gifts to her pensioners—some of whom she had never even seen—standing at the side, half-dazed with illness and physical pain, with her heart aching, wondering half vaguely " if it was worth while going on," then gathering together every bit of her strength, and going on to make her audience rock with delight at her audacity and her glorious comedy.

I wonder if you had told her that for the last years of her life she played *Pagliacci* magnificently what she would have said ? Probably told you not to talk like a fool.

It was never easy to offer her sympathy, she resented it and resented the imputation that she was incapable of managing her own affairs.

So, if I seem to have avoided the real issue, if I have said very little of anything except the physical decline of Marie's magnificent health and physique, it is because Marie would have forbidden it. I remember soon after her death I was asked to write an " Impression " of her for a well-known paper, who assured me that they wanted something " written with the gloves off." I wrote it, and I was satisfied with what I had written. It was bitter, hard, very frank, and it showed Marie Lloyd as I had known her during those last years—a terribly unhappy, heart-broken woman.

Then I remembered an incident when I had tried to interfere in Marie's defence, when I had said a good deal that was possibly true, but which was neither pleasant nor particularly refined. I remembered that Marie had scowled at me and that all the thanks I got was : " Who made it your bloody business, anyway ? "

Not because she didn't know in her heart of hearts that I was right, not—I think—that underneath those words there was not a certain acceptance of what I had said, and even a sense of satisfaction that I should have dared to say what I did, but that Marie hated interference, Marie brooked no criticism, and she liked to keep up that elaborate fiction of hers, that she was perfectly capable of running her own life.

So, as I read what I had written over again, some of my satisfaction evaporated, and I became less and less certain that Marie would have done anything but scowl if she had read it. I could even fancy that I heard her old question : " Who made it your bloody business, anyway ? " I decided to tone down all I had said ; then I decided to tear the whole thing into little pieces and tell the editor who had demanded the " Impression " that I couldn't write it at all.

Remember that it is not your woman who assumes an attitude of defiance, who can hold her own verbally, who can swear and who does swear if she wants to, who " lives her life," who is the best fitted to face unhappiness. Nine times out of every ten it is your little thin-lipped, meek, drab, utterly conventional woman who can go on, day after day, and never let life break her. Your Marie Lloyds of this world are far too vulnerable, their hearts are far too soft. They have no idea of " hedging," all their money is put on one horse— to win or lose. All their eggs go into one basket. All their money into one bank—and when that bank breaks, they are ruined.

Had Marie been the woman so many people believed her to be, she might have been here to-day, for she would have been able to fall back on her gambling, on those mythical men who were supposed to matter so much, she could have found

distraction in extravagances of many kinds. She never was
what so many people believed her to be. She was far more
simple than they supposed, and so at fifty-two she became a
poor, disappointed, lonely woman, fighting against ill-health
and desperate unhappiness.

Her pride—and, as I have said, Marie was tremendously
proud—was wounded. Like other famous people, the Queen of
Comedy could not hope to keep her private affairs from the
public. What had at first been the conviction that : " Alice
knows, Gracie knows, the whole family know——" became,
" the whole world knows what my life is, my audiences whisper
among themselves, and—pity me !" She called to her aid a series
of masks, and wore them ; she " played pretend " ; she was
still Marie, the Pet of the Public, she was still the Creator of
Magnificent Clothes, she was still the Greatest Comedienne
on the Stage—and all the time it was " Laugh, Clown,
laugh ! "

Blame Marie for being too " soft," blame her for not having
the ability to shrug her shoulders in everyday life as successfully
as she could on the stage, blame her for being—Marie Lloyd.
Only, in common fairness to her, remember that during those
latter years of her life *something* had changed her whole outlook.
Something had broken her courage, had smashed her faith,
changed her from the brilliant, laughing creature she had been
into a woman with " the saddest eyes in the world and a smile
which never touched her eyes."

In her last song, " One of the Ruins that Cromwell knocked
about a bit," she sang : " Them that studies 'istory—sings an'
shouts of it "—very well, do that, and if you will study, if you
will judge impartially, you will be able to satisfy yourself in
what and where lay the real tragedy of Marie Lloyd.

Her own physician knew, though he gave—as doctors always
do—a Latin name to her illness, her brothers and sisters knew
though they wrote down the name of her malady for me when
I asked for it, but they told me this as well. When, at the
eleventh hour, a great specialist was sent for, he came and ex-
amined her as she lay there almost unconscious, and later stood in
Marie's drawing-room and talked to her family. They asked :
" What is it—what does it mean—this long, elaborate Latin
name ? "

He glanced at the words written on a piece of paper which lay
on the table. " That's one of the things that is killing her," he
said. " We use these long names, you know, we doctors.   But,

to put it quite simply, I can give you a name that is not in any medical dictionary, which never appears on any death certificate—and in this case it happens to be what is really going to end her life. She is dying of a broken heart, she obviously doesn't care to live."

CHAPTER TWO

" THE LAST STAGE OF THIS STRANGE EVENTFUL HISTORY . . ."
SHAKESPEARE

" A LITTLE TRUST THAT WHEN WE DIE
WE REAP OUR SOWING, AND SO—GOOD-BYE "
DU MAURIER

The Alhambra—October the seventh—Tragedy at Edmonton—
" To-day we are going to Marie's funeral "—Little 'Eart of
Gold—The call boy of the stars.

DURING the rehearsals of *The Young Idea* I went
down on to the stage one evening and found Noel
Coward, the author, who was also playing in the
play, seated at a piano. He was playing a tune which he had
written, and it struck me as being beautifully catchy, and
I asked if he had written a lyric for it as well as the music. He
had. He sang it over to me.

It was a typical " Marie Lloyd " song, about a young French-
woman who, filled with patriotic fervour, gave of her very best
to the soldiers who passed through her village. I cannot
remember the name, I can only remember that the last line
was something like this :

" She loved them, and they left her—much wiser than
before," that was at the beginning of her career : in the last
verse the refrain was :

" She loved them and they left her—much richer than
before." I said : " Marie Lloyd ought to sing that song ! It
would suit her marvellously."

Noel Coward liked the idea, he admired Marie's work, and I
said that I'd mention it to her. I didn't do so, for when I saw
her she was too ill to discuss songs.

The Young Idea went on a five-weeks' tour before its production at the Savoy, in London. The tour opened at Sheffield
on October 2nd.

While I was rehearsing, I went into the Alhambra one evening, accompanied by a north-countryman, a successful, hardheaded man of business ; he wanted to hear Marie Lloyd, who was appearing there.

The hall was packed, and Marie was on the top of her form ; she sang her brilliant " talkie " song, " Woman's opinion of man," a second number which has escaped me, and finally, " One of the ruins that Cromwell knocked about a bit." She was magnificent, and the man who was with me said : " It's fifteen years since I saw her last, and she's better than ever." The audience went crazy, they would have kept her there all night, singing song after song, had it been possible. As it was, the applause continued after the tabs had fallen. After a moment or two they parted and Marie came out. Not the Marie of her last song, not the smart " woman of umpty-eight " of her first song, but the real Marie. Looking ridiculously young, wearing a dressing-gown, her fair hair rather untidy because she had had no time to arrange it after her last number, and in that dear husky voice she made us a little speech.

She reminded us that she had sung here at the Alhambra when " the managers first began to think that, perhaps, I was rather a clever girl." She had sung a song then, " and it wasn't rude " ; and now she asked us to sing it with her : " Oh, Mr. Porter."

" Oh, Mr. Porter, what shall I do,
    I want to go to Birmingham, they've put me out at Crewe,
    Oh, take me back to London, as quickly as you can,
    Oh, Mr. Porter, what a silly girl I am ! "

The audience sang it, Marie sang it ; though her sister Alice, who was with her, tells me that she stumbled over the words, it was so long since she had sung that song. Though they sang ; though everyone in that audience wanted to show Marie—Our Marie—that they remembered her song, there were many, very many, people who wiped their eyes. I know the man next to me had tears running down his cheeks as he sang those silly words. Not, as you may have read, because " we realized that this was an old woman "—that's sheer rubbish. I think because she looked so exactly like the Marie we had known years ago. She looked young and rather uncertain, just a little confused and shy ; her hair looked so very " youthfully " golden and her voice—well, we'd always adored it ! Then, by that time, many of us knew quite a good deal about the Marie Lloyd who didn't sing " naughty " songs. We knew—because she was our friend and because she had always " belonged to us "—many things, and it seemed so impossible that life—fate—people—circumstances, could have used her hardly. " A star without an enemy," and yet we had heard, read, been told—and it hurt us to remember those things. If an audience ever proved their love, their personal affection for an artiste, the audience at the Alhambra proved theirs for Marie that night, when they sang with her, the tears running down their cheeks.

The song ended, the tabs closed and Marie disappeared. I went round to see her afterwards. She was sitting in a chair and looked cold and as if she was " huddled " together. Underneath her make-up she looked ghastly and dreadfully tired. As usual, her first question was : " How was I ? "

" Grand," I said. " Better than ever ! " And I meant it.

I told her that I was going on tour ; she shook her head.

" You ought to stop in London ; don't go into the provinces. They're no good for the legit."

" Only for five weeks, then we come back to the Savoy to open."

" The Savoy, eh ? Five weeks. Right, I'll be there. Yes, I will—for the first night." It struck me that she wasn't getting her breath easily, almost as if she had a touch of asthma.

She said : " Good night, Micky, and good luck. Don't forget—I'll be there ! "

Sheffield, October the second. Matinée on Saturday, October the seventh. I was in the same rooms with dear Robert Arthur and the stage manager, Teddie Lytton. I ran upstairs to get those extra bits of grease-paint off that always seem to take more removing after a matinée than at any other time, and presently someone knocked at my door. It was Teddie Lytton. He had an evening paper in his hand.

I said : " Teddie—what's wrong ? You're ill ! "

He shook his head and pointed to the crumpled newspaper.

" No, I'm all right," he said, his voice very shaky, " only—only—Marie's dead."

I remember Robert Arthur, who had known her, sitting there making no attempt to hide his tears ; Teddie Lytton, who scarcely knew her at all, wiping his eyes so that he could read what they had written of her in the paper. That night in the theatre—and remember this was a theatre, not a music-hall— I have never felt such depression. Everyone felt it : the audience, the stage hands, everyone in the place. Something had gone, something which had not only belonged to the music-halls, but which had belonged to England.

The next day, in Leeds, I listened to a Mass said for the repose of that generous, gallant, great-spirited soul which had inhabited the body of Marie Lloyd, the Queen of Comediennes.

The story only came filtering through in little patches. It came through people who had been present, through the news-papers, through sentences invariably spoken unsteadily, by her friends. The Alhambra had been followed by Willesden, Willesden by East Ham.

On the Monday evening she played both houses, and played with her usual brilliance, on the Tuesday it was obvious that she was very ill indeed, and after the first house—when she had worked splendidly, though with a certain effort—the manager, Mr. Leon Pollack, was sent for to her dressing-room. She was in a state which almost amounted to collapse. Against Marie's wishes, for she protested again and again : " I'll be all right in a minute ! There's nothing really wrong—a bit tired, that's all ! "—a doctor was sent for. He " strongly advised " her not to play the second house, but to go home immediately. That was when Marie heard the audience coming into the hall. She shook her head. " Hear that ? The boys and girls coming in. They're coming to hear me ! " That splendid arrogance of a great artiste ! " I'm going on."

She dressed and went down to the side, scarcely able to stand, having to lean on the arm of her dresser and the manager. The moment came for her to go on, and with a supreme effort she straightened her shoulders and made her last entrance.

No one in the audience realized that she was ill. Leon Pollack continues : " It was the ' Pagliacci ' business over again. Marie and I were the only people who knew the tragedy which was being enacted. Her last song was ' One of the ruins that Cromwell knocked about a bit,' in which she imitated the staggerings and clumsy buffoonery of a drunken woman. She staggered from sheer weakness, and the audience imagined that they were watching her usual, fine comic acting. As she fell, they shrieked with laughter." The tragedy which had been drawing nearer and nearer for the past years reached her and laid its hand on her shoulder. She was helped back to her dressing-room, scarcely able to speak, but still protesting that all she wanted was " a little rest."

And as I write this a curious little fact strikes me. I remember Marie's second song—the one which came between, or after, " Woman's opinion of man " and " One of the ruins " —it was the " Cosmopolitan Girl." That is curious, because never was an artiste less cosmopolitan than Marie Lloyd ; never was any artiste more typically and entirely British. Her winks, nods, gestures, and smiles, were never international ; they were never in the least like the winks, nods, gestures, and smiles of Alice Delysia and Mistinguette. Marie's gestures were born in London ; they were understood by Londoners, and the man I have quoted before, who stated that Marie was not a mere music-hall artiste, not a comedienne, but an Institution, was right. She was Piccadilly, Trafalgar Square, the Strand, the Mile End Road—never was she the Champs-Élysées, the Corso Vittorio Emmanuele, or the Kurfurstendamn.

While she was carried home, while she lay there, assuring everyone that she was only " a bit tired—that was all," the bills outside the Alhambra were still showing a reminder : " Week after next, welcome return visit of Marie Lloyd."

Wednesday, Thursday, she was growing weaker, and at midnight on Friday, Marie Lloyd died in the arms of her sister, Rosie. Her family were with her ; they had always been united : when Marie had been appearing, when she had enjoyed her greatest triumphs, her sisters, her brothers and her mother had always been near at hand, and they were there when she took her last call.

When they left her bedside they found the house filled with weeping men and women, fellow-artistes who had come to hear the latest news of the Queen of Comedy. Next morning England woke to find the placards bearing the words : " Death of Marie Lloyd."

I have been told that never since those same placards carried the words : " Lord Kitchener drowned," did any announcement of a death make such an impression. Harry Tate, who owed it to Marie's encouragement that he followed a career on the Variety Stage, said : " Out Croydon way the bills were headed with her name ; she was due to appear there next week. I arrived in Trafalgar Square to see the posters announcing that she was dead. It didn't seem possible."

That was the feeling everywhere—it was not possible. She had reigned for so long, she had held her undisputed sway over the hearts and imaginations of her audiences, she had become— yes, just that—an institution, and it was impossible to think that we should never watch her, listen to her, laugh with her again.

There were those who attempted to make capital over her death, the same type of person who had invented stupid and utterly impossible stories concerning her while she was alive. As always happens when the great die—and I use that epithet advisedly—they are forbidden by the verbal vultures and emotion mongers to enjoy their last privacy.

That united family, who had always stood shoulder to shoulder, who had been so loyal to each other, who had never failed in love and devotion to her, read : " Marie Lloyd dies in her husband's arms." They had to read imaginary death scenes, imaginary last words, when only they knew how peacefully and quietly Marie had slipped away with her sister's arms round her.

The newspapers were filled with "impressions," with "tributes," some very splendid, some fulsome and stupid. There were impertinent anecdotes, impudent suggestions, written by people who would never have been tolerated by Marie Lloyd for an instant. On the whole, putting aside the typical " gutter Press," there were some noble and brilliantly written notices of her life, her art and her character. Many of them written by men who were stylists, who wrote with great understanding and who used phrases which were exquisite and beautifully expressed. True, once or twice as I read them, with their classical illusions, with their French idioms, and even here and there a Latin tag, I wondered what Marie would have made of it all, and how much she would have understood. She'd have liked it—she would have loved it—it would have given her real pleasure, actual satisfaction, and one of the most satisfying things about these appreciations was this—the better the newspaper or periodical, the finer the words of the tribute to Marie, the more laudatory were the sentiments.

Men whose opinion counted in the world of criticism, men whose judgment was cool, admirable and reliable, these were the people who did not hesitate to use such words as artiste, supreme, magnificent.

I should like to quote here an extract from *The Stage*—after all, the artiste's own paper—*The Stage* and *The Performer* are the two papers which deal exclusively with matters appertaining to the Stage and the Music-halls. This article struck me at the time as being so admirable, and yet so beautifully simple, that I should wish to include it at this place in Marie's story.

"' Marie,' an appreciation, by A. C. A.

Marie Lloyd's crowning triumph in life, and the one that she herself loved best, was that everyone known or unknown called her ' Marie.' That, after all, is her noblest epitaph, for it means that everyone loved her—even those who were inclined to criticise her. Perhaps those who criticised her loved her best of all, for criticism implies a loving interest. Probably we loved Marie most of all, however, and quite apart from her supreme qualities as an artiste, because she was, before all things else, a perfect human being ; and no really human being can be perfect without some little imperfections. Odd as it may seem there was a ' mothering' quality about her too ; one seemed to catch it coming over the footlights even in her most frivolous songs. That was because she always had her brain in her heart and her heart in her brain. It is the perfect harmonious combination of the two that makes the supreme artiste. And Marie was certainly that. She was among the big people of the earth, those people who were big because they had big hearts and everybody loved them. It is almost unnecessary to speak of her splendid generosity. It has become traditional. She had a whole host of retainers and kept open house. No one ever solicited her help in vain. Her eyes would brim over at a story of misfortune, and she regarded everything she had as belonging to somebody else. She was Marie always, Marie she always will be, and to-day we are going to Marie's funeral.

Sarah Bernhardt had the happy intuition of genius when she said that Marie was the most exquisite artiste of the British stage. It would be easy enough to prove—but this is neither the time nor the place—that her art ranked all the higher for its lack of education or artificial culture. She had not been dulled by hothouse intellectuality, thank Heaven ! The aggressively intellectual, shrivelled up in her presence like autumn leaves in a furnace.

She was as much part and parcel of her time as were Dickens and Thackeray a part and parcel of theirs : and in her and all about her was the glorious atmosphere of London on the Thames ! In her vivacious, rather stubby little body, she carried about with her all the compact delights of sunlit comedy, and the humour and the pathos of tragedy ; and when she was not saying things to us with her eyes, she was speaking volumes to us with her hands. No other artiste of our time, not even Irving, had more eloquent hands, and after she had waved them to us for the last time, Marie's wonderful hands turned over a fresh page in music-hall history. The older regime owed its life and its success to the genius and ability of the individual artiste. The question is not who is to take Marie's place. It might be that the present generation will account itself fortunate if there is any such place as Marie's left available. When we say good-bye to Marie to-day, we shall remember that good-bye means ' God be with you,' and we shall hope that this Queen of Comediennes, who has so completely won our hearts, will in some brighter clime bid us good morning."

It is almost thirteen years ago since that was written. This morning as I sit writing these pages in Italy, with the bright autumn sun shining over everything, it is the second of October; and still those words : " To-day we are going to Marie's funeral " make me feel, as Harry Tate did thirteen years ago : " It doesn't seem possible."

Coldly, calmly considered, we know that no one is indispensable ; that no one is essentially necessary to the happiness and welfare of a nation ; but the fact remains that there have been spirits so bright, characters so gallant, hearts so kind that the whole nation is the poorer for their loss. That is what the public felt about " Our Marie." She had been " ours," she had confided her audacities and verbal naùghtiness to us over the footlights, and we had roared back our approval. We had seen her on the race-course, elegant and exquisitely gowned, and she had still belonged to us, though she might be " among the swells " and we were just " the crowd." She had travelled to the other end of the earth, travelling first class while we sweated in the steerage, but she still belonged to us.

We had known of her marriages, we had our own private opinions about these very personal matters, not that any of her husbands were overwhelmingly interesting to us as personalities. They were only our concern because they were " Marie's husband " ; and, after all, the role of Prince Consort to the Queen of Comedy is a secondary position to hers. We had recounted her sayings, retold her stories, and there were several thousands of people who had learnt to know you had only to preface an old chestnut with the words : " As Marie Lloyd said the other day—— " to gain an immediate and attentive audience. Later we had known that she was ill, known that life was not all " beer and skittles " for her any longer. You see, if you occupy a place in the heart as well as the eye of your

public, nothing can happen to you that is not of importance
to them. It was a tribute to her, a proof of the love and
affection that we had for her that made us talk of her as we did.
We frowned and muttered : " Blimy, ain't it a ruddy shime !
Marie—mind yer ! Never 'urt a fly in 'er life, didn't Marie.
Never played the gime like wot some of 'em 'as neither. Not
like X, or Y, or Lidy Z ! If she'd 'a bin like them trollops,
well—someone might 'a said suth'in. Little 'Eart of Gold,
thet's Marie. A proper pal, thet's wot she's bin."

And that was what we'd, every one of us, lost—Our " Little
'Eart of Gold."

And so London went to Marie's funeral.

Never since the day when William Terriss was buried have
there been such crowds, never since " Breezy Bill " took his last
journey have there been such masses of people coming from all
parts of London to pay tribute. And what crowds ! Costers,
street hawkers, taxi-drivers, old men and women who had
started early in the morning to walk to Golders Green because
they hadn't the price of a bus ticket in their pockets. Street-
corner bookies, tipsters, race-course touts, old cabbies, stage
hands, down-and-out jockeys ; all those rather threadbare
members of the " Village Blacksmith " company, dock hands,
waiters, bar-tenders, all came on foot. Her fellow-artistes,
managers, celebrated jockeys, orchestra leaders, members
of the great Bohemian clubs, successful agents—all the
" upper ten " of the theatrical world—all came to pay their
tribute.

From early morning the people began to gather. Their
numbers were judged to be fifty thousand. What an audience
for Marie's last appearance ! Flowers—and it needed more
than a dozen cars to carry them—many of them must have
cost enormous sums of money, and among them little pathetic
bunches tied with a piece of string, carried in hot hands all
the way from the East End.

" I'm over seventy," said one old fellow. " I sang with
Marie—on the same bill when she was just a kiddie. I've
walked for miles to say good-bye to her. Please let me in—
just for a minute."

Women stood whispering memories of Marie to each other,
men recounted how she had " stood by Bill when 'e was in
trouble," or told how " Marie come along an' cleared the bums
art—paid up the lot, so she did." Always the same story,
always, in implication, that line which Marie once declared

she would have liked to say—Poor Joe's line—" 'E was very good to me, 'e was."

That's what they all said : " She was very good to me, was Our Marie."

When Marie made her last appearance, when the coffin was carried out, the people who waited looked, half astonished, at the little casket. They had never realized what a little woman Marie was. The realization brought with it an additional touch of pathos.

In the church they sang two hymns which could not have been more wisely chosen : " Onward, Christian Soldiers," and " Peace, Perfect Peace." How the robust, healthy sentiment of the former would have appealed to Marie ; how she would have enjoyed the swing of the music and the words, and how she would have understood the full beauty and meaning of that second hymn. Poor Marie—she hadn't known much peace for the latter years of her life, even though she had held up her head and marched like a good—and God knows—Christian soldier.

All day the crowds passed the grave ; all day Marie held her last reception, gave her last audience to her vast throng of friends. The flowers drooped and died, the newly broken earth was trampled by many feet, the gates were closed, the curtain had rung down for the last time, and Marie was getting what she had said she needed so badly—" Just a little rest, I'm only a bit tired."

The *Referee* printed the following verses, written by Hartley Carrick. I don't know if they are great poetry or not, what I do know is that they express what most of us felt, and what we should have liked to be able to say :

" ' Hail and farewell ! ' Marie. We simple men,
    And women too, sat spellbound, 'neath your spell ;
Our one and only—our Comedienne,
    We bid you last farewell.
Dear Marie (dear again), supremely great,
    Freed from life's turmoil, fretfulness and jars,
We know in all serenity you wait
    The Call Boy of the Stars."

That is what we all felt—what we still feel. You who didn't know her perhaps cannot understand—it's your loss. There was something about her that caught and held you, something which was not due to her brilliance, to her wit or her artistry—

those things go. There is nothing so ephemeral as the art of the stage. Once a song, a speech, is delivered—it is ended, and lives no more except in the memory of those who heard it. Marie's songs, Marie's smiles, winks, her expressive hands, they can only live in the memories of those who knew her, and after thirteen years those memories begin to grow a little dim. The essentials that were Marie, don't die. That is the reason why, after all these years, I am writing this, conscious that my eyes smart and that my throat aches, conscious that I would give a great deal—a very great deal—to have the door of my study open and hear her cry : " It's all right— Marie's here."

Little Tilley Wood, Matilda Alice Victoria Wood, who in your utter simplicity thought that you would take the name of Bella Delmare, and who became Marie Lloyd, Our Marie, what a grand woman you were. Working to earn money to give away, with your hand for ever in your pocket, with your heart always open, with your stubbornness, your love of adulation, your inability to differentiate between gold and gilt, your tempers, and your disregard of convention !

Dan Leno, Harry Tich, Gene Stratton, Paul Cinquevalli, Chirgwin, Fragson, Sheridan, Dick Knowles, and you, Marie, could have saved the music-halls : the " Old Guard " carry on grandly, but they needed you, all of you, to beat the drama which will never be anything but a " shadow drama " ; you gave us flesh and blood, real laughter, and real tears.

Miss Catherine Geere, the principal of the Clarence House School, Brighton, where Marie's daughter, Marie Courtney, went to school, and also where several of the younger of Marie's sisters were educated, wrote the epitaph for the grave. Here again I am not quoting it as great poetry ; I only record it because it does seem to fit the purpose for which it was intended. Marie would have liked simplicity, because she would have understood it ; she would have liked sincerity because she was, herself, essentially sincere, and this little verse is both those things.

" Tired she was, although she didn't show it,
Suffering was she, and hoped we didn't know it,
But He above—and understanding all,
Prescribed ' Long Rest,' and gave the Final Call."

But best fitted to Marie, beautifully simple and simply

beautiful, are the verses of Matthew Arnold's, which might have
been written for her :

> " Her mirth the world required :
> She gave it in smiles of glee.
> But her heart was tired, tired,
> And now they let her be.
> Her life was turning, turning,
> In mazes of heat and sound.
> But for peace her soul was yearning,
> And now peace laps her round.
> Her cabin'd, ample Spirit,
> It flutter'd and fail'd for breath,
> To-night it doth inherit
> The vasty hall of Death."

CHAPTER THREE

"AND TREAT THESE TWO IMPOSTORS JUST THE SAME"
                                            KIPLING

The Times—Sheffield Daily Telegraph—" Carados " of the *Referee*
—" A true, loyal V.A.F."—James Agate—The *Manchester
Guardian*—. . . the others—" He broke the die."

THE tributes to her in the Press were extraordinary and
it is my purpose to record some of them here for two
reasons : First, that never was praise given so unstintingly by papers of standing and weight ; and, secondly,
that there were various silly errors, misstatements, made which
ought to be corrected. Corrected for those people who were
Marie's friends, admirers ; to say nothing of those members of
her family who must have suffered hurt from these printed
impertinences.

The Times devoted a whole column to her art and her
achievements. " In her the public loses not only a vivid
personality whose range and exceedingly broad humour as a
character actress were extraordinary, but also one of the few
remaining links with the old music-hall stage of the last century.
. . . It is a great tribute to her powers that she maintained her
popularity to the end, being indeed ' booked up ' for several
years ahead. But she did not presume on her fame, for she
was a very hard worker, always studying touches from real life
wherewith to build up her inimitable impersonations."

That is merely an extract to show that *The Times*, the most
famous newspaper in the world, was ready to devote both time
and space to Marie Lloyd.

The *Sheffield Daily Telegraph* said : " London's cleverest, and
most typical, comedienne died yesterday, and for very many
Londoners her death is the most serious news of the week-end.
I call Marie Lloyd a comedienne, rather than a music-hall
artiste, because any actor or dramatic critic will tell you that,
had she chosen to play broad comedy parts in drama, she would

have been supreme in them. Her ambition did not rise beyond music-hall songs with ' patter ' and ' business,' but that she did with an incisiveness and art which made her one of the three or four great favourites of the Halls for something like thirty years. Her singing voice was good, though not exceptionally so. Her songs were generally lively, though, as often as not, vulgar. But even when her voice was tired and her song a repetition of conventional jokes, her exuberant enjoyment and her gift of ' characterization ' gave her turn on the Halls an attraction which no other woman artiste could rival. If I had to compare her with other artistes, I should turn to the legitimate stage and cite Miss Connie Ediss, Miss Mary Brough, Miss Lottie Venne, or Miss Marie Tempest. Miss Lloyd, at her best, seemed to capture a portion of the art of each of them."

The *Referee*—a newspaper which has always been Bohemian in the best sense of the word, said :

" All England is the sadder for her passing. This passing will be felt not only by the public to whom she was ever the most loyal of servants and the most lively of influences, but also by her brother and sister theatrical and Variety artistes, for by all of these who knew her she was deeply beloved.

It will be by the poorer and more struggling of professionals, however, and by similar members of the outside public that Our Marie will be mourned. For that gay and often giddy ' serio ' (as they would call her in the days when she came out) would ' give her heart away '—not in the sordid sense, lamented by Wordsworth, but in the most benevolent and charitable form. . . . As to my Dear Old Friend, Marie, I finish as I began. Throughout both her Variety and theatrical career, Marie Lloyd—whatever her little failings may have been—was the soul of honour and true charity. And so, as I bend in reverence, in memory of this often foolish, still more often misled, but always dear, brave, lovable little woman, I am impelled to think of Him who said : ' She hath done what she could.' "

That extract is from the column written for Marie by " Carados " of the *Referee*.

Here is the *Observer* ; and from the initials " H. G.," which are the signature, I imagine that this is written by that admirable critic, Mr. Hubert Griffiths.

" The most recent memory of her is as the charwoman who, moving house, had lost her way," says this extract. " Lost the furniture cart, mislaid her husband, and was wandering bewildered in company with a pet canary in a cage—the sole survivor of a disastrous day. The sketch was introduced by the verse of a song, and concluded by the verse of a song, but in between whiles Miss Marie Lloyd talked, and in that wonderful monologue told us all there is to be known about the souls of charwomen, of a life where a little too much beer is drunk, where husbands are hasty, where 'shooting the moon' is a constant preoccupation, and where a black eye may be either a corrective or a compliment. This sketch *that was never played the same way twice, that was varied and enlarged to suit the taste of different audiences* (the italics are mine.—N. J.) was character acting, and something cleverer than that, character study—of a kind that neither the music-halls nor the legitimate theatre shows us often. Miss Lloyd was not less than a great artiste. She never played 'Lady Wishfort' in Congreve's *Way of the World*. Had her thoughts turned towards the 'legitimate,' there was a part waiting for her.—H. G."

The music-hall's own paper said : " A true, loyal V.A.F." (That is a member of the Variety Artistes Federation.) " One who went out on strike, who harangued, and did picket duty for the righting of contractual wrongs of her less fortunate brother and sister artistes. She answered the ' strike call ' though it lost her hundreds of pounds. Marie lived and died for her work, she represented true ' Variety ' and—when God made her He broke the die."

Mr. James Agate, in the *Saturday Review*, wrote a magnificent appreciation, which was later included in his book, *Half-Past Eight*.

" When, in the Tottenham Court Road, I saw, tucked under the newsboy's arm, the sheet which announced that Marie Lloyd was dead, everything around me became still. The street lost its hubbub, and for a space I was alone with a personal sorrow. . . . It was not, however, from a world of bullies or the lower deck that Marie Lloyd drew her chief support. She was enormously popular with the class which lives in villas and makes a fetish of respectability. To placate these, would-be apologists would have pleaded that ' whilst many of the songs were in themselves offensive, the manner of their delivery took away the offence.' This is the purest nonsense. The genius of the *diseuse* consisted in the skill and emphasis with which she drove home the ' offensive ' points. She employed a whole armoury of shrugs and leers, to reveal every cranny of the mind, utilized each articulation of the body. Frank in

gesture as Fielding was in phrase, her page of life was as outspoken and as sure. . . . She reduced to the comprehension of
butcher's boy and clerk those limbs moving ' as melodies yet '
to quite unpardonable music, all that meaningless tosh about
' curing the soul by means of the senses.' Little patience, we
may be sure, had the comedienne with the original form of these
nostrums for sick minds. She translated them into tonics for
the healthy body, she preached the world and the flesh, and
gloried in their being the very devil. . . . There was no decadent
Latin taint about Marie, she was almost saltily British. . . .
Was Marie Lloyd vulgar ? Undoubtedly. That jovial
quality was her darling joy. She relished and expounded those
things which she knew to be dear to the common heart. Marie
had the *petite frimousse eveillée*, the wideawake little ' mug ' which
Sarcy noted in Réjane. Her dial, as the Cockney would put it,
was the most expressive on the Halls. She had beautiful hands
and feet. She knew every board on the stage and every inch of
every board. In the perfection of her technical accomplish-
ment she rivalled her great contemporary of another stage, Mrs.
Kendal." (With all respect to Mr. Agate, they could scarcely
be called contemporaries. Mrs. Kendal passed away at considerably over eighty, only last year. Marie died in 1922, at
the age of fifty-two. Marie would only have been sixty-six in
1936.) " Briefly, she knew her business. But it is not my
purpose to talk now of her technical excellence. Rather would
I dwell on the fact that she was adored by the lowest classes,
by the middle people, and by the swells. . . . Marie broadened
life and showed it, not as a mean affair of refusal and restraint,
but as a boon to be lustily enjoyed. She redeemed us from
virtue too strait-laced and her great heart cracked too soon."

Here is a report which seems to me to miss the point pretty
badly : " Nothing like the crowds have ever been known in the
quiet cemetery, and the police have been hard at it for three
days making the pilgrims ' pass along there, please.' Those
who come seem by their appearance to be comfortable folk
of the lower middle class, but a number of private motor cars
and taxis were drawn up waiting for their occupants when I
passed, and I was assured that a good many had come up from
the country. Almost opposite is the wide grave where the
soldiers who died in Hampstead Hospital during the Great
War are buried. But not one eye in a thousand glanced that
way. Marvellous ! "

Apart from the fact that the construction leaves one in doubt

as to whether the " almost opposite " refers to Marie's grave, or
to the " country " or the taxicabs, why should it be so " marvellous " that people, having made a pilgrimage to Marie's
grave, should not turn their eyes from what they had come to
see ?

The *Manchester Guardian*—and here again note that the
greater the standing the paper possessed the greater respect and
admiration it paid to Marie Lloyd.

" Over a hundred thousand people are said to have passed
the grave of the great artiste. Nothing of the kind has been seen
in our time in London. The people were mostly of the humbler
classes, whose lives always entered into her songs and patter—
costermongers, people connected with the licensing trade, char-
women, bookmakers and horsey men and women of all
descriptions, taximen and cabmen, small shopkeepers and com-
rades of the music-hall stage and all connected with it. A
correspondent who was in the cemetery for some time gave me
this analysis, but he also mentions the large number of middle-
aged people of a richer class who seemed to come along and
appeared genuinely distressed. The passing of anyone whose
personality and energy warmed the life of her generation
strikes sharply on those who have lost their youth, and the
world seems colder and emptier. The death of a great laughter-
maker seems to many like the end of laughter.

Marie Lloyd's funeral was honoured in many curious ways.
I have heard that in some taverns crape was put behind the
bar and that nearly everyone in Leicester Square district
seemed to be wearing a black tie on that day."

And now for the rest, who, unlike James Agate and Hubert
Griffiths, unlike *The Times* and other papers of note, tried to
make capital out of Marie and her passing. First of all this, to
use Mr. Agate's word, " tosh " about Marie " showing herself
for what she was—an old grey-haired, weary woman." Marie
looked as she had always looked, magnificent. Marie's voice—
except possibly on that last tragic evening at Edmonton—was
as good as ever, her inflections as just, her enunciation as perfect
and her gestures as admirable. Listen to this : " It was
pitiful. She was incoherent. The audience rocked with laughing. Obviously she was unfit to go on the stage. ' I'm
one of the ruins that Cromwell knocked about a bit,' she sang
and leered at us. The clothes she wore were those of an old
hag."

On Mr. Leon Pollack's showing she gave a " brilliant first

performance " at Edmonton, the last night she ever appeared.
Even after a doctor had " strongly advised her to go home,"
she went on and, though evidently ill, got through. " Sang
with a leer " ! She was playing the part of a drunken charwoman—what was she to do : smile like an advertisement for
some tooth-paste ! As Marie, herself, would have said : " Have
a heart ! " Her clothes were those of an old hag. Is she, then,
to play a charwoman in silk, and pearls, carrying her diamond-
headed stick !

Another paper records the fact that she often put on three
new songs in one evening because she did not know what nerves
were. Well, Marie was an astonishing woman, but I should
consider any artiste who embarked on three new songs in one
evening not only astonishing, but astonishingly silly. Unless
the reference is to pantomime or a new musical show. As for
Marie's nerves—well, she might never have actually " dried
up "—she was too good an artiste, but nerves—well, she knew
all about them.

" . . . Led her to that extravagance which brought her in
recent years to poverty." You get a mental picture of Marie
sitting in a dingy attic with a crust and lacking a penny for the
gas-meter. Such an implication is not only untrue, but it is an
insult to her whole family. Admittedly, Marie ran into debt ;
we know that she entirely lacked the ability to save ; but she
lived in an exceedingly comfortable house, bought by her two
sisters, who let it to her. To imply that she was " poverty-
stricken " is utterly untrue. To lack capital, to possess no bank
balance, is not to be without the means to live, and Marie
would never have been that so long as her brothers and sisters
were alive.

Another brilliant suggestion is that " if she had consented to
take a farm and live in the country, her life might have been
saved." Well—Marie on a farm ! Marie, who was the very
soul and spirit of London, who had been born in Hoxton and
lived all her life, if not within the sound of Bow Bells, then at
least within reasonable distance of Big Ben !

The patronizing tone of one smaller journal, whose reporter,
had he ever been admitted to Marie's dressing-room, would
have considered himself more than ordinarily fortunate, is
almost amusing. " She had many faults, but—to some extent
at any rate, they were compensated for by her virtues." You
don't hear the people who knew her chattering about " faults "
—failings, possibly, and " some extent "—well, that fifty-odd

thousand who came to pay their last respects to her don't seem to have been deeply concerned with her "faults" after all.

Another journal—the name is entirely unknown to me—adopts a tone of pity. When, having been the Star of Stars, she drifted, driven by circumstances, domestic and otherwise, for a while to music-halls of second rank."

Why should her "domestic" circumstances drive her to inferior halls? And what were those halls? Is the Alhambra an inferior hall? Can the Holborn be considered a second-rate place of entertainment? You have had the figures, you have read what her salaries were—do second-rate halls pay three hundred pounds a week, four hundred, and even five? What do they know of Variety business, who only the Palladium know?

Then you can turn back and read the words of the far from "second-rate" critics, and note that, in their opinion, "she never lost her hold on the public"—and they are right.

And, lastly, one report in which the writer appears to take it as a personal affront that Marie did not leave a fortune, when he says with quite deplorably bad taste: "Forty-seven members of the Wood family were mixed up with the overpaid ones of the stage; and amid loud lamentations they read the will, etc. etc." That old sneer at the "overpaid ones of the stage" has been argued out long ago. If it comes to that, then Marie herself must have fallen into that category, for no one earned a higher salary, and I should like to write that word *earned* "very large and clear." Artistes are worth what they can bring into the house, and though an inflated salary may be paid, it very soon begins to drop off when an artiste cannot justify it. Managers are not fools, on the contrary, they are remarkably smart and businesslike people, and they know—it is part of their job to know—what an artiste is worth to a penny. You may cheat some of the managers some of the time into believing that you're worth fifty pounds a week, when your real salary ought to be a fiver; but you can't deceive all of the managers, all of the booking offices, and all of the agents, all of the time.

"Loud lamentations" is not a particularly pretty way in which to refer to the family of a woman who has recently died; it smacks somewhat of that overstatement which is slightly derogatory. In fact, in that particular report of Marie's funeral only one person is mentioned as being obviously distressed; that is her husband. There is no mention of her

devoted father and mother, of her sisters and brothers—those
people who had loved her so deeply are ignored. Even her
friends, and we know how great were those people who came
to pay tribute to her, are not credited with having shown
the slightest emotion.

So it is pleasant to know, as I said before, that the better the
paper, the finer the writer, the better the critic—then, automatically, so much more careful, respectful, kindly, and
affectionate were the comments made concerning Our Marie.

And out of her vast earnings, what did Marie leave behind ?
She left practically nothing. Her property was mortgaged ;
she had sold a certain amount of her jewellery, and when
everything was sold in accordance with the will, the whole sum
was about one thousand pounds, and she had earned, at *a low
estimate*, £250,000.

She made only three definite bequests : three hundred
pounds to her brother, Johnnie, one hundred pounds to her
maid, Mrs. Wilson, the rest—whatever it was—she ordered
was to go to her daughter, Marie Courtney, for her use during
her life-time. At her death it was to go to the poor of Hoxton.

She had paid her bequests while she lived ; she had given all
her legacies while she was still working and moving among her
fellow-men, and by those she will be remembered. You can't
eat your cake and have it ; you can't give away thousands and
die leaving a sum which will materially benefit the Death
Duties. In addition, putting aside all Marie's extravagances,
all her generosity, remember that the greater the Star, the
greater the Star's expenses.

Your small artiste can afford to dissipate energy, and travel
from Brixton to Islington by 'bus or tube ; your star, who
carries the greatest weight of the programme on his or her
shoulders, dare not waste that precious vitality. A car is not a
luxury, it is a necessity. Clothes must be expensive, beautiful,
and constantly renewed. Songs have to be bought and paid
for ; your two hundred pound a week artiste can't offer " free "
songs to a critical public. Your star can't spend the week on
tour in cheap rooms, in some little back-street : it isn't politic.
People would soon begin to say : " So-and-So must be going
off ! Know where she's staying this week—same place as the
first turn stayed last week, and they were only getting a
fiver ! "

Think of the tips which must be given every week ; think of
the applications for local charities, footballers, hospitals, any-

thing that happens to want a presentation or a subscription—
the Star will contribute. There are Music-Hall Charities,
Music-Hall subscriptions to the various Unions and Societies.
It's pay, pay, pay, all the time, and pay they do, these Stars.
What did it matter after all? Imagine if Marie's will had
been published in the daily papers, with the heading : " Marie
Lloyd leaves sixty thousand pounds "—who would have
remembered that in ten years? But Marie Lloyd left nothing,
because she gave it away as fast as she earned it. Well, that's
not going to be forgotten, and it's a better recollection than
that of having been niggardly and mean.

She used to sing : " Lost me purse, lost me way—still that
don't matter to you ! "—and all that concerns us is that no
one ever told " the hard luck story " to Marie and found that
she didn't listen and didn't offer practical help.

Marie—well, she *mattered* to people. She wasn't just a name,
or a number at the side of the stage. She was just a little of an
enigma to many people, rather like a firework, apt to blow up
unexpectedly, but a figure always. That was why you found
a woman like Clarice Mayne—not over-emotional, not given to
exaggeration, writing on the wreath which she sent : " To the
greatest woman of our time." " I loved her. She had no
professional jealousy, and was the very soul of generosity," is
what Connie Ediss said of her. Harry Tate's comment was :
" She was the finest artiste and the biggest hearted woman in
the music-hall profession." That is why among the flowers
which poured into the house at Golders Green there was a
wreath inscribed with the words : " To a great artiste. She
has given lightness of heart to many a heart bowed down.
Ellen Terry." Hetty King, who remembered a scene in the
dressing-room at the Old Met., when a little fair-haired woman
stood up for a frightened child, Fred Terry and Julia Neilson
sent their tribute to the woman who had " loved their plays."
Steve Donoghue, Willie Clarkson, who had introduced Sarah
Bernhardt to Marie, Cissie Loftus—and the others, the flower-
seller at Swiss Cottage, " a flower boy," dressers from almost
every hall in London, taxi-drivers, and " an old cabby," all
sent their tributes. Those messages from these simple people—
from people who wished to remain anonymous, because their
names would have meant nothing to anyone, people whom
Marie only knew as " the poor old bloke," or " this down-
and-out fellow," or " nice, cheery little cock, that ! "—they
were part of the reason why Marie left under a thousand pounds.

"Nothing," wrote one of those ignorant, would-be-clever people of Marie, "would have ever made her a lady." The reply is that, on the contrary, nothing could have ever made her anything but a lady. That lovely thing implied by that word which has become pinched and impoverished, which has come to mean everything but a " gentle woman "—was what Marie *was born*. Marie could give, without humiliating the recipient of her charity ; Marie could entertain, so that for the time you felt that her house and everything in it was yours ; Marie " spoke no scandal, no, nor listened to it," Marie fought for the under-dog, and Marie did her work to the very best of her ability and was the Faithful Servant of her public. And if that is not a lady—tell me what is.

The insertion of your name in Burke's Peerage won't make you a lady, and being born in Hoxton won't prevent your being one. Having a passion for winkles argues no lack of aristocratic taste, nor does the ability to drink champagne prove its existence. I ónly know that I dined at a well-known restaurant when I was in town, and enjoyed the delightful spectacle of an expensively dressed woman at the next table, who had the dirtiest shoulder-straps I have ever seen. Marie could never have worn soiled clothes ! Marie, the whole family for that matter, was always exquisite in her dress. Her house was meticulously clean, her taste admirable.

Let's have done with this rubbish about ladies, and these silly questions as to " what were her people," and admit that Our Marie could talk like a coster to costers, and like a great actress to Sarah Bernhardt ; she could talk like a mother to some crying child, and she could talk—like Marie Lloyd, which not another soul in the world could have done, or will ever be able to do. She could be witty, she could be Rabelasian, she could swear like—as Langley Levy says—" the British Army in Flanders," and she could prohibit the mildest of bad language in a dressing-room if she thought that it hurt anyone who was young and immature.

" What the hell's the matter with you ? " she asked another artiste one day, because she had seen a girl flush painfully at some " broad " remark, " No need to talk like a damned cesspool with the b—— lid off, is there ? "

And, because I am " on my finish "—remember that Marie's broad, Elizabethan comedy never degenerated into " personal exploitation of her own physical charms." That's a long and rather ponderous way of saying a very simple thing, but I wanted to make it clear. Other artistes, French and English, will make their appeal directly to the audience, show off their physical attraction as Marie never did. Marie's humour was always about " Flossie," or " Gertie," or " Mrs. What's-It, next door." She betrayed the secrets of an imaginary husband— " 'e struck up a new idea when 'e saw the ladies bathing in the sea. 'E said : ' What a man requires is change of—everythink—ah, an' 'e ought ter tike 'is 'olidays alone,' " but she never betrayed herself, Marie Lloyd. Her references were always oblique, never personal. At least, never when she embarked on songs which were audacious.

" See the twinkle in me eye ? " she would sing, but when it came to " intimate details "—then it was " Bertie and Gertie have just tied the knot."

There was any amount of impropriety in Marie's songs ; there was any amount of " naughtiness "—but there was never the least bit of dirt, never any personal " sex appeal."

I have tried, with the help of others who knew and loved her, to show you what she really was, and if I have not succeeded, it is not because she was so complex, but because she was so full of that essential simplicity which is terribly difficult to convey, because most of us have got so far from it—more's the pity.

No saint, and certainly no sinner, possessed of many failings, but no real faults. Living in the world for fifty-two years, and with one enemy—herself.

Dear Marie, you were a grand woman !

The man who wrote in *The Performer* was right :

" When God made you, He broke the die."

FINALE

"FOR IT IS A PLEASURE, TOO, TO REMEMBER"

OVID

An "imagination" party—The Grand Old Man of Variety—
Maidie Scott—Bransby Williams—George Wood—Johnnie tells
a story—Clarice Mayne—George Mozart—Songs—Marie in
the Law Courts—Ring down!

HAVE you ever given an "imagination" party? It
has always been one of my favourite ways of "awake
dreaming"; to sit back with a cigarette, and knowing that I have ample time to prepare a—let's say—cocktail
party, invite all the people I should like most to see at that
particular moment. Space and time are eliminated, places and
positions are disregarded. I can gather together exactly whom
I want and yet know that the people who are not invited
"because they might not mix very well," cannot be offended,
because they will never know anything about it.

No need to send out invitation cards, no need to worry that
anyone will refuse, that the ice won't be delivered on time, or
that the vermouth will run out at the crucial moment. Everything runs smoothly at these "imagination" parties of mine
and they are always a success!

And now, without the trouble of announcing and opening
doors, the room is full and you must stand back well and
prepare to listen.

Here is an elderly gentleman—you can't say that he is an old
gentleman, although as a matter of fact his real age is over
eighty—with bushy eyebrows and a quick alert manner. He
is talking to a pretty, vivacious woman with very bright eyes.

"And last night was your first appearance before the microphone? Really, is that so? I wondered if you were going to
give us 'Green Apple Pain' when Brian Mickie announced
you."

She shakes her head. "No—I don't know that the B.B.C.

would quite approve of it ! I remember once Marie denounced that song to a manager as being far more improper—well, the word she used was——" and here she whispers and I can't catch the word, but I suspect that I know it ! " than her own numbers."

The man nods. " I saw her first when she was just beginning—" he says. " I knew then that she was destined to be a star."

Another man with wavy black hair has joined them. He smiles, showing very white, even teeth.

" There are some songs and some people," he says, " that always keep their place in the affections of the public. Your own song, ' The Man who Broke the Bank,' is one of those songs ; Marie was one of those artistes."

Maidie Scott, the woman who spoke first says : " Well, your own old ' Penny Showman ' was rather like that too—I often wonder why you never do it now."

" Too old ! "

" Too old ! " she echoes, ' the Showman ' or you ? Rubbish, Bransby Williams. What have you and age to do with each other—nothing ! "

" Old songs—how good they were too ! " They turn and greet a tall, thin fellow whose name I cannot remember ; but they all seem to know him. " I used to do a turn of the old songs. Playing them at the piano. You know, I did yours, Mr. Coborn : the old ' Man who broke the Bank ' ; I did ' Waiting at the Church ' and ' Three pots a shilling ' ; you know all the old favourites. I remember at the Oxford ; oh, this must be quite ten years ago and the audience sang every chorus—loved it, let their voices really go ! Then, right at the end, I said : ' I'm going to play you one of the songs sung by a great little lady—someone you and I all knew and loved.' I played ' One of the ruins that Cromwell knocked about a bit.' The result was almost uncanny. No one made a sound. You could have heard a pin drop in the auditorium. When I came to the last bar I stopped and waited. Then—the applause came ! No singing, they didn't want to sing Marie's song, they just wanted to listen and applaud. I never hope to come across a finer tribute to a great artiste."

Someone says to a short man whose face still retains the " chubbiness " that earned him the name years ago of : " Wee Georgie Wood " : " You used to do an imitation of her, didn't you ? "

" Years ago. I was just a little boy. There's the person—the only person—who can really imitate her—Clarice Mayne."

Lovely, pink and white, with something that is almost spring-like about her, a tall woman joins them.

" Who is taking my name in vain ? " she asks. " My imitation of Marie ! How funny she used to be over it too. You know, Marie did like to be consulted and conferred with. She gave me permission to do this imitation ; indeed, she always wanted me to do it. After four or five weeks I'd have a telegram from her, telling me that she wouldn't allow me to go on doing it. Then I'd go and see her, ask what was wrong.

" ' Oh, well—I do so-and-so when I sing it ! ' very indignant.

" ' Well, so do I,' I'd protest. ' I do so-and-so always.'

" ' Do you ? Oh, well ; that's all right then—go on doing it.'

" Marie wanted knowing. Like all great artistes she had her little vanities and that was one of them. She did like being consulted from time to time. She loved simple things, though. I remember once she asked me to go motoring with her. We drove for hours, singing the choruses of popular songs all the time.

" Once in her dressing-room someone came from one of the big shops selling evening capes. Lovely things. If they hadn't been Marie wouldn't have looked at them, because she had the most wonderful taste. She bought three ; all different colours. Then called in two of her sisters and another girl who was with them and threw one to each of them." She breaks off and says suddenly : " Oh, there's Alice ! Isn't she like Marie ? It's almost startling. Alice ! " she calls, " do you remember the day Marie wanted to come back home and put that vest slip in her dress ? "

A voice which is almost precisely like Marie's, without that husky quality, says : " Of course I do ! Hello, Bransby, how are you ? "

" What about the vest slip ? " someone asks.

" It was when we all wore vest slips in the front of our dresses. Modesty vests they were called. Marie was driving somewhere with Clarice. Very smart, beautiful dress and a lovely hat. Just as she's getting into the car she said : ' Lord, I've forgotten my vest slip. I must go back and put it on.' We all said that it didn't show, that she'd soon be back to change to go to the theatre. Marie considered a moment. Then she said to the chauffeur : ' All right, only whatever you do, don't drive past Buckingham Palace, the King might see me. Awful if he spotted that I wasn't properly dressed.' "

"She was ' wery good to me, she was '—' when I was a little boy.' "

Bransby swings round : " Hello, George, you know your Dickens ? "

The thread of the conversation is lost. They begin to talk of Dickens and we move on to another group. You hear the name—Coram. A man and his wife are talking to a little crowd of people. Mrs. Coram is speaking, with great animation.

". . . The dearest, sweetest thing that ever happened. Her generosity—but you know all about that ! She didn't know how to say ' No.' You might remonstrate with her : ' But you can't give to that person again. You gave to them last week.' Her answer was always the same : ' What's that got to do with it ? The poor devil's hungry ' ; and out of her money would come. There were thousands of other things she did that no one ever heard about. Down-and-out artistes couldn't get jobs. She'd take infinite trouble to get them a hearing, to persuade agents to come and hear them at some obscure hall. And her courage ! I've known her doubled up with pain, many many times—but she always went on."

Coram chuckles. " And her stories ! I've seen people get positively hysterical when she told stories about ' Aunt Betsy.' "

" Yes, and her own special rather-near-the-knuckle stories," his wife adds, " but she never told them to the wrong person ! You see, in addition to everything else she *knew* her audience, whether that audience was composed of two people or two hundred. I can hear her now. The first thing she said when she entered the hall where she was working was always : ' How long have I got,' wasn't it, Johnnie ? "

Johnnie Wood—Marie's elder brother—nods and says in that quiet, rather temperate voice of his : " Always. I remember hearing her say it once, quite calmly, when the whole staff of the Hippodrome at Southend was standing on its head."

Someone cries : " Go on, Johnnie, tell us about it ! "

" It was in the war. I'd been dashing about trying to find a chauffeur for her. You remember, as soon as you got one, they were called up ! I met her for luncheon. We were all going down to Southend by train. Her maid, luggage and her usual crowd of friends had gone down before. Marie arrived at the restaurant where we were to lunch, with her husband, Bernard Dillon, who was in khaki. He was in not the best of tempers."

" What did you say, Sid ? "

" That's not part of the story ! She was trying to calm him down and not making too good a job of it. Luncheon was, to say the least of it, not an easy meal, and I could see that Marie was getting nervy and worried.

" Suddenly she got up, said that she was going to have a wash and tidy up and then we'd get along. Off she went. We sat there and waited. No sign of Marie. Closing time came, still no sign of her. Dillon said that he'd go and find her, and in spite of my protestations off he went into the Ladies' Cloakroom. The woman hadn't even seen Marie. That didn't improve matters and he was annoyed about it. I left him and off I went down to Southend, worried to death. First house had started. No Marie. Maid, friends, relations all waiting to dress her. Telegram for me. ' I am at Colchester. Coming on by car. Don't worry. Marie.' Forty-three miles from Southend !

" I went round to all the artistes and asked them all as a great favour to spin their acts out as long as they could. Ten minutes before she was due to go on up rolls Marie. In a ' Tin Lizzie ' she'd hired at Colchester, paying a fiver for the drive. You could have bought the thing for that !

" ' Here I am ! How long have I got ? ' Oh, the relief !

" Then I asked questions. Where had she been, how did she get to Colchester, and all the rest of it.

" ' Look here, Johnnie,' she said, all the time making up and getting dressed for the stage, ' I don't often bother to keep my temper. I felt that I wanted to this afternoon. I'd done my best to smooth things down, and—I got sick of it ! I knew you'd come down all right, and I thought : " Damned if I don't travel down alone, all nice and peaceful ! " I went to Fenchurch Street—oh, yes, I know now that I ought to have gone to Liverpool Street—bought a book, sat back and read it, forgot that I had to change and landed at Colchester ! That's where the oysters come from, isn't it ? I might have brought a few along with me—still, never mind, nothing like the old Southend winkles ! There, I'm ready ! '

" On she went, quite happy and not a bit disturbed. She'd got there all right ; that was all that mattered ! "

" Ah, Alice has always been like that too ! " An elderly, very neat little man speaks : George Mozart. Someone laughs and says that " he has always had a great admiration for Alice Lloyd."

"For the whole family !" he protests. "The father and mother were brilliant—well, happily, their father is still with us. Look at your three sisters, Johnnie. How clever ! How very, very clever. I'm seventy-two——" There are cries of : "No, George, you're not !" He nods : "Indeed I am, though. I can remember Marie when she was singing ' Wink the other eye.' Marvellous ! There's no one—no, not even present company excepted—to-day who can put over a song as she could ! And always nervous ! ' If anyone comes to me and tells me that they're not nervous,' she said once to me, ' I don't want to see their show. I know that it's no good !'

"I'm a Catholic, you know—well, she lived opposite to the Catholic Church at Golders Green. I honestly believe that she helped to build that church, although she wasn't a Catholic. People tell you that she was vulgar. Rubbish ! I listen to vulgar turns to-day—Marie was, if I might coin the expression, artistically vulgar.

"I remember once someone came and told her that some poor old woman was at the stage door asking for half a crown. ' And I've got no money on me !' Marie said, disturbed and upset at once. Those two words—' poor ' and ' old ' never failed to touch her. A man standing near said : ' I'll lend you half a crown, Marie. Here you are !' She turned on him : ' Half a crown !' she said. ' How would you like to have half a crown banged at you ? Lend me a b—— quid, you miserable swine. To hell with half a crown ; what good is that to any-one !' Believe me, no one was more surprised than the old woman who, mark you, had *asked* for half a crown. But, there, that was Marie ! Ah, Sid "—to Sidney Wood, Marie's younger brother, who is standing near, " you belong to a unique family. I've seen Alice standing at the side, down at the last minute, buttoning a pair of those long white kid gloves ladies used to wear, as cool as a cucumber and only about one minute before she had to go on. Mind, never late ! Only—always down at the last minute."

"She used to make me shine my leather suit all over with Nugget when I drove her car for her at one time," Sid says. "Awfully particular about clothes, always. I've gone into her dressing-room, perhaps taken a friend with me. I might have a new suit on, something that I rather fancied myself in, you know. Marie'd stare at me, frown, then say : ' Don't like that suit you've got on. Looks like a damned horse-cloth,' or ' Looks like a hearth-rug,' or ' somebody's twenty-five shilling touch.'

I'd protest that I liked it. ' Well, I don't Don't wear it again. Give it to him.' Pointing to whoever was with me. ' I'll buy you a new one to-morrow.' I swear that in her time she bought me literally dozens of new suits, just because the ones I bought didn't suit her fancy ! "

" She's become almost a legend," George Mozart says.

Johnnie laughs. " I should think so ! The things some of them say ! Not long ago an old friend of hers sent me a picture taken from a book of *London Recollections*, or some such name. Underneath this picture, it said : " Marie Lloyd in 1894."

His sister, Daisy, stands beside him, listening. " Yes—Marie in 1894, and in reality it was *Mother*, taken about 1874 ! We all had a good look at it, not one of us could tell where this man had got it for his book—we'd never seen it before. I never know where these people get these photographs——"

" Or where they get their information from, either ! " Rosie Lloyd adds. " Stories about Marie—about all of us for that matter ! Our ages have been everything from seventy-five to a hundred and seventy-five. When Marie was fifty—and mind, her birth certificate was kept at the Referee Offices—there were lots of people who used to swear that she was seventy——"

" Fierce is the light that beats upon the throne ! " a man suggests.

" And I suppose that you are to English Variety what the Barrymores are to the American stage."

Rosie shrugs her shoulders. " Oh, I don't know. Audiences are very nice to us, I admit. Last week, you should have heard how they applauded Daisy——"

To which Daisy promptly replies : " Nothing like they brought down the house for Alice, when she sang ' Good old Iron.' "

" What's that ? " Alice asks, coming forward from the other end of the room. " Me ! Nothing like they applauded you and that new song of Rosie's ! I never heard anything like it. It was a riot ! "

" New song, Rosie ? " Clarice Mayne asks. " And aren't they difficult to get in these days ! "

There is a stir near the door and a tall woman comes in.

An unmistakable voice says, " Well, well, me dear, Violet Loraine ! " She answers : " Well, if it isn't George Graves ! Who was talking about songs ? "

" Ah ! There aren't any songs like that classic of yours me dear ! "

" What—' The only girl in the world ' ? Oh, that wasn't only my song. George Robey had as much right to the success —it was *our* song, not *my* song. I remember once at the Tivoli, and I was just a beginner in those days, I was in Marie's dressing-room, and word was brought that a gentleman wanted to know if she'd see him for a moment. She turned to me ' I'll bet it's a song-writer—and that there's no second verse ! ' It *was* a song-writer, and there *was* no second verse. Judging by the first it was just as well, for even Marie would have blushed to sing it ! Marie, with her unending generosity and dry humour, gave him some money, and said : ' Now, go and get yourself a beefsteak—without a cork in it, mind—and when you do write that second verse, well, let it be meaty, but not too fruity.' "

" Marie's humour was like good champagne, dry and not a headache in the bottle ! " George Graves says. " No, I'm wrong, me dears—it was like Imperial Tokay ! "

" Why ? "

He laughs : " It's practically unobtainable now—finished, no more to be had, a thing of the past ! "

By this time the room is full, almost too full, only when you give these imaginary parties your rooms automatically expand to suit the number of guests, and so now, when Mrs. Dick Burge enters with Mrs. Gunnup and Kate Carney, who has just celebrated her—no, when I look at her I know that it can't be possible, know that this talk of fifty years celebration is sheer nonsense and that the time cannot be more than five years since she first delighted us with " Three pots a shilling " —there is still plenty of room. There, too, is Mrs. Egerton, who used to keep the American Bar at Liverpool. She is like Marie in one thing, at least ; her heart is always ready to beat in sympathy with " hard luck stories." Her hands are always ready to offer help and kindness. No wonder Marie and she were friends. Mrs. Egerton's friends are like the sands of the sea.

There is " Billie " Boardman, who used to be the popular manager of the Hippodrome, Brighton. He is listening to one of Johnnie's stories of how Marie served—or didn't serve —on a jury.

" When was it, Johnnie ? "

" The end of 1921," he says. " She was appearing at the Palladium, and one evening there she received this summons to appear on the jury at the High Courts of Justice ! Marie read it, and passed it on to me. You know how much Marie took in those things—they were Greek to her. I was amused at this, surprised, too, and rather stupidly couldn't resist showing it round, among others, to the Publicity Manager. He asked if he might keep it for a little time ; I consented, little dreaming the bother and trouble my consent was going to cause. The next night all the papers were full of it. Placards read : ' Marie Lloyd summoned on the Jury.' Bookings went up, newspaper sales went up, and it meant a pat on the back for the Publicity Manager. He didn't get one from me, though ! For there was Marie, pestered with reporters, all wanting to know what she thought about it, how she felt, what she was going to say, and all the rest of it.

" Then—to make matters really terrible—the date was fixed. She was ordered to appear on a day when we were due in Cardiff, and she was on a percentage basis, not a salary. The *South Wales Echo* had got the story ; there were a great many enquiries, questions as to whether she'd be able to be back in time for the show and, honestly, it all made Marie quite ill. You know how nervy she was about her work ! I tried every way to get her exemption. But I suppose the authorities thought that it was just unwillingness to lose a few pounds and refused to listen. The day came. I went with her to the High Courts, with her own doctor and a trained nurse, both ready to certify that she was not physically fit to go through the ordeal. They wouldn't listen ! By this time Marie was really getting angry about it all, and showed it pretty plainly.

" She was sworn in, took her seat, and I sat in the Public Gallery where I could see her. The case came on, a dispute over some property between two of the Chosen People—again, all so much Greek to Marie. What did Marie know about leases and dilapidations, and repairing clauses ?—not a thing !

" I managed to catch her eye, and pulling out my handkerchief, held it to my mouth, making certain unmistakable movements. Marie understood like a flash. Out came her own handkerchief, up to her mouth it went, and believe me, she never gave a finer ' 'mime' show in all her life. The Judge noticed, and stopped the case, Marie still looking piteous and pathetic. He said : ' It is evident that a member of the jury is ill. She will be allowed to retire ! ' She retired in double quick time. I felt like ' giving her a hand,' I can tell you. Within ten minutes she was having a glass of wine in Romano's to restore her to something like her old self. We were surrounded by camera men, one of them even rode on the back of her car all the way to Golders Green, trying to make her 'give him a story.' Everyone heard how she 'got on the jury,' but until now, Billie, no one ever knew 'how she got off the jury'!"

"Expensive business for her, I suppose. She couldn't play the week out at Cardiff, eh?"

"It cost her—" Johnnie does a little mental arithmetic, "it cost her—three hundred pounds!"

"And a jolly good 'turn' in the Law Courts—for which there was no money paid on Friday night, eh?"

The piano is playing, and Billie Boardman says: "Hello that's Daisy singing, isn't it?" Johnnie nods. "She's a little like Marie sometimes, isn't she?"

As you listen you hear that she is like Marie. There is the same clear diction, there is the same knowledge as to which words are of real value, and which may safely be unstressed.

> "The old gang won't care whether,
> You're broke or in the dough.
> You'll find dreams left behind,
> In the old familiar places——"

The old familiar places, Manchester, Liverpool, Leeds, "King Pantomime," and Daisy Wood his very admirable Prince.

The song ends, and another begins.

Someone says: "Now, *Rosie's* like Marie—no, not in looks, but in the tone of her voice. Now and then, if you shut your eyes, it might be Marie singing."

Johnnie tells them: "There's a certain likeness runs all through the family."

> "I filled your heart with hope and glory,
> When you told me the hard luck story——"

How often did Marie do that? How many "hard luck stories" did she listen to, and send the people who told them away filled with, if not actually "hope and glory," at least with the assurance that the world still held "hearts which were kind and fair"?

"But Alice is most like her! Look at her now. That's exactly how Marie used to stand when she was going to sing!"

She sings: "Good old iron, never been known to rust," and ends by telling us: "Don't forget, the older the fiddle the sweeter the tune."

It's an old saying ; it has become trite and threadbare, but it's true. The fiddle may lie in its case for years, but when you take it out, the music will be as sweet as ever.

The crowd fades away, and one by one they pass through the door and I am left alone, sitting and staring, rubbing my eyes, because my " dream party " has been so real, so vivid, that I can scarcely believe it wasn't really true. Words of the songs I have heard come back to me—" Old friends are treasures, one should never lose "—there is no need to lose them, either, if you'll only " work at friendship " and not regard it as something which can be taken up and thrown down at will.

It is exactly thirteen years ago since Marie left us, and here are memories of her crowding in on us, here are people still wishing to talk of her, to recount her kindnesses, her wit, and her genius. Yes, I know, that's a big word, a misused word in these days when everyone who makes a momentary success thinks that it applies to them, only in this case, applied to Marie Lloyd, it is just and right.

As I turn over the pages which I have written, I am almost certain that I can hear a husky, lovable voice say : " What's all that about ? "

" It's about—well, it's about you, Marie."

" Me ! Blimy, whatever have you said about me ? " The voice is incredulous, amused. It is obvious that she suspects me of making fun of her, trying to have a joke.

" I've said that you were the kindest-hearted woman in the world."

" Rubbish ! What's money for, except to give away. It's round and it's made to go round ! What else ? "

" I've said that you were a genius."

This time I " get a laugh," a delicious, chuckling laugh.

" People 'ul laugh at you, they'll think you're balmy ! Go on——"

" It's not only me ! " I protest. " It's everyone—look here, at these letters ; dozens of them, all about you."

" All about me." There is a little pause. " Nice letters, eh, Mick ? "

" Wonderful letters, my dear."

" That's nice. From my pals, are they ? " I nod. " And—" her voice shakes a little, " my ' boys and girls ' too ? "

" Lots of them."

" I'm glad of that. They count, you know, the pit and the gallery. Their sixpences and shillings mean more to them

than the half-crowns and five shillings, quids and fivers do to
the stalls and boxes. If they like you—the ' boys and girls '
—they can make you ! "

There is a long silence and then I fancy that I can hear
her say :

" Don't make me too nice, cocky. Make me just what I was
—y'know. Patchy—like most of us. No one's all white or, for
that matter, all black. If you splash too much whitewash
over me they won't recognize me."

" I haven't done that," I answer. " I—I've just tried to
show them—Our Marie."

Then, I am staring in front of me, my eyes smarting a little,
because " Our Marie " did *matter* so much to so many of us, and
even after thirteen years we still miss her—miss her acutely.

It's almost a relief to turn to a letter from America, written
in the characteristic scrawl of Nigel Bruce, who started his stage
career with me, when we were both so bad that, mercifully,
we didn't realize just how bad we were. He writes from
Hollywood, where he is achieving the success he deserves—he
has changed from a very bad actor to a very brilliant one. He
says : " Marie Lloyd represented pre-war England, the real
England of the Man-in-the-Street, as nobody I have seen did
—before or since. She had a great, God-given vulgarity that
always put one in a better mood with oneself and one's
surroundings. It was so absolutely healthy ; and when one
thinks of the post-war type of suggestive, sensual filth, one is
so damnably sorry for the stage—and the public who have no
Marie Lloyd.

" I remember so well the buzz of anticipation during the
latter part of the turn of some poor devil who was ' on ' before
Marie Lloyd. How it rose until the audience almost ' got
rid ' of him—or her—and sat back ready for Marie's entrance.
The lights would go up, on the side her number appeared,
there were three seconds' sudden hush of expectation, and
then—that huge roar of welcome as she walked on to the
stage.

" It's awful to me to think what we have lost with those
artistes who were such a personal matter of interest and
affection to us all—and she was unquestionably the greatest
of all those great people. Try to tell the post-war generation
what she meant to us all. They ought to know."

That goes in here because Nigel—" Willie "—Bruce is not
only a name we are all coming to know and look for, but he is

" The Man-in-the-Street," and I felt that he had a right to say a word to you.

I shuffle my papers together, blink my eyes again because they are smarting rather badly and hope, with real sincerity, that I have done justice to—Our Marie.

CURTAIN

MERANO,
   ITALY.
  1935–1936

CHAPTER TWENTY-TWO

"MY SISTER ! MY SWEET SISTER ! IF A NAME
DEARER AND PURER WERE, IT SHOULD BE THINE "
                                          BYRON

Her sisters' letter.

"DEAR MICKY,

It must be three years ago since you wrote to us asking
for a photograph of our beloved sister, Marie, because you
wanted to include it in a book which you were then writing,
called *Me*.

When you sent us a copy of the book, and when we read
the chapter which you called ' Our Marie,' I think we all
realized that you understood her character very fully and
that you had a real and genuine affection for her.

Then, this summer, when you came over that evening to
Epsom and proposed that you should write a book which
should be entirely devoted to Marie, our feeling was that—
possibly—it might be difficult, after so many years, to gather
up sufficient material for a full-sized book. However, writing
is *your job*, and we felt that it was not for us to bring forward
suggestions and so forth, any more than you'd come round after
our show and begin to show us how to do *our work*.

One thing, as we told you at the time, and as we said to
Sadie Robinson when she came to see us after you had gone
back to Italy, we all wanted it to be a *real* life of Marie. Not
just a beautifully written, delightfully expressed, faultless
picture ; but something which was real. Marie, with her
generosity, her open-handedness, her loyalty and her tempers
and little faults, all complete.

To draw her as a woman whose character was made up of
nothing but nerves, tempers, storms and irritabilities, would
be just as wrong as to draw her faultless, always gentle, always
smiling on life.

That's what we wanted, Micky—a *Life of Our Marie*. A life

which will show her to everyone who remembers her as something real, as a thing of flesh and blood, and to those who do not remember her as a woman who is worthy of reading about.

Talking about her—as we often do—we are not certain that she was not made more lovable by those faults, certainly they made her terribly human.

You were right to ' begin at the beginning,' because no life of our family could be complete unless our father and mother were included and shown as what they were—the people who gave us all a splendid start in life. We never have ' *pretended* ' and none of us want to start doing so now. It's something—as we see it —to be proud of, that father and mother worked for us and strove hard to give us the best of everything. Even now, we can remember that we were always the best-dressed children in the school. Not because our parents were rich, but because they worked hard and because mother would sit up until all hours of the night, making clothes for us. We always had splendid food, always plenty of it, and because of that we all grew up strong and so very well able to fight our way in the world.

You say in this book that you wanted it to be ' everyone's tribute to Our Marie '—well, this little bit is *our* tribute to *mother and father*.

We wrote just now that we had never ' pretended '—and that is the answer to a question you put to us a few weeks ago. Do you remember asking : ' Why have the public always felt a kind of personal affection for you all ? ' This is the real answer—because we have always tried to be just ourselves because we have never tried to pretend that we were any better than anyone else, and have always been ' hail fellow, well met.' That was why her public loved Marie, and that is why—as we say in our own act now—' Alice, Daisy, Rosie ' have kept a hold on the affection of their audiences—just ' being ourselves.'

And another thing, and Marie felt this too, it's no use looking back and whining and pulling a long face about what is over and done with. Marie made a fortune and lost it ; we've all done the same—though we haven't all lost money for the same reason that Marie did. We don't get the salaries we used to get—*no one does !* Those days are over for *everyone* in the business. One has had to face disasters, financial crashes, investments that turned out badly, the loss of those one loved very dearly —but it's no use whining and grousing. There are lots of good times left, lots of good friends and, after all, as Daisy sings, one's real friends don't care ' if you're broke or in the dough '—and so life goes on and we can still sing that ' everything at Lloyd's is still A.1.'

No one and nothing can take from you the good times you've had, can they? Time can't rob us of those nights when audiences stood up and shouted their applause, when the stage was covered with flowers and every performance was a riot ! Time can't take from any of us some of those letters which you have included in this book, time can't prevent our dressing-room still being filled, whenever we are working, with friends who are real friends.

Thinking it all over we came to the conclusion that Marie, bless her, is as rich now as ever she was, because the appeal which you made for stories, recollections and photographs of her have called forth such a grand response from people who, after thirteen years, still want to prove their love and admiration for her.

And the public treats us just the same. Everywhere we go, and work comes in splendidly, almost surprisingly when you remember at what a low ebb the Variety stage is in these days, we get constant reminders that people don't forget the old days. We're still—not ' The Sisters Lloyd '—we're ' Alice,' ' Daisy Wood ' and ' Rosie Lloyd,' and every week people come round to talk to us, and their conversations all begin in the same way :

' Do you remember when——'

While we have been getting material for you for this book it's queer how almost always when we talk about Marie—we laugh. The things which come back to us are amusing things, funny little incidents which have been buried in our minds and half forgotten, and they come to the top, and we tell them —laughing.

There was a great deal of sadness in her life, and we, her sisters, saw it and hated it for her.

That seems to have gone now and we remember the things that made us all laugh together !

There is one other thing—and we say this because we know that you, like us, like most people who have lived part of their life among stage people, or have earned their living on the stage, feel pretty strongly about those matters which affect the people you love, or have loved. We didn't want—and you have evidently felt the same from the book—anything said that was not *just*.

We didn't want Marie made into a ' plaster saint ' at the expense of anyone else, *neither* did we want anyone else ' nicely laundered ' at *Marie's* expense. We want honesty, and that's what you've given us !

Mr. Robertson, a great friend of ours from South Africa, and a great admirer of Marie's, said something very illuminating the other day. He said : ' She wasn't a star, she wasn't a music-hall artiste, she was an—institution.'

So let the public who knew her, and the public who wish to know something about her, see her and get to know her as she was, truthfully drawn, not over-coloured, just—life-like.

No one is all good or all bad, no week is all sunshine or all clouds, no life is all smiles or all tears, and Marie's was no exception to the rule.

We don't know if this letter will be all right to go into the book. We have just written it down as the thoughts came into our minds—when we've been talking at home, sitting between the first and second house at the theatre, when we've been going home at night after the show. Possibly it is very disjointed, and maybe we have not said half the things we wanted to say—it's written as we talk !

There may even be little mistakes in the stories of Marie which we have told you. We may have said : ' Once when she was at Brighton—' when it ought to have been : ' Manchester,' or ' Liverpool.' Those little things don't matter—the essential things are all true, and the ' trimmings ' don't affect the stories.

After all, ' the play's the thing '—and this is a play written round the life of Marie Lloyd, and the little bits of scenery don't affect it, do they ? It's the truth that matters—and you've got that all right !

You have, we know, thanked all the people who have come forward, who have offered you material, who have written their recollections of Marie, sent pictures and so on—well, we want to add our thanks, too, and particularly to those old people to whom writing letters is not a very easy business—to them we send our love and thanks.

We're glad that you have written this book, Micky.

We're glad that everyone has rallied round you so well.

We're glad that we are associated with it, and—we know that *Marie will be glad, too*.

And, in our hearts and yours, we know *that* is the most important thing of all.

        Love to you, dear,

           (Signed) ALICE, ROSIE and DAISY.

PS. We all know just what it has meant to a busy person like yourself to have to sort and answer all the letters you have had and go through paper cuttings, send out appeals and all the other little things which are quite apart from your job of writing. We know, too, how much you loved her and how loyally you have tried to present a *real Marie*, and so, for this, your own personal tribute to her, we all, Alice, Rosie, Daisy and all the rest of the family, including Marie's daughter, if she were here, say : ' Thank you, Micky Jacob, and God bless you.' "

INDEX

A

Adair, James, 17, 130, 131
Adeler, Edwin, 141
Adeson, Mrs. Martin, 145
Agate, James, 198, 255, 257
Albert, Lottie, 141
Albini, Lieutenant, 57
Archer, Matilda Caroline (Mrs. John Wood), 27, 28 *et seq.*, 70, 101
Arthur, Robert, 224, 243
Austin, Charles, 19, 107

B

Barclay, George, 171
Bard, Wilkie, 19
Barnes, Fred, 92, 176
Bass, George, 89, 222, 237
Bastow, George, 18
Belmont, George E., 55
Bendon, Father, 159
Bently, Walter, 150
Bernard, Clara, *see* Adeson, Mrs. Martin
Bernhardt, Sarah, 111, 124, 247, 261, 262
Blanche, Ada, 81
Boardman " Billie," 53, 112, 170, 271
Boganny, Joe, 162
Booth, J. B., 110, 111
Braithwaite, Lilian, 199

Broadfoote, Marguerite, 128, 154, 171, 187
Bruce, Nigel, 275
Burge, Dick, 150, 211
Burge, Mrs. Dick, 58, 78, 99, 123, 126, 140, 212, 213, 271

C

Campbell, Herbert, 81
Campbell, Mrs. Patrick, 111, 199
Carados, 252
Carney, Kate, 171
Carrick, Hartley, 250
Chevalier, Albert, 83
Chirgwin, 18, 251
Cinquevalli, 18, 106, 110, 150, 251
Claff, Harry, 17, 19, 131, 134, 162, 171
Clarkson, Willie, 124, 261
Coburn, Charles, 19, 55, 192
Coburn, Mrs. Charles, 141
Collins, José, 131
Collins, Lottie, 70, 130
Cooper, Gladys, 199
Coram, 267
Coram, Mrs., 267
Corin, Winnie, 92
Corti, Luigi, 27, 169
Courtneidge, Robert, 216, 224
Courtney, Marie, *see* Lloyd, Marie (Junior)

PORTWAY & NEW PORTWAY

NON-FICTION

Anderson, Verily	Beware of children
Anderson, Verily	Daughters of divinity
Armstrong, Martin	Lady Hester Stanhope
Arnothy, Christine	It's not so easy to live
Asquith, Margot	The autobiography of Margot Asquith
Barke, James	The green hills far away
Bentley, Phyllis	The Pennine weaver
Bishop, W.A.	Winged warfare
Blain, William	Home is the sailor
Brittain, Vera	Testament of experience
Brittain, Vera	Testament of friendship
Brittain, Vera	Testament of youth
Buchan, John	The clearing house
Cobbett, William	Cottage economy
Crozier, F.P.	Ireland for ever
Day, J. Wentworth	Ghosts and witches
Dunnett, Alastair M.	It's too late in the year
Edmonds, Charles	A subaltern's war
Evans, A.J.	The escaping club
Falk, Bernard	Old Q's daughter
Fields, Gracie	Sing as we go
Firbank, Thomas	A country of memorable honour
Gandy, Ida	A Wiltshire childhood
Gary, Romain	Promise at dawn
Gibbons, Floyd	Red knight of Germany
Gibbs, Philip	Realities of war
Gough, General Sir Hubert	The fifth army
Grant, I.F.	Economic history of Scotland
Hart, B.H. Liddell	Great captains unveiled
Hart, B.H. Liddell	A history of the world war 1914—18
Hart, B.H. Liddell	The letters of private Wheeler
Hart, B.H. Liddell	The other side of the hill
Hecht, Hans	Robert Burns: the man and his work
Holtby, Winifred	Letters to a friend
Huggett, Renee & Berry, Paul	Daughters of Cain
Jones, Ira	King of air fighters
Jones, Jack	Give me back my heart
Jones, Jack	Me and mine

PORTWAY & NEW PORTWAY

FICTION

Albert, Edward	Herrin' Jennie
Aldington, Richard	All men are enemies
Aldington, Richard	Death of a hero
Anand, Mulk Raj	Seven summers
Andersch, Alfred	Flight to afar
Anderson, Verily	Our square
Anderson, Verily	Spam tomorrow
Anthony, Evelyn	Imperial highness
Anthony, Evelyn	Victoria
Arlen, Michael	Men dislike women
Arnim, Elizabeth von	Elizabeth and her German garden
Arnim, Elizabeth von	Mr. Skeffington
Ashton, Helen	Doctor Serocold
Ashton, Helen	Family cruise
Ashton, Helen	Footman in powder
Ashton, Helen	The half-crown house
Ashton, Helen	Letty Landon
Ashton, Helen	Swan of Usk
Barke, James	Bonnie Jean
Barke, James	The land of the leal
Barke, James	Major operation
Barke, James	The song of the green thorn tree
Barke, James	The well of the silent harp
Basso, Hamilton	Pompey's head
Bates, H.E.	The purple plain
Baum, Vicki	Berlin hotel
Benson, R.H.	Come rack come rope
Benson, R.H.	Lord of the world
Bentley, Phyllis	Love and money
Bentley, Phyllis	A modern tragedy
Bentley, Phyllis	The partnership
Bentley, Phyllis	Sleep in peace
Bentley, Phyllis	Take courage
Bentley, Phyllis	Trio
Birmingham, George A.	General John Regan
Birmingham, George A.	The inviolable sanctuary
Blackmore, R.D.	Mary Anerley
Blain, William	Witch's blood

Blaker, Richard	The needle watcher
Bottome, Phyllis	Murder in the bud
Bromfield, Louis	Early autumn
Bromfield, Louis	A good woman
Bromfield, Louis	The green bay tree
Bromfield, Louis	The rains came
Bromfield, Louis	Wild is the river
Brophy, John	Gentleman of Stratford
Brophy, John	Rocky road
Brophy, John	Waterfront
Broster, D.K.	Child royal
Broster, D.K.	A fire of driftwood
Broster, D.K.	Sea without a haven
Broster, D.K.	Ships in the bay
Broster, D.K. & Taylor, G.W.	Chantemerle
Broster, D.K. & Forester, G.	World under snow
Buchan, John	Grey weather
Buchan, John	The Runagates club
Buck, Pearl S. *(Trans.)*	All men are brothers (2 vols.)
Buck, Pearl S.	Fighting angel
Buck, Pearl S.	The hidden flower
Buck, Pearl S.	A house divided
Buck, Pearl S.	Imperial woman
Caldwell, Erskine	Place called Estherville
Caldwell, Taylor	The arm and the darkness
Caldwell, Taylor	The beautiful is vanished
Caldwell, Taylor	The final hour
Caldwell, Taylor	Let love come last
Caldwell, Taylor	Melissa
Caldwell, Taylor	Tender victory
Callow, Philip	Common people
Chandos, Dane	Abbie
Chapman, Hester W.	To be a king
Church, Richard	The dangerous years
Collins, Wilkie	Armadale
Collins, Wilkie	The dead secret
Collins, Wilkie	The haunted hotel
Collins, Wilkie	Poor miss Finch
Common, Jack	Kiddar's luck
Comyns, Barbara	Our spoons came from Woolworths
Cookson, Catherine	Maggie Rowan
Cookson, Catherine	Mary Ann's angels

Cookson, Catherine	Rooney
Cookson, Catherine	Slinky Jane
Cooper, Lettice	Black Bethlehem
Cooper, Lettice	The new house
Cooper, Lettice	Private enterprise
Cooper, Lettice	We have come to a country
Cordell, Alexander	Race of the tiger
Cost, March	The dark star
Cost, March	The year of the yield
Costain, Thomas B.	The tontine
Crockett, S.R.	The black Douglas
Crockett, S.R.	The raiders
Croker, B.M.	The youngest miss Mowbray
Cusack, Dymphna & James, F.	Come in spinner
Dane, Clemence	The arrogant history of white Ben
Dane, Clemence	The Babyons
Dane, Clemence	The moon is feminine
Davenport, Marcia	East side, west side
Davies, Rhys	The black Venus
Davies, Rhys	Honey and bread
Davies, Rhys	Jubilee blues
Davies, Rhys	The red hills
Davies, Rhys	Rings on her fingers
Davies, Rhys	The trip to London
Deeping, Warwick	Apples of gold
Deeping, Warwick	Doomsday
Deeping, Warwick	Lantern lane
Deeping, Warwick	Martin Valliant
Deeping, Warwick	Old Pybus
Deeping, Warwick	Orchards
Deeping, Warwick	Suvla John
Dehan, Richard	The dop doctor
Dehan, Richard	The man of iron
Dehan, Richard	That which hath wings
Douglas, George	The house with the green shutters
D'Oyley, Elizabeth	Play me fair
Dumas, Alexandre	The Corsican brothers
Fanu, Sheridan Le	In a glass darkly
Feuchtwanger, Lion	The day will come
Feuchtwanger, Lion	The Jew of Rome
Feuchtwanger, Lion	Jew Süss
Feuchtwanger, Lion	Josephus

Field, Rachel	Time out of mind
Field, Rachel & Pederson	To see ourselves
Firbank, Thomas	Bride to the mountain
Fletcher, H.L.V.	The devil has the best tunes
Fletcher, H.L.V.	Forest inn
Fletcher, H.L.V.	The rising sun
Fletcher, H.L.V.	The whip and the tongue
Gibbs, Philip	The ambassador's wife
Gibbs, Philip	The battle within
Godden, Rumer	A fugue in time
Golding, Louis	Camberwell beauty
Golding, Louis	The dangerous places
Golding, Louis	The loving brothers
Goodrich, Louis	By Greta bridge
Goodwin, Geraint	Come Michaelmas
Goodwin, Geraint	Watch for the morning
Goodwin, Geraint	The heyday in the blood
Goodwin, Geraint	The white farm & other stories
Graves, Robert	'Antigua, penny, puce'
Graves, Robert	Proceed, sergeant Lamb
Graves, Robert	Sergeant Lamb of the ninth
Graves, Robert	Seven days in new Crete
Graves, Robert	Wife to mr. Milton
Greenwood, Walter	His worship the mayor
Griffith, Wyn	The way lies west
Griffith, Wyn	The wooden spoon
Gristwood, A.D.	The Somme/the coward
Grun, Bernard	The golden quill
Gunn, Neil	The key of the chest
Gunn, Neil	The well at the world's end
Herbert, A.P.	Number nine
Herbert, A.P.	Why Waterloo?
Hichens, Robert	The Bacchante and the nun
Hichens, Robert	The garden of Allah
Hodgkiss, Louis	Deep shafts
Hodson, James Lansdale	Harvest in the north
Holtby, Winifred	The land of green ginger
Holtby, Winifred	Mandoa, mandoa!
Holtby, Winifred	Poor Caroline
Home, Michael	God and the rabbit
Houghton, Claude	I am Jonathan Scrivener
Jefferis, Barbara	Half angel

Jenkins, Elizabeth	Robert and Helen
Jenkins, Elizabeth	The tortoise and the hare
Jenkins, Robin	So gaily sings the lark
Jones, Jack	Black parade
Jones, Jack	Choral symphony
Jones, Jack	Come night: end day
Jones, Jack	Lily of the valley
Jones, Jack	Lucky Lear
Jones, Jack	The man David
Jones, Jack	Off to Philadelphia in the morning
Jones, Jack	Rhondda roundabout
Jones, Jack	River out of Eden
Jones, Jack	Some trust in chariots
Jones, Jack	Time and the business
Kersh, Gerald	Nine lives of Bill Nelson
Keyes, Frances Parkinson	All that glitters
Keyes, Frances Parkinson	The ambassadress
Keyes, Frances Parkinson	The career of David Noble
Keyes, Frances Parkinson	Christian Marlowe's daughter
Keyes, Frances Parkinson	If ever I cease to love
Keyes, Frances Parkinson	Larry Vincent
Keyes, Frances Parkinson	The letter from Spain
Keyes, Frances Parkinson	Madame Castel's lodger
Keyes, Frances Parkinson	The old Gray homestead
Keyes, Frances Parkinson	Queen Anne's lace
Keyes, Frances Parkinson	The river road
Keyes, Frances Parkinson	Steamboat gothic
Klingman, Lawrence, & Green, Gerald	His majesty O'Keefe
Knight, Eric	This above all
Knight, L.A.	Conqueror's road
Knight, L.A.	Deadman's bay
Knight, L.A.	High treason
Knight, L.A.	Judgment rock
Knight, L.A.	The brazen head
Knight, L.A.	The dancing stones
Knight, L.A.	The Viking feast mystery
Lawrence, Margery	Madonna of the seven moons
Lawrence, Margery	Number 7 Queer street
Lewis, Hilda	A mortal malice
Lewis, Hilda	Call lady Purbeck
Lewis, Hilda	The day is ours

Lewis, Hilda	I, Jacqueline
Lewis, Hilda	No mate no comrade
Lewis, Hilda	Pelican inn
Lewis, Hilda	Penny lace
Lewis, Hilda	Wife to great Buckingham
Lindsay, Jack	Caesar is dead
Lindsay, Jack	Last days with Cleopatra
Lindsay, Jack	Lost birthright
Lindsay, Jack	Men of forty-eight
Lindsay, Jack	1649 A novel of a year
Lindsay, Jack	Rome for sale
Lindsay, Philip	The gentle knight
Lindsay, Philip	Here comes the king
Lindsay, Philip	London bridge is falling
Lindsay, Philip	Love rides to Buttermere
Lindsay, Philip	Pudding lane
Lindsay, Philip	The queen's confession
Lindsay, Philip	Sir rusty sword
Lindsay, Philip	They have their dreams
Llewelyn, Michael Gareth	The aleppo merchant
Llewelyn, Michael Gareth	Angharad's isle
Lofts, Norah	Requiem for idols
Lofts, Norah	White hell of pity
Mackenzie, Compton	The altar steps
Mackenzie, Compton	Poor relations
Macminnies, Mary	The visitors
Marton, Francesca	Attic and area
Marton, Francesca	Mrs. Betsey or widowed and wed
Masefield, Muriel	Seven against Edinburgh
Mason, A.E.W.	The truants
Maturin, Henri	Melmoth the wanderer — 3 vols.
Meredith, George	Diana of the crossways
Morrison, N. Brysson	The gowk storm
Mundy, Talbot	O.M. — the secret of Arbor valley
Mundy, Talbot	Purple pirate
Mundy, Talbot	Queen Cleopatra
Mundy, Talbot	Tros of Samothrace
La Mure, Pierre	Beyond desire
Myers, Elizabeth	A well full of leaves
Myers, L.H.	The near and the far (2 vols.)
Neill, Robert	Hangman's cliff
O'Brien, Kate	The ante-room

O'Brien, Kate	The flower of May
O'Brien, Kate	The land of spices
O'Brien, Kate	Mary Lavelle
O'Brien, Kate	Pray for the wanderer
O'Brien, Kate	Without my cloak
O'Flaherty, Liam	The assassin
Oliver, Jane	Crown for a prisoner
Oliver, Jane	Isle of glory
Oliver, Jane	The lion and the rose
Oliver, Jane	Queen of tears
Oliver, Jane	Sing morning star
Oliver, Jane	Sunset at noon
Onstott, Kyle	Drum
Onstott, Kyle	Mandingo
Ouida	Moths
Page, Gertrude	Paddy-the-next-best-thing
Pain, Barry	The exiles of Faloo
Pargeter, Edith	The assize of the dying
Pargeter, Edith	The city lies four-square
Pargeter, Edith	The eighth champion of Christendom
Pargeter, Edith	Holiday with violence
Pargeter, Edith	A means of grace
Pargeter, Edith	Most loving mere folly
Pargeter, Edith	Ordinary people
Pargeter, Edith	Reluctant odyssey
Pargeter, Edith	The scarlet seed
Pargeter, Edith	The soldier at the door
Park, Ruth	The harp in the south
Prior, James	Forest folk
Porter, Jeanette Stratton	Freckles comes home
Proctor, Maurice	No proud chivalry
Prouty, Olive Higgins	Now voyager
Pym, Barbara	Jane and Prudence
Pym, Barbara	Less than angels
Raymond, Ernest	Child of Norman's End
Raymond, Ernest	Daphne Bruno
Raymond, Ernest	The five sons of le Faber
Raymond, Ernest	The fulfilment of Daphne Bruno
Raymond, Ernest	For them that trespass
Raymond, Ernest	A song of the tide
Renault, Mary	The friendly young ladies
Riley, William	Jerry and Ben

Riley, William	Laycock of Lonedale
Roberts, Kenneth	Arundel
Roberts, Kenneth	Oliver Wiswell
Roche, Mazo de la	Delight
Roche, Mazo de la	Growth of a man
Roche, Mazo de la	The two saplings
Sandstrom, Flora	The midwife of Pont Clery
Sandstrom, Flora	The virtuous women of Pont Clery
Seton, Anya	The mistletoe and sword
Seymour, Beatrice K.	Maids and mistresses
Shellabarger, Samuel	Captain from Castile
Sherriff, R.C.	The Hopkins manuscript
Shiel, M.P.	Prince Zaleski
Sienkiewicz, Henryk	The deluge (2 vols.)
Sienkiewicz, Henryk	With fire and sword
Sinclair, Upton	Boston
Sinclair, Upton	The flivver king
Sinclair, Upton	The jungle
Sinclair, Upton	Oil!
Sinclair, Upton	They call me carpenter

WORLD'S END SERIES

Sinclair, Upton	World's end
Sinclair, Upton	Between two worlds
Sinclair, Upton	Dragon's teeth
Sinclair, Upton	Wide is the gate
Sinclair, Upton	Presidential agent
Sinclair, Upton	Dragon harvest
Sinclair, Upton	A world to win
Sinclair, Upton	Presidential mission
Sinclair, Upton	One clear call
Sinclair, Upton	O shepherds speak
Sinclair, Upton	The return of Lanny Budd
Smith, Betty	A tree grows in Brooklyn
Smith, Eleanor	Caravan
Smith, Sheila Kaye-	The children's summer
Stone, Irving	Love is eternal
Stone, Irving	Lust for life
Sue, Eugene	The wandering Jew (2 vols.)

Sutcliffe, Halliwell	A man of the moors
Sutcliffe, Halliwell	Pedlar's quest
Sutton, Graham	Fleming of Honister
Sutton, Graham	North star
Sutton, Graham	The Rowan tree
Thane, Elswyth	Young mr. Disraeli
Thomas, Gwyn	A frost on my frolic
Thomas, Gwyn	Now lead us home
Thomas, Gwyn	The world cannot hear you
Thompson, Morton	Not as a stranger
Tibber, Robert	Love on my list
Tilsley, Frank	Champion road
Trollope, Frances	The life and adventures of Michael Armstrong
Trouncer, Margaret	Madame Elizabeth
Trouncer, Margaret	Oriflamme
Tunstall, Beatrice	The dark lady
Turnbull, Agnes Sligh	The rolling years
Turnbull, Patrick	Red walls
Turner, Sheila	Over the counter
Tutton, Diana	Guard your daughters
Viereck, G.S. & Eldridge, P.	My first two thousand years
Walpole, Hugh	Fortitude
Walpole, Hugh	Wintersmoon
Watson, Winifred E.	Fell top
Watson, Winifred E.	Odd shoes
Weidman, Jerome	I can get it for you wholesale
Werfel, Franz	Embezzled heaven
Wilkins, Vaughan	And so — Victoria
Wilkins, Vaughan	A city of frozen fire
Wilkins, Vaughan	Fanfare for a witch
Wilkins, Vaughan	Husband for Victoria
Wilkins, Vaughan	A king reluctant
Wilkins, Vaughan	Lady of Paris
Wilkins, Vaughan	Seven tempest
Vachell, H.A.	Vicars' walk
Zweig, Arnold	The case of sergeant Grischa

PORTWAY JUNIOR

Armstrong, Martin	Said the cat to the dog
Armstrong, Martin	Said the dog to the cat
Atkinson, M.E.	August adventure
Atkinson, M.E.	Going gangster
Atkinson, M.E.	The compass points north
Aymé, Marcel	The wonderful farm
Bacon, Peggy	The good American witch
Baker, Margaret J.	A castle and sixpence
Blackwood, Algernon	Dudley and Gilderoy
Coatsworth, Elizabeth	Cricket and the emperor's son
Edwards, Monica	Killer dog
Edwards, Monica	Operation seabird
Fenner, Phyllis R.	Fun, fun, fun
Haldane, J.B.S.	My friend mr. Leakey
Hill, Lorna	A dream of Sadler's Wells
Hoke, Helen	Jokes, jokes, jokes
Hoke, Helen	Love, love, love
Hoke, Helen	More jokes, jokes, jokes
Hoke, Helen & Randolph, Boris	Puns, puns, puns
Hourihane, Ursula	Christina and the apple woman
Lemming, Joseph	Riddles, riddles, riddles
Lyon, Elinor	Run away home
Parker, Richard	The sword of Ganelon
Pudney, John	Friday adventure
Pullein-Thompson, Christine	Ride by night
Pullein-Thompson, Diana	The secret dog
Pullein-Thompson, Josephine	Janet must ride
Pullein-Thompson, Josephine	One day event
Pullein-Thompson, Josephine	Show jumping secret
Manning-Sanders, Ruth	Children by the sea
Manning-Sanders, Ruth	Elephant
Saville, Malcolm	All summer through
Saville, Malcolm	Christmas at Nettleford
Severn, David	Burglars and bandicoots
Severn, David	Dream gold
Severn, David	The future took us
Sperry, Armstrong	Frozen fire
Sperry, Armstrong	Hull-down for action
Sperry, Armstrong	Thunder country
Stucley, Elizabeth	Springfield home

PORTWAY EDUCATIONAL & ACADEMIC

Abbott, W.C.	Colonel Thomas Blood
Abrams, Mark	The condition of the British people 1911–45
Adams, Francis	History of the elementary school contest in England
Andrews, Kevin	The flight of Ikaros
Balzac, Honoré de	The curé de Tours
Bazeley, E.T.	Homer Lane and the little common-wealth
Bowen, H.C.	Froebel and education by self-activity
Braithwaite, William J.	Lloyd George's ambulance wagon
Brittain, Vera & Taylor, G. Handley	Selected letters of Winifred Holtby and Vera Brittain
Cameron, A.	Chemistry in relation to fire risk and extinction
Clarke, Fred	Education and the social change
Clarke, Fred	Freedom in the educative society
Caldwell-Cook, H.	Play way (1 map, 14 illustrations)
Crozier, F.P.	A brass hat in no man's land
Crozier, F.P.	Angels on horseback
Crozier, F.P.	The men I killed
Dewey, John	Educational essays
Dewey, John	Interest and effort in education
Duncan, John	The education of the ordinary child
Fearnsides, W.G. & Bulman, O.M.B.	Geology in the service of man
Ferrier, Susan	Destiny (2 vols.)
Galt, John	The provost
Gates, H.L.	The auction of souls
Gilbert, Edmund W.	Brighton old ocean's bauble
Glass, David V.	The town — and a changing civilizatior
Gronlund, Norman E.	Sociometry in the classroom
Geological survey	The geology of Manchester and the south-east Lancashire coalfield (H.M.S.O.)
Hadow report 1933	Report of the consultative committee on infant and nursery schools (H.M.S.O.)
Harrison, G.B.	The life & death of Robert Devereux Earl of Essex